THE
NEXT
AMERICA

THE
NEXT
AMERICA

Moving Beyond a Fragile Economy

DON A. HOLBROOK

THE
UNBOUND
BOOKMAKER

ISBN-13: 978-1466416987/ISBN-10: 1-466-41698-X

Cover design by Jamie Zvirzdin
jamie@unboundbookmaker.com

Edited and typeset by The Unbound Bookmaker
www.unboundbookmaker.com

CONTENTS

Section One
Refining and Bolstering Our National Government

Section Two
Rethinking and Fortifying Our International Policies

Section Three
Recovering and Jump-Starting Our Local Economies

Section Four
Building Utopgrilotis: Existing in Harmony with Our Environment

Section Five
So What Now?

Dr. Matthew Gardner

Director of Sustainserv and Former Executive Director of the
Earth System Initiative, Massachusetts Institute of Technology

Humanity faces challenges unlike any others we have ever seen before. Our planet is changing in unpredictable and often deteriorating ways before our eyes, our social fabric is fraying, and our economies are stressed. More importantly, our faith in the institutions that have formed the bedrock of our societies, government, the private sector, and religions has been tested by numerous scandals and acts of malfeasance.

Many things have led to this point. Our ever-increasing appetite for natural resources; the dysfunction of global, regional, and local governance systems; our insatiable demand for energy of all types; and at times our insistence on growth and expansion regardless of cost have all led to a point where the Earth system and all of its components are wavering between stability and instability. The direction our planet takes depends upon the choices we will make now and in the near future.

The crisis that we face with respect to energy is a case in point. We are in an era of skyrocketing demand for energy. As the economies of China, India, Indonesia, and other developing nations continue to expand, these countries' needs for energy expand as well. Where that energy comes from—and how can we deal with the fact that most energy sources produce greenhouse gases, the source of global climate change—is a paradox today. Renewable energy can be part of the solution we seek, but renewable energy will not supplant fossil fuels any time soon. The answer lies in a portfolio approach, in which a mix of technologies, renewable and nonrenewable, is deployed to supply our energy needs. This approach, coupled with robust research and programs that develop new climate-neutral energy generation technologies and vigorous efforts to conserve energy, can get us over the hurdles we face.

Complicating things even further is the fact that we live in an era of global connectivity and instantaneous communication. Information travels around the globe at light speed, enabling commerce and discovery, but it also clouds our ability to differentiate between fact and fiction, hype and reality. People and institutions have learned to take advantage of this capability, for better or worse, in ways that we are only now beginning to understand.

Most illustrative of our challenges are those who are presented by the reshaping of the global financial industry. All of the factors described above have contributed to an environment in which the financial markets are viewed with skepticism but also as a potential opportunity. Despite the controversies of the past decade or so, the global economy remains the engine that drives economic and social development. It is the rocket fuel that can launch our society to better places, as long as it is guided appropriately with a sufficient level of oversight and with a compass that considers a wider range of inputs than simply financial gain. These higher-order considerations are what have been missing.

The challenge will be to introduce these higher-level principles, such as environmental protection, social value, ethics, and morality, into an industry that has not been compelled to do so up to now. Throughout history, for the most part, the only metric that mattered was a return on investment. But we are starting to see a shift—a shift from activities focused entirely on investment returns to activities that consider at a more granular level how economic activity will affect various stakeholders.

The activity of economic development is where the rubber meets the road. This discipline, whereby jobs and value are created in regions, cities, or neighborhoods, needs to integrate the higher-order concepts of environmental protection and social value into its framework. No longer can projects be selected or solicited simply because they create jobs;

communities need to consider whether the projects introduce undue environmental risk into a community or whether the projects will bring long-term social value.

There is much to encourage us. The concept of corporate social responsibility is rapidly becoming a concept familiar to all industries across the globe. Companies realize that in order for them to stay in business, regardless of their sectors, they will need to consider a wider range of issues in order to avoid negative publicity and to take advantage of the benefits that come with good corporate citizenship. As companies seek to expand their activities, to move into new communities, to tap into well-trained workforces, and to take advantage of natural resources, they will need to demonstrate transparently and credibly their commitment to operating under a new set of rules. It is this fact that gives us all reason to be hopeful. It is this fact that will allow us to continue to leverage the opportunities that solid, ethical, and truly sustainable economic development offers.

Dr. Matthew Gardner
April 14, 2011

ACKNOWLEDGEMENTS

This book is the culmination of a three-book series that I started over five years ago as a professional journey of enlightenment for myself. I also wanted it to awaken my own colleagues, friends, neighbors, and others I encounter to the dire situation I feel our country is in and how we all have a voice and are accountable to step up and take action. I could not have started or completed this monumental task without the undying support of my family: my lovely wife, Laurie; my two boys, Ian and Aidan; my parents, Floyd and Elizabeth Osman; and my father-in-law, Gary Lutz.

Furthermore, my friends took great efforts to keep me focused, sane, and healthy during this time frame. I owe a special thanks to Doug Taylor, Greg Owens, Bill Barber, Frank McCrady, Jeff Finkle, Don Lessem, Roger Reynolds, Karin Richmond, Simon Millcock, Steve Chapple, Kane Martin, Steve Carne, Leon Cubillas, and Gordon and Mary Neufang.

In addition, my editor, Jamie Zvirzdin, and her awesome team at The Unbound Bookmaker did a great job of organizing my hodgepodge of thoughts into a sensible and readable manuscript; they deserve many thanks and have my deepest appreciation. I want to thank all my colleagues for their input and commentary, which have helped me shape this book to the times. While my thoughts will be challenged by many and are imperfect, I hope they will inspire some; it is my best effort to describe my own experience and beliefs on how to turn our nation around and make it the strongest, safest, and best place to live in the world, without question. Thank you to all my family, friends, and colleagues for all your support.

Saving Humanity
One Community at a Time

On account of us being a democracy and run by the people, we are
the only nation in the world that has to keep a government four
years no matter what it does.

                    —*Will Rogers, American Entertainer and Humorist*[1]

From reading the newspaper, watching television, or listening to the radio, it should be clear that the unsettling situation America finds itself in today has presented us with several conundrums. We are concerned about where our nation is headed, how to make a living, how to prepare for retirement, how to create a better life for our families today, and how to leave our posterity with an inheritance of economic opportunities.

The global economy has created more chaos and hardships than most of us have previously experienced. Not since the Great Depression have folks been so beleaguered by so many tumultuous problems. Even more devastating is the degradation of our main pillar of humanity, our core: the family unit. With the massive amount of unemployment and underemployment that has arisen in this perfect economic storm, many of us have burned through our benefit claims, extensions, and options. We face loss of income and also hope and self-dignity. These immense

---

[1] Ketchum, *Will Rogers, His Life and Times*, 280. From a column sent from his *Daily Telegrams* to the *News Wires*, February 21, 1930.

problems have made many of us rethink our values and dreams. In the worst of cases, we have given up the ideal of aspiring for a better life—not only for ourselves, but also for our children. The economic pressures are not the only problems in this perfect storm. We face burgeoning pressure from religious zealots who are not tolerant of religious differences. We face environmental calamities, both natural and man-made. In addition, the resources that we depend on to fuel our global economy, such as energy, are peaking in costs and diminishing in availability.

To further frustrate and annoy our already overloaded psyches, we have a complete lack of trust in our governmental systems. People are weary of the either/or partisan politics and government's failure to look out for our best interests. Many folks see the crazies and zealots at each end of the political spectrum as a gridlock that cannot be resolved. Our politicians continue paying more attention to the special interests that most folks feel helped create the economic chaos. The real and perceived corruption of those who claim to create the jobs, make the policies, and take our hard-earned money through taxes for governance have led us to distrust politicians.

Along with our distrust of government, we distrust employers and other institutions, such as the media, banking, and health care organizations. The blame game is running rampant, and still no economic changes have taken hold to correct our course. We are quickly approaching the tipping point, and without a major overhaul, the American Dream could become a real-life nightmare. We could see the flow of money drying up, people losing their buying power, businesses folding at a record pace, and possible food rioting in the streets.

How am I different from other doomsayers? I feel that fear is not what inspires men and women to action; although it is helpful to recognize potential consequences, men and women must be inspired by higher motives than fear to rebuild a fractured economy and society. So more than simply pointing out the problems, *The Next America* contains solutions to troubles that beset us today. *The Next America* suggests that although inconvenient, we can rebuild our economy. We always have.

Rebuilding our society to be responsible for the future and to create economic opportunities today so we can support a sound and happy family core tomorrow must be the main objective. Humanity deserves to have access to quality education, affordable health care, economic opportunities, and recreational activities. Rebuilding our country to include these privileges comes with risks, but the risks of failure far outweigh the risks of not acting at all. Rebuilding does not require a shift to bigger government or a more socialistic government; rather, it requires a better, more honest government that is in tune with economic realities, moral convictions, and our spirit of capitalism.

It is good to remember that humankind makes its decisions based upon three sides of human nature: fear, greed, and natural honor or bravery; the decision-making process is additionally affected by the caliber of the moral compass an individual possesses and by his or her underlying belief in God's own requirements of us all. If it were not for these counterbalances, our world would quickly revert to the dark ages of savagery and warlords. The recent corruption of our political systems threatens to undermine our common voice, a voice trying to make sure that all are treated equally and are equally able to pursue life, liberty, and happiness.

> *Three things prompt men to a regular discharge of their duty in time of*
> *action: natural bravery, hope of reward, and fear of punishment.*
> —*George Washington, from a Letter to the President of Congress,*
> *February 9, 1776*[1]

In order to establish our collective best interests, we have to start at the grassroots level—within our own families, communities, and companies—and make strategic decisions about how to create the future we want not only for us but also for our children.

I have often discussed in my previous books my mantra that world-class communities of all shapes and sizes are possible today.

---

[1] Washington, *Maxims of Washington*, 154.

World-class communities are not determined by population, geographic location, and/or availability of natural resources. They are created by the quality of the local community's vision and the mindset of the local leaders and decision-makers who set the policies that will determine the course of the community. Communities must focus on charting their own courses and investing in themselves; they must not wait for outside assistance. The communities that act locally will win globally in the twenty-first-century economy.

This book is for those communities.

Refining and Bolstering Our National Government

The first section of *The Next America* will focus on the national or federal government challenges that confront us all. We will look unabashedly at the consequences of remaining at the status quo. We cannot—we must not!—languish in a state of chronic denial regarding these important matters.

The most crucial issue here will be to determine how government can act as a catalyst while simultaneously avoiding heavy-handed, oppressive oversight that stifles growth, innovation, and entrepreneurial opportunities. Just as we know that a fine line exists between calculated and reckless risk, we now know, with grim hindsight, that government should not give the markets free rein to wheel and deal as they please. Transparency, appropriate oversight, and effective checks and balances are essential tools to be used wisely in the protection of our economic, political, and environmental decisions and investments.

Cleansing a Corrupt Political System

Corruption has its own motivations, and one has to thoroughly study that phenomenon and eliminate the foundations that allow corruption to exist.

—*Eduard Shevardnadze, President of Georgia (1995–2003)*[1]

The majority of promises made by our political leaders are hollow, superficial ruses. They alone are not at fault: we voters don't hold politicians accountable in fulfilling the promises they make. Each election, we forget that politicians are feeding us propaganda and that they scoff at their promises as soon as they are elected. Each election cycle, political machines become bolder in their attempts to control the election process. Nothing is above their consideration—they look for ways to rig the system and fix the outcomes. An example of this is the infamous 2000 election of George W. Bush: the gerrymandering of political boundaries reduced voter diversity so those elected had the greatest chance of being reelected.

Over the last decade or so, we have seen countless examples of our political leaders' lack of accountability to and isolation from their constituents. All too often, our elected officials behave like pampered rock stars rather than guardians of the public trust: they take private jets on all-expense-paid junkets, trade in-kind legislative favors for

---

[1] Campos, *The Many Faces of Corruption*, 267.

large political donations, and push aside or forget the needs of the people they're supposed to be representing. They have also embraced the fallacy that they and their staff are members of a privileged class and are thus exempt from the laws that govern the rest of us. Examples range from President Clinton's total disregard for sexual harassment laws to the abuses of power by former Governors Spitzer, Sanford, and Blagojevich.

Let's examine some examples in more detail. Why? When we pay attention to how small infractions of the law turned into major scandals, we can use this awareness and vote more wisely for leaders who will uphold our own laws.

On September 28, 2005, House of Representatives majority leader Tom Delay and two political associates were indicted by a grand jury in Austin, Texas. It was but the latest in a series of misadventures in the spectacularly checkered political career of "the Hammer." Delay earned the nickname while he was GOP whip from 1995 to 2002 because of the tight discipline he imposed on his Republican colleagues in the House.

Just two months after the indictment, Michael Scanlon, a former Delay aide, pleaded guilty to bribery related to lobbying activities associated with the notorious Jack Abramoff. That same month, Representative Randy "Duke" Cunningham pleaded guilty in a federal court to tax evasion, a conspiracy to commit bribery, mail fraud, and wire fraud. Cunningham admitted he accepted multiple bribes, including an inflated price for his home, free use of a yacht, a used Rolls Royce, antique furniture, Persian rugs, jewelry, and a $2,000 contribution toward his daughter's college graduation party.

Unfortunately, 2005 proved to be merely the first act; the guilty pleas that rained down in 2006 made that year a thunderously memorable second act. The downpour began on January 3 when, appropriately attired in a black hat and raincoat, the mighty Jack Abramoff pleaded guilty in federal court to charges of conspiracy to bribe public officials, tax evasion, and mail fraud. In return for informing on fellow conspirators, Abramoff was sentenced to a maximum of ten years in the slammer. Not bad, considering that he could have faced up to thirty years of jail time.

It continues. On June 4, 2007, Representative William J. Jefferson was indicted by a federal grand jury. This indictment came almost two years after an FBI raid on his home netted $90,000 in cold, and presumably hard, cash found in his freezer. The sixteen-count, ninety-five-page indictment charged Jefferson with bribery, racketeering, money laundering, obstruction of justice, and related charges. True to form, Jefferson, who was known to many as "Dollar Bill," claimed he had done nothing wrong, despite two associates (including one of his former congressional aides) having previously pleaded guilty to related corruption charges. Jefferson's attorney said his client would continue fighting and that the FBI "picked the wrong congressman, and they picked the wrong facts."[1]

Jefferson did indeed fight on, even though he was videotaped putting a cash bribery payment, which included the previously mentioned $90,000, in the trunk of his car. His fight continued even after his August 5, 2009, conviction on eleven of the sixteen counts: after the conviction, Jefferson's attorney said the ex-congressman (he lost a December 2008 bid for reelection) would appeal the conviction.

While the Jefferson fiasco was playing out, so was Rod R. Blagojevich's extravaganza. It began on December 9, 2008, when the Illinois governor was arrested on federal corruption charges. These charges were related to his attempts to profit financially from his power to appoint someone to the Senate seat vacated by Barack Obama after being elected US president. Reacting with unaccustomed swiftness, the Illinois legislature voted 114 to 1 for a bill of impeachment. After a one-week trial, "Blago" became the first Illinois governor to be removed from office. Blago protested, of course, that he was a victim of his political enemies, an innocent lamb thrown to the wolves. But the facts pointed to him actually being the head wolf of a ravenous pack. For example, in one of the

---

[1] Weiner, "Prosecutors: Congressman Took $400K in Bribes," June 7, 2007.

wiretaps that led to his arrest, he characterized the Senate appointment as a potential "gold mine." On June 27, 2011, the court-appointed jury convicted Blago on seventeen of twenty counts; he will now, supposedly, be off to prison.

One of the most recent examples of government corruption is that of Charles Rangel, whom the House Ethics committee has charged with numerous ethical violations related to donations from corporations; not disclosing his assets and income to the IRS, including a luxurious beach house in the Dominican Republic; and many other financial improprieties. Rangel taunted his fellow legislators to "bring it on," but he did so during protected House proceedings, where the facts could not be used against him—yet another example of a politician using the system to his advantage.

Low-Hanging Fruit of Corruption

As we are now all too well aware, the "Low-Hanging Fruit," as I call it, of political corruption has proved an irresistible temptation to politicians of every stripe. But the temptation does not stop with politicians. It extends to all associates: lobbyists (the number of which has grown exponentially over the past decade), staff members, fund-raisers, and other political activists. And the problems don't stop at the federal or state level. Countless local politicians ignore conflict-of-interest laws and roll out the welcome mat for special interests, especially those with deep pockets. These special interest groups can easily finance dummy corporations and fill foreign bank accounts, all for the purpose of padding the pockets of politicians willing to do the bidding of the special interest groups.

> *This country has gotten where it is in spite of politics, not by the aid of it. That we have carried as much political bunk as we have and still survived shows we are a super nation.*
>
> —*Will Rogers*[1]

---

[1] Rogers, *Will Rogers*, 282.

I have touched on the dreary reality of politicians' cheating, bribery, extortion, fraud, and lying not merely to describe the current state of American politics on all levels but also to sound a loud emergency alarm—a call to take action against the corruption resulting from the tainted cash flooding our political system. While our country has seen explosive growth in the middle class in the post–World War II period, especially in the past twenty-five years, this expansion of prosperity has brought with it more cash to fund corruption. The result is a continuous incoming wave of corruption, engulfing every part of the country, straining our legal system, depleting our resources, and challenging our democratic institutions. What can we learn from this, and what can we do about it?

Undeniably, from its earliest days, our nation has been threatened, attacked, and made to suffer grave injuries from repeated onslaughts of corruption. We would do well to pay attention to the following excerpt from George Washington's Farewell Address:

> However combinations or associations . . . may now and then answer popular ends, they are likely, in the course of time and things, to become potent engines, by which cunning, ambitious, and unprincipled men will be enabled to subvert the power of the people and to usurp for themselves the reins of government, destroying afterwards the very engines which have lifted them to unjust dominion.[2]

If we want to eliminate the rampant corruption and restore confidence in how we are governed, we must act boldly and effectively, raising the bar regarding what is acceptable conduct for our politicians. We should not let them slip through the legal system, and we should not tolerate their unapologetic behavior after their misconduct has been made public. As Theodore Roosevelt said in his speech "The Man with the Muck-Rake":

---

[2] Washington, "George Washington Farewell Address," http://www.earlyamerica. com/earlyamerica/milestones/farewell/text.html.

At the risk of repetition let me say again that my plea is
not for immunity to, but for the most unsparing exposure
of, the politician who betrays his trust, of the big business
man who makes or spends his fortune in illegitimate or
corrupt ways. There should be a resolute effort to hunt every such man out of the position he has disgraced. Expose
the crime, and hunt down the criminal; but remember that
even in the case of crime, if it is attacked in sensational, lu-
rid, and untruthful fashion, the attack may do more damage to the public mind than the crime itself.[1]

Recently, Delay was dancing around like a rock star after he was
cleared of federal charges. In fact, he is free enough to appear as a con-
testant on the television series *Dancing with the Stars*. Blago was charged
with just one count of criminal conduct, and he seems to be making the
most of his celebrity status, including through the promotion of his autobiography, *The Governor*. Our criminals are now celebrities.

What of the politicians who refuse to clean up their acts? Perhaps
our current fixation on reality TV could be our weapon for change.
Why don't we create a reality-TV version of what the ancient Romans
did in the Colosseum (a nonviolent version, of course)? When a politician is accused of corrupt actions, we could televise the situation and
then have the general population determine the verdict through on-
line voting. If the politician were found guilty of the accusations, the
people would decide the appropriate punishment. Not only would
such a TV show have a huge viewership, it would give us all a glimpse
of just how untrustworthy and unscrupulous our political representatives are.

In addition to boosting viewership through the roof, providing the
media with skyrocketing advertising value, such a show might begin to
restore some valuable investigative journalism. We could then expand
the show to include those involved in corporate crimes. Just another

---

[1] Roosevelt, "The Man with the Muck-Rake," April 15, 1906.

twist on the success of letting the population be the judge in real time and with immediate results. Now, that would be TV worth watching.

As I close this chapter, I am watching Donald Trump create a platform for a possible presidential bid. Trump as president? Now, that would be entertaining! It can't be any worse than a beauty queen or professional actor running for office.

In sum, we have seen even in recent presidential elections how the media can be used to destroy or build up the public opinion of public personas and their stated objectives. President Barack Obama used social media better than anyone could imagine; he inspired us to believe that change, hope, and progress would be possible under his direction. I would now make the case that his campaign was just another version of unaccountable rhetoric. President Obama went into office and immediately started with the disclaimers of "I inherited this problem from former president George Bush." While this excuse might be true, he made the situation worse through his own decisions—influenced by political junkies, special interests, and corporate investors—which resulted in the recovery plan only helping institutions, not citizens.

Now many of us feel betrayed and disgruntled that, yet again, we were led to believe another media-induced fantasy of rebalancing our great country. Rather than obtaining the progress we'd been promised, we see the stark realities that public confidence is horribly low, unemployment is stubbornly high, inflation is just around the corner, the deficit is growing exponentially, and tax reform and workforce improvements are nonexistent. In fact, the United States now has the highest taxes in the world, but with the least results to show for it. Politicians think that the solution to our country's problems is to increase taxes even more, rather than to embrace true government reform and adopt a balanced budget. People are seeing the energy beast devour their cash at the gas pump, with no hope of a strong renewable and energy-efficient policy to incentivize true energy reform. Bankruptcies and mortgages in default remain in favor of the bankers and not those bilked out of their earnings, savings, and investments in their homes.

In short, our country is a gigantic mess. What we need is benevolent and selfless leadership from people who want to make this country great again—even if it means through their own sacrifice. Our founders built this country at immense personal risk, knowing that if they failed, it would mean probable death from the ruler of the day. Despite this knowledge, our founders undertook this enormous task because they were true leaders who cared more about the welfare of the country than themselves.

The next chapter will focus on changes that we can make to fix the system, rooting out the bugs that are corrupting the government's programming so that it will function correctly again.

CHAPTER TWO

Changing the Political System

The price of apathy towards public affairs is to be ruled by evil men.
—Plato[1]

Political corruption is not the only problem with our government. Even the politicians who are not engaging in underhanded deeds are out of touch with the people they represent. Their lifestyles contrast so greatly with the general population that our politicians don't understand our needs, and they certainly don't make the effort to understand. When our elected representatives are questioned about their decisions, the subtexts of their statements—underneath all the dignified-sounding, self-serving puffery—consist of the following:

- They know what is best for us and therefore are acting in our own best interests.

- There are some things they must do in private, shielding us from hard, unpleasant facts. Otherwise, progress in every sphere of government would be impeded, our national security would be jeopardized, and our national economy would be left broken beyond repair.

- Their high standards of patriotism explain their actions.

A similar theme is that we, as voters, just don't possess the intelligence to grasp the deep complexities of the problems our hard-working

[1] Archer, *The Quotable Intellectual*, 93.

legislators and members of congress must wrestle with on a daily basis. Thus, we are unable to appreciate, much less comprehend, the actions they take to address the problems of our state and country.

Our founding fathers formed this country over two hundred years ago as part of their struggle to free themselves from tyranny, taxation without representation, and the aristocrats and monarchs who wanted to suppress them. Yet, it seems that today we are once again in that same plight, only we're not struggling against rulers in a faraway country— today's tyrants live within our country and try to make us believe they are working for us.

William Barber, a retired member of the US Marine Corps and an entrepreneur, said, "There is a Marine Corps saying, 'Presumptions and assumptions get you killed in combat.'" He suggests that the same goes for the political combat that goes on between civilians and politicians:

> Our United States of America has over the last century (or more) developed and in the main established a government whose process of operational scope is not of the people, by the people, nor for the people; indeed, there is evidence that the 1789 constitutional intent has perished from reality. We the people can no longer presume nor assume that our representative republic is in fact representative, that our federal system of power sharing between the government of central and state is intact, nor that our republic functions within the lawfulness of the Constitution.[1]

We are not stupid, and we are not serfs of despots; we have a voice. Reform of our political system from top to bottom—on national, state, and local levels—remains the only viable option for fighting the erosion of our democratic values wrought by special interests and holier-than-thou political leaders.

---

[1] Barber, "In the Interest of Sensibility," June 19, 2011.

Suggested Changes to Limit Corruption

When this reform is achieved, our elected officials will have little, if any, excuse for not getting on with the people's business; they will neither waste countless hours bemoaning the rise of partisan politics nor practice those same partisan politics to the fullest extent possible.

> *The Greatness of America lies not in being more enlightened than any other nation, but rather in her ability to repair her faults.*
>
> *—Alexis de Tocqueville*[2]

It is time to address the fundamental reforms for our elected officials at all levels of government. I recommend taking the following actions to restrict corruption in our elected offices and to enforce accountability:

- Establish term limits of no more than three terms. Further, move from two-year terms to three-year terms for representatives (which will allow them to get out of campaign mode) and from six-year terms to five-year terms for senators. I would apply these same terms to our state legislatures as well. It is a fallacy that the longer someone is in office, the better he or she is in effectively serving constituents. In reality, allowing politicians to stay in office for long periods opens the way for politicians to receive greater lobbyist donations and special interest favors that totally contradict what is in the best interests of constituents. Extended time in office has nothing to do with effective management and representative capabilities. It does, however, increase a politician's power, which almost always whittles away the politician's personal resolve and convictions, leading the politician to embrace the dark side of the lucrative lifestyle driven by special interests, both during and after the time in office.[3]

---

[2] Semas, *Reason, Justice, and Common Sense*, 235.

[3] For more information on this topic, please see Thompson, *Just Elections*, 233.

- One might argue that if our plight were improving, perhaps our political leaders would deserve more terms. But this argument is irrelevant because our situation is worsening. Our politicians are ineffective because of their own gamesmanship in the halls of government. Even relationships between the federal and state governments are dysfunctional. States such as Arizona are filing suit against the federal government regarding their inability to protect their citizens from the perils of illegal immigration. Federal and state officials need to work together, not against each other. A house divided against itself cannot stand.

- Pay politicians salaries equal to the wages of comparable positions in the private sector. Include allocations for travel and campaigning, and require full transparency regarding expenditures. We can gain insight from Singapore, which pays its elected officials in this manner. Singapore's reasoning is that the country will attract the brightest citizens to run for office and these individuals will represent the best interests of their constituents. Further, aligning salaries with private-sector wages will debunk the claim of politicians that they are poor public servants making sacrifices on our behalf—a claim they make to cover up the reality that they are cheating us out of indirect benefits, power, and needed opportunities.

- In addition, require politicians to be audited. If all politicians are required to submit to full IRS audits each year, politicians will understand just how misguided and wasteful this form of taxation oversight is and the need to completely overhaul and simplify our tax codes.

- End the special treatment—provide elected officials with the same benefits (insurance, 401(k) plan, unemployment, etc.) that employees in the private sector receive.

Eliminate lavish numbers of holidays and vacation days, luxurious retirement packages, extravagant health care programs, and other hidden perks. Require politicians to set aside retirement funds, and make politicians pay the same costs as other citizens pay. As a result of this equalization, politicians will be more mindful when deciding whether to increase taxes or change benefits levels—they will have to experience the ramifications of their decisions. Then, perhaps, we can get started on true reforms to the tax system and workforce benefits—a new, true, and realistic contract with America.

- Prohibit organizations—including corporations, unions, and citizens' groups—from donating money for election campaigns. Though the McCain-Feingold Act, which took effect January 1, 2003, helped to regulate campaign financing, three of its provisions have been overturned by the Supreme Court. The last vestige of the campaign finance reform was shot down by the Supreme Court in 2010; many believe this opened the floodgate for corporations to invest in special interests, further reducing the voice of those with a small pocket book—that is, the common citizen. The only donations allowed should come from citizens entitled to vote in the election in which the candidate is running. Donations should be limited to $2,000 per individual or $3,000 per household if more than one member of the household chooses to donate.

- Forbid corporations and special interest groups from paying for travel, meals, hotel accommodations, education events, and any other events designed to promote their agendas. This ban should apply not only to the politicians but also to their staff members and family members. Require expenses related to such events to be posted publicly and to be paid for from the funds citizens donate. We must endeavor to eliminate the poisonous power of special interests with the same intensity that we strive to destroy deadly viruses. By doing so, the voice of the people will once again be established as the great influencer of politicians' decisions.

• Ban elected officials and their families from lobbying or working for companies that are negotiating for or benefiting from any type of governmental contracts. We must completely break any ties to financial gains associated with the indirect influences of politicians. If a conflict of interest arises, the company must disclose the conflict and the elected official must resign from office and/or the employee must be terminated. We must allow zero tolerance regarding indirect financial gaming of the system.

• Require politicians, their staff, and their family members to wait at least five years after leaving office and/or public service before seeking employment at organizations lobbying any level of government. Implementing this policy will minimize the potential benefits of such relationships, which will greatly reduce political corruption.

• Looking to Singapore again as an example, implement a zero-tolerance policy regarding breaking laws. When a politician is tried in court, require the trial jury to consist of ordinary citizens rather than other politicians, and enforce serious punishments for convicted political corruption, including mandatory jail time and the revocation of retirement and all other benefits. This would include steep financial penalties that are not dischargeable via bankruptcy.

To be sure, the changes I advocate will undoubtedly cause an outcry from all elected officials, their staffs, and special interests because they will immediately recognize the extent to which their powers will be limited. However, these changes are vital if we really want to regain our power, which has been usurped by these violators of the public trust. You see, public service is not a career—it is a calling. It should be a true sacrifice based on a true desire to serve the people. We are the rightful owners of this country and its government and must have the power to run it in a way that will meet our needs.

The Need to Limit Spending and Government

As one of our past presidents said,

> *A government big enough to give you everything you want, is strong enough to take everything you have.*
>
> *—Gerald Ford*[1]

Over the last forty years, like the erosion of sand from the shoreline of our great nation, many of our individual freedoms have been gradually taken from under us by various forms of justification. Since this has been occurring slowly, tax-by-tax, law-by-law, it was not noticed by many. During this time, the federal government, through the actions of Congress and the courts, has significantly expanded its powers, interfering significantly with state and local governments and limiting our ability to control our own government by way of our electoral system. In reality, they have used the political game to game us. For more than forty years, the Congress of the United States has borrowed money to fund its programs (many unnecessary and often blotted with pork barrel political paybacks) and gerrymandered boundaries to ensure the re-election of its members. Congress has looted all of its trust funds and amassed a crushing debt, which it does not intend to repay, leaving this responsibility to future generations.

---

[1] Steele, *Right Now*, 83.

This massive debt is consuming the wealth of America, stealing our future ability to invest in ourselves, and has placed our country in dire financial jeopardy. In addition, by borrowing from foreign entities, we have become commercially and politically dependent upon other nations for our own solvency. Amendments are needed to prevent the federal government from continuing to borrow money and to force it to begin repayment of its debts, not burdening our great-great-grandchildren with this obligation. Worse yet, the size of government has grown so large that none of the people within the government can comprehend the Byzantine maze of connections within the system that suck productivity, transparency, and accountability from public view and from the alleged intended outcomes. They are, in effect, running their own version of the Wizard of Oz: "Pay no attention to that man behind the curtain . . . You are too dumb to understand anyhow!"

The federal government has expanded the federal courts well beyond the borders of the authority granted in the Constitution. The federal government has invaded our daily lives and with its treasury is usurping the power of state and local governments. Now the federal government is empowering lobbying, reducing the restrictions we had already placed on lobbying, and has overturned recent advances made in restricting such lobbying efforts.

Let's make one thing clear about lobbying: corporations are not citizens and do not have the same rights—only our citizens who vote are true citizens. It is in our best interest to create a business climate that enables corporations to profit and grow economically, but it is *not* in our best interest to serve their needs uniquely or individually as a government.

In addition, through legislation and decree, the federal government is gradually taking ownership of more and more private entities, causing what is known as socialism, which is the absence of economic freedom. This trend is likely to continue if not stopped with an amendment. The amendment would rein in the powers of the federal government, prevent it from nationalizing private businesses, and restrain it from meddling with our belief that capitalism needs to rightsize itself—it is the free market that will restore local control of our state, county, and city governments. This, of course, would be balanced by true regulatory oversight to set limits and boundaries for the activities of these corporations so they do not abuse the trust the citizens, customers, and shareholders place in them. That is the proper role of government. Balancing these regulatory reforms so they are not unjustly bureaucratic or harmful to making a reasonable profit is the most difficult task of our elected officials.

Much of the abuse in the legislative process is caused by the extreme difficulty of changing the members of Congress and our state legislatures. Because of the trappings of office, the distance from their voters, and the ability to raise money to fund their reelections, senators and representatives not only seek continual reelection but are virtually assured of it. Two current members of Congress first took office during Dwight Eisenhower's first term as president. The seniority system within Congress enables those who have served the longest to have the most power. Today, only a small group of legislators controls Congress, making our nation more of an oligarchy than a democratic republic. It is so easy for members of Congress to be reelected that a Constitutional amendment to limit the terms of office is needed to limit the powers of all levels of government.

The Need to Amend the Constitution

Recently, there have been movements advocating that we convene a Continental Convention as a means of amending the Constitution to address the size of our federal government. Our founding fathers saw the benefits of holding Continental Conventions and outlined, in Section V of the Constitution, the process of convening a convention to add an amendment to the Constitution. Our country is not the only one that allows for such conventions. Conventions such as those used in Switzerland add power to the voice of the people. And we shouldn't stop at the national and state levels. Town hall meetings would also strengthen the voice of the constituents and give us an opportunity to address government's problems.

To restore control over our government, we need to consider suggestions such as the "10 Amendments for Freedom," sponsored by a non-profit movement led by a former mayor from Ohio, Bill Fruth, as a viable grassroots-driven agenda that merits some attention. Those who support this group want their ten amendments added to the Constitution of the United States by way of a convention of the states as allowed in our Constitution.[1] The Constitution has been amended twenty-seven times; Congress proposed each of these amendments. Since the propositions within the "10 Amendments for Freedom" will restrict the federal government, it is not likely Congress will take any action to propose them.

In order for an amendment to be added to the Constitution, three-fourths of the states must ratify the proposed amendment. There are two ways to propose an amendment: (1) by Congress, via a vote of two-thirds of its members, and (2) by way of an Amendments Convention called by the state legislatures.

Through our state legislatures, we can vote to hold an Amendments Convention, which will then propose the "10 Amendments for Freedom" to the other states for ratification. Once thirty-four states have ratified these ten amendments, we can then, by the power of the people's voice, amend our Constitution appropriately. It can be done in the spirit of open debate over each proposed amendment for consideration. The following excerpt is from a document produced by 10 Amendments for Freedom, Inc.

> The Freedom Amendments Resolution provides for a convention that is expressly limited to the following four subjects:
>
> - **Improving the fiscal management of the federal government** by imposing requirements, with any stated ex-

---

[1] PR Newswire, "Congress Is Looting Federal Worker," February 2010.

ceptions, that federal expenditures during a fixed time period not exceed federal revenues or anticipated revenues
during that time period; imposing prohibitions and/or
limits on federal debt; and/or imposing limits on expenditures, revenue, and/or taxes.

- **Improving the legislative process** by requiring that
all bills, orders, votes, and resolutions introduced in
and passed by Congress contain only a single subject
and/or by providing a minimum time period before
passage for bills, orders, votes and resolutions to be re-
viewed by members of Congress and members of the
general public.

- **Restraining the powers of the federal government**
by clarifying that the Constitution does not authorize
Congress to employ its spending power to regulate activities otherwise outside its enumerated powers and/or
prohibiting mandates or requirements on any state, sub-
division of any state, or any official thereof, unless the
federal government fully funds the cost of compliance.

- **Empowering the legislatures** of the several states,
with stated exceptions, to repeal all or certain acts of Congress and/or administrative regulations.[2]

A Note about God and the Constitution

Throughout the history of humankind, government has looked upon
the people's belief in God as an obstacle. As long as the people believed
in a Higher Being, the government could not have total authority. Both
Congress and the courts have embarked on a path to disassociate government from God Almighty, forgetting from whom we derive our freedom and moral compass.

---

[2] 10 Amendments for Freedom, Inc., *America's Freedom Amendments*, 3.

The federal courts, teeming with atheists and agnostics, are systematically removing all references to God in the public sphere. As a result, a Constitutional amendment is necessary, not to allow religion in government, but to acknowledge that God, not the government, has given us our rights and freedoms. Our nation was founded as a Christian nation, a nation that has developed tolerance for other religions and will continue to do so, but we will not allow God to be struck from our heritage. However, we must provide a caveat here: under no circumstance should religious beliefs be allowed to obstruct the rights of citizens. There is a current movement to outlaw Sharia law, but to deny Muslims the freedom to worship as they choose is unconstitutional and extremist.[1] Newt Gingrich, a conservative extremist, said that we should have a federal law prohibiting any court in the United States from recognizing Sharia law.[2] Gingrich also said, in a speech given at the American Enterprise Institute in July 2010:

> How we don't have some kind of movement in this country on the left that understands that Sharia is a direct mortal threat to virtually every value that the left has is really one of the most interesting historical questions.[3]

Though Gingrich was pandering to the extremely conservative Christian movement, we must recognize that Muslim religious beliefs in turn should not encroach on others that do not hold those same beliefs. Muslim religious views must not be presented and forced upon those who do not share those beliefs. Moreover, I would like to stress that we should not ignore the fact that our nation was founded on—and remains openly supported by—a Christian-based belief system. In the 1780s, Americans used the metaphor of a melting pot to describe how different cultures could melt together and thereby live together in the

---

[1] See Mandaville, *Citizen-Soldier Handbook*, 239.

[2] McMorris-Santoro, "Gingrich Calls for Federal Law Banning Shariah Law in US," September 18, 2010.

[3] Robinson, "Sharia as the New Red Menace?" September 21, 2010.

same land. In the last forty years, however, people have started to value cultural and religious differences and thus have used the metaphor of a salad bowl—the ingredients are all mixed together, and together they make an excellent, healthy dish. This is America; I have no doubt that if we keep respect at the forefront of the discussion, problems between Christians and Muslims will abate.

However we may worship God, it is when we remember him that He can help us as a nation to overcome our challenges—in particular, managing a government that is good but needs pruning. Our founders felt so strongly about the statement "In God We Trust" that they imprinted it on all the nation's currency. That was no mistake; their intentions were clear.

Summary

As Thomas Friedman wrote about in his *New York Times* article entitled "Really Unusually Uncertain,"[4] a structural reformation of our entire governmental system is long overdue. As Friedman says, in America our two biggest parties are still clinging to their core religious beliefs as if nothing has changed and without regard for our real economic and civic situation. Republicans try to undermine the president at every turn and offer their vision of tax cuts that they decree will solve everything— without ever specifying what services they'll give up to pay for them, how they can balance the budget, and how to realign our social expectations as well as pay heed to their corporate special interests. President Obama gave us expanded health care before expanding the economic pie, Friedman says, and providing realistic and sustainable financial tools to sustain it. This has occurred before requiring private sector collaboration and cooperation through new competition measures.

In fact, today we still don't sense that our politicians understand our deep American desire to right our own ship, balance our own financial affairs, and secure our own economic opportunity for our own

---

[4] Friedman, "Really Unusually Uncertain," August 17, 2010.

employment. Politicians must understand that giving us meaningful ways to achieve retirement, protecting us when unemployed, and enabling us to become reemployed in a dignified occupation and/or endeavor is what we would like. The list can go on to include providing a reasonable insurance product to cover us when we are ill and/or disabled. We owe this rebuilding not only to those who work diligently toward solving these problems but also to our future generations. The fact remains that our country elected Obama to invoke meaningful change, and I believe our country understood that this would require immense sacrifice but with measurable outcomes and a realistic time line. Instead, Obama has failed at that mantra; he has squandered his presidency. There will be little chance for a real recovery until we require our elected leaders to address these economic issues. As this book goes to press, our politicians have made little progress, our country remains snarled in the longest and deepest recession since the Great Depression, and unemployment refuses to relent.

Let us not be stubborn. Let us see the writing on the wall and choose to act together with our state legislatures and Congress to trim the fat off the government. How we elect those who serve us, what we expect of government by way of our social contract, and how we voice our approval and disapproval of new laws needs to be restructured. Our own will, voice, and uniquely American mind-set must be reflected in all actions of all levels of government in this century; only then will the American Dream be reborn and flourish again as a beacon of hope and opportunity to all those desiring to live within our nation as responsible citizens.

CHAPTER THREE

Tackling the Tax Code: The Key to Strengthening Capitalism and the Economy

Our tax code is the 21st century version of slavery. We will replace oppression with prosperity. If 10 percent is good enough for God, then 9 percent should be just fine for the Federal Government.

—*Herman Cain*[1]

C apitalism is on the operating table with grave injuries. If left untreated and our leaders are unprepared to conduct the surgery that would revive it, capitalism will suffer and be permanently crippled. This chapter focuses on why and how a revision of our tax code would reinvigorate our economy and keep capitalism alive and strong.

Goal: Help Shareholders Invest in US-Based Jobs

The new goals of US capitalism in the twenty-first century must include, first and foremost, creative economic incentives that promote fiscally prudent spending—within reason—among our fellow citizens once again. The bolstering of consumer confidence will not be easy. Consumers have been continuously sold a bill of goods that has only exacerbated their own personal situations and cause them to feel like indentured servants to banks and credit card companies.

---

[1] Bingham, "Herman Cain's 9-9-9 Plan: Buy Less, Pay Less," September 27, 2011.

This goal will remain out of reach and unachievable unless there is broad-based investment in viable living wage jobs here in the United States. In order to attain this investment, we must help citizens achieve personal financial stability and wealth accumulation and preservation. We can do this through a modern, restructured tax system. This favorable investment climate would unblock and free up innovation capital. Investors would then be drawn to new opportunities; for example, they would be encouraged and motivated to update our transportation networks as well as additional infrastructure improvements; to expand green-energy alternatives and medical innovations; and to speed up other technological advances such as those promoting even more widespread personal and commercial use of the Internet both here and abroad. In essence, the economy is tied to the following major components:

- Consumer goods,
- Energy,
- Mobility and transportation,
- Housing,
- Health care services,
- Computing/technology,
- Banking/finance,
- Tourism/leisure,
- Entertainment (including sports), and
- Communications.

These are the foundations of most of our economic growth and the underpinning issues that in most cases are woefully out of whack with how we pay for them as consumers. The investment of new and better capabilities in all these areas will be the hotbed for growth this century. Entrepreneurs are constantly trying to come up with products and services that will give them a competitive edge within these fields.

The Power of the Tax Code

There are so many opportunities that await us in our economic future, but unfortunately it is easy to get confused and take our eyes off these prizes. Restoring confidence in the markets is our ticket to keep investors working. The way to stimulate the economy is through capitalism, not socialism and a big central government (often called "the Nanny State"). Too often we get caught up in the partisan approach of either/ or politics. Cut taxes, say the Republicans, and the Democrats answer by spending more money on the safety net of entitlements for individuals. Of course, both approaches are unrealistic or they both would have worked. What I mean is we have tried both and neither has kept us out of economic harm's way. Because we tilted too far to the Republican agenda, with less regulation, fewer taxes, and the market-knows-best mentality, in 2008, we had one of the biggest economic meltdowns in history followed by the 2010 BP Gulf oil fiasco. This ushered in the Great Recession and the much-anticipated but completely absent "Great Recovery/Reboot/Renewal" — you can pick the optimistic term.

In all cases the preliminary architects were Republicans, the critical care responders were Democrats, and the results were less than impressive. The meltdown, in my opinion, was answered with an impressive array of well-meaning federal bailouts to maintain buoyancy in the economy, but these had absolutely no ability to stem job losses or to rebuild consumers' battered balance sheets. In fact, the corporations involved got the economic salvation holy water while the consumers and small businesses got their economic brains bashed in. Even today we are on the eve of yet another seismic economic shock as the thrill ride for the bailouts' lingering effects wear off and the economy begins to shed more jobs, housing begins to slump, construction remains stalled, and new investments go the way of the dodo. So first, let's fix things by providing jobs for Americans. We do this by easing up on the tax regulations for investors. If we do, the investors will invest; jobs will be created; and, in the end, tax revenue will be enough to cover our needs.

The fiscal problem today within government is rooted in our expectations of what we expect from government in the form of services; in many cases the cost of entitlements is built upon the sinking sand of our progressive, highly inefficient, underperforming, and abusive tax code. This tax code penalizes investment and the accumulation of wealth, and it does not provide for the fair and equitable funding of the needs of our workforce on a proportional basis. In short, it is a tax code that reflects a socialistic approach to governance more than the capitalistic foundation that our republic was built upon. This tax code has been like a cancer within our business climate and has done more to harm American jobs and thus economic security. The end result is that it has eroded the American Dream more than any other aspect of all levels of our government. In simple terms, when government tries to enjoy the fruits of our labor we have the basis for a real concern, the same concern that led our country to break away from Europe over two hundred years ago. It is a burden and a yoke of a highly repressive and costly government that negatively affects the quality of life of its citizens more than it promotes net benefits, especially to those who are trying to work productively within the boundaries of the country. We have replicated the plight that drove so many immigrants to our shores in the first place.

Why Raising Taxes Won't Help Us

The problem with raising taxes is that eventually it just drives the wealthy out of the risk market. So investments just dry up, and investors move to better business climates with modest or reasonable taxes on corporate profits. Raising taxes therefore will only provide a very short-term economic boon; if enacted, higher taxes will be followed by a major bust in growth, decreased productivity, and even sharper job losses. The investment into entitlements and big government comes with tons of legacy and sunk costs that we simply cannot afford. If people believe that the government is the management answer to lowering costs and balancing the situation, they need look no further than the current sad state of social security, Medicare, and Medicaid to show them the error of their ways. If they looked a little longer, they might also see the failure of Fannie Mae and Freddie Mac. The list goes on and on. And then, of course, there is Europe; need I say any more on this subject?

The current scare has people looking to the government to restart the economy, but that does not mean we are ready to embrace socialism or become a Big Brother–based Nanny State. But we are Americans. We stand for freedom from oppressors. We possess the greatest ability to create, reinvigorate, and renew.

> *History suggests that capitalism is a necessary element for political*
> *freedom.*
>
> —*Milton Friedman*[1]

This is the time to make systemic structural changes that over a decade will put America squarely back in the ring as a champion economy—an economy that is economically vibrant, world class, and visionary in its response to both challenges and opportunities. As Raghuram Rajan, a University of Chicago Economist, said:

> The bottom line in the current jobless recovery suggests
> the US has to take deep structural reforms to improve its
> supply side. The quality of its financial sector, its physical
> infrastructure, as well as its human capital, all need seri-
> ous economic and politically difficult upgrades.[2]

These times require us to look at several major lingering issues to restore economic order to our house and thus increase investments— investments which will begin to create jobs once more. Most of us common-sense Americans already know the roots of the problems. We have even been telling ourselves for years that these problems would be our burden to bear. We can no longer afford the old dinosaur Social Security and other socialized entitlement benefits for the masses based

---

[1] Friedman, "Economic Freedom, Human Freedom, Political Freedom."

[2] Rajan, "Bernanke Must End Era of Ultra-Low Rates," July 28, 2010.

on their inept concepts. Social Security and other entities are historical sunk costs that our nation is desperately trying to capitalize through new taxes, increased taxes, and reduced benefits. We have to sunset these entitlements and cross over to a fiscally sound system for this century. All of this adds up to less worthwhile programs; less disposable income; and less motivation to make money that benefits the government more than the less-productive masses, more than the most productive members, and more than the greatest innovative wealth creators. If we therefore can reduce taxes and the federal deficit but increase surety of transparency; increase access, choice, and accountability for the quality and solvency of our workforce benefits; and increase disposable income, all the while increasing personal wealth and jobs, who would be against it? Nobody, in theory, would be against such objectives, at least not the typical American taxpayer. In fact, citizens needs to take this position exactly. We believe there is a methodology that is uniquely American and that can and must balance those goals while keeping our reward— achieving the American Dream—alive and well.

How we restructure our tax code and target high growth in the key economic components mentioned earlier are linked. For example, we need to come up with financially prudent solutions that allow the average consumer to afford to drive a modern, clean, fuel-efficient vehicle; to own his or her own house; to accumulate wealth without risk of seizure due to excessive taxes and health care costs; to have enough money to heat, cool, and operate his or her home and business, if applicable. The average consumer needs access to capital for reasonably priced goods and services with terms and conditions that are not subsidized by our own tax dollars. So the path to progress, in my mind, is a hybrid of tax reductions; tax increases on targeted inefficient technologies; and tax relief on investments that will quickly build the kind of highly efficient, new technologies that a progressive and profitable society can sustain within their own fiscally prudent capabilities. These increases and decreases need to be phased in aggressively but without partisan interruption no matter which party is in power . . . in other words, they need to be our national resolve, the will of the public.

Rebuilding our tax code is the spark that will ignite job creation and new investments, and thus it is the greatest catalyst to a healthy economy. The new regulations must create a spirit of can do, must do, and will do among our people, a spirit of collaboration. We need to concede that the next ten years will not be easy, but they will become the cornerstone for a stronger, more vibrant future for us and for our children.

> We won't find solutions if our pundits, politicians, and business leaders are still caught up in parochial arguments about debt and deficits and how to bring back the housing industry. We can't neglect the present, but we also have to think beyond it. If we keep spending on the old economy and our old ways of consumption and living, a new, post-industrial society may still emerge, but it will take longer to do so and it may not be one that most Americans will want to live in.
>
> —Dr. Richard Florida, American Economist[1]

The fundamental problem with our current tax code is that it is counterproductive to growing the economy and does not serve the purposes that it was allegedly created for. There is a direct correlation between the amount of taxes and the economic prosperity of a country; where taxes are repressively high, economic vitality goes missing. Furthermore, high taxes breeds a new level of acceptable corruption within the government and in the general population in the form of black market trading of goods and services. I am not advising that we should not pay a fair tax to our governments; I just want it to be a fair portion of our income, no matter how much or little we make. America is about individual accomplishment and was not designed to be a welfare or entitlement bureaucracy.

---

[1] Florida, "The Road Map to a High Speed Recovery," August 10, 2010.

You don't pay taxes — they take taxes.
— Chris Rock, Actor[1]

How to Restructure the Tax Code

Our entire premise as a republic was the opportunity for self-initiative and the pursuit of economic opportunity, coupled with a broad set of civil liberties. Nowhere in the Constitution did our founders say, "and please provide a safety net for those who try and fail." Therefore, a flat tax on all persons is fair and equitable. As Steve Forbes said, "The flat tax would be so simple, you could fill it out on a post card. A post card that would say, in effect, having a wonderful time; glad most of my money is here."[2] At this point it would be wise to discuss the purpose of taxation in general, our expectations, the various types of taxes, and the good that can come from handling these taxes the right way.

Taxes do have a place in our system; they are a necessary part of our existence as Americans. The tax money, used appropriately, enhances our quality of life. In this regard I agree with Justice Oliver Wendell Holmes, former Chief Justice of the US Supreme Court. In response to a secretary's query of "Don't you hate to pay taxes?" Justice Holmes said, "No, young fellow, I like paying taxes, with them I purchase civilization."[3]

But while necessary, we must proceed cautiously when it comes to taxes. Fiscal irresponsibility largely lies in how we collect our taxes and what we use them for. The most efficient source of collecting taxes is at the point of transactions for services such as labor (and contract obligations in the case of 1099 employment). The following is a conversation about such considerations.

---

[1] Deuch, *Surviving the Coming Tax Disaster*, 29. The quotation from Chris Rock was taken as an excerpt from his HBO special "Bigger and Blacker," aired in 1999.

[2] Forbes, "PBS New Hour Interview of Steve Forbes," October 9, 1995.

[3] Szenberg, *Eminent Economists*, 201.

Workforce Benefits

One of the biggest breakdowns in our financial system today is how our workers are treated and taxed. The way the system is now makes it more difficult for workers to transfer their skills, going where they can earn the best wages and taking their hard-earned benefits with them. In light of how much the current pension and retirement systems have failed workers and how frequently the flight of jobs overseas has affected workers, it is no wonder that they are a little paranoid about the loss of jobs. Unions are no better. They represent an old strategy that is antiquated today; their outdated methods drive up costs while failing to benefit the productivity and profitability of the workers. This causes American workers to be less competitive in the global marketplace, to say nothing of addressing their desire for workforce security. The answer to this conundrum lies in true skill competition, which produces highly productive labor and allows funds to support a bundle of benefits that are portable and controlled by the workers themselves.

I come back to discussing the value of a set of taxes that are fixed and not capped at any point. They float with earning power, but as such, they allow the workers to control their own choices for how to best take care of their needs with items such as disability, retirement, unemployment, sickness, and general health care. Coming up with a simple cost allocation for such is a great approach. Then, no matter whether self-employed as 1099 workers or employed by corporation, the workers can purchase their benefits as part of a structured cost of using people to perform productive tasks for business enterprises. An example could be a simple 12 percent employment and/or personal productivity tax that is then given to each employee to purchase these items from private providers. The responsibility of the federal government at that point is to make sure that such insurance providers are legitimate and solvent, meeting stringent financial requirements to be in this type of business. The competitive nature of the system allows us the best choices no matter what our wage levels are.

When we look at our current out-of-whack and unfunded Social Security mess that was set up by our short-sighted government during the Great Depression, we can see at its base that it is flawed: it allows us, after about $100,000 per year, to opt out of paying any further. If members of the government really wanted to make the system work, they could just remove the cap and freeze the maximum payment distribution, calling it what it really is: an income redistribution tax for the aged. While I am not in favor of this approach, it is a current remedy for the short-term cash flow. What we have to realize is that if we did make that switch, the federal government would simply use the net proceeds for other matters and not as the funds were intended, so the problem would just continue. This is why I believe that adjusting to an economic security benefits plan that is a 100 percent private option, independent, and portable is essential for every American. It builds upon our capitalistic roots and our entrepreneurial spirit; it provides us with solvent and government-guaranteed choices for our coverage. Most importantly, it frees us from the shackles of oppressive government misspending and debt, allowing us to invest in the fruits of our own labor, not toiling away for the collective good as somebody else sees it. Nonetheless, we will have to make life more difficult for those currently on Social Security and other entitlements; this includes those so close to retirement (say ten years away) that the new system will not have enough time to remedy their situations. In these cases, we should place a 4 percent Social Security sunset tax on all income for a defined period of no more than ten years. We should uncap the tax so that it is paid on all income regardless of how much a person makes. This huge boon will pay down the Social Security deficit and allow the government time to prepare fiscally for the winding down of the remaining obligations.

Small Business Finance and Investment Tax Credits

The core of America's competitive stature is our ability to efficiently raise and loan out capital for new business needs. This cannot be jeopardized. Providing adequate capital for all levels of business in the most cost-effective manner is essential. The Small Business Administration; CDC Development Solutions; and venture, seed, community future funds, and angel capital networks need to be formalized and regulated to make sure that the flow of capital remains available. In addition, these networks need incentives to open local capital markets again for new and existing business investment; this will create jobs and begin to renew growth in our local economies. For example, banks must be required to invest a percentage of their holdings in small businesses, microenterprises, and large businesses on a model basis in order to receive federal insurance on their products. Investment tax credits for small businesses[1] should be used to create a secondary market for new investments into local job creation projects. Since tax code reform is highly unlikely as of the publication of this book, we need to work to create meaningful tax credits for high-income investors that will renew investment and growth in our nation. Since these credits can be sold and even traded in some cases, they would act as catalysts to get equity funds back into projects so that nervous banks might begin to lend to those with small businesses. This would supplant their current focus on disposing toxic assets and would manage their draw down on federal government bailouts for the sale of such toxic assets.

Allowing individual investors to get investment tax credits for making such investments would be a good basis to build upon so that we can put more capital to work for us. Again, if we understand and believe that we need an equitable income tax with a method to reduce it by investing in the toils and fruits of others (for the benefit of the economy, not to increase government programs), then this method would be highly effective. We must have the energy of capital to fuel business; to attract such energy we must coax it from folks who have more than they require for their own uses.

---

[1] See Novogradac, *New Markets Tax Credit Handbook*, 641.

Flat Taxes versus Progressive Taxes

Let's be clear on this issue: we cannot tax our way to a good business climate or overall wealth as a nation—in fact, taxes have just the opposite effect. The increase in taxes reduces jobs, inward investment, and economic freedoms. Only those who will benefit from increased taxes (those who have paid entitlements not received by the fruits of their own earning powers and those who benefit from the insider circle of power) are in favor of increased taxes. A progressive income tax is purely a means of redistributing wealth, and thus it is just a glorified name for socialism. In fact, I believe taxing us on our property is just another feudal tyranny held over from the concept of medieval monarchy. True flat taxes would be a capitalistic approach . . . all members pay their pro rata (proportional) share of the collective no matter what rank they are or income they have. This would also ensure that all members of our American society pay the cost of living here. My consternation is that those who favor progressive taxation say how unfair it is to those in the lower income levels. I do not believe that our country's founders meant that if someone is a US citizen then he or she is entitled to the same amount of opportunity with regard to his or her own efforts to attain a fair share.

In fact, I think that our country should be based on the belief that all are entitled to the same processes and infrastructure. This allows us to better ourselves; protect ourselves from financial harm; increase our education; invest our monies and fruits of our know-how; attain capital for our innovation and entrepreneurial efforts; invest in our health; provide for our own welfare; and prepare for economic hard times, which includes unemployment and/or disability. This lengthy list does not mention that we owe those who do not strive to improve themselves a disproportionate compensation just because they are citizens. It is this list of entitlements that causes me to rely on my belief that fair taxation should be largely based on the consumption of goods, services, and licensing for the use of assets such as transportation and other items that require licensure. This means that I am in favor of a more aggressive approach to corporate taxation than just taxing corporate profits and using a horde of deductions from which to minimize the taxes owed. I believe a flat corporate gross receipts tax would be more fair and useful to ensure that taxes are paid. I do not think such a tax should be excessive—perhaps 3 percent on the first $1 million, which would cover most of the self-employed, and then 5 percent of gross revenues above $1 million. By far the most concerning topic to me is not just how we tax ourselves (I oppose wealth taxes on capital gains), but how the government spends our monies gained from taxation, how the government can function within a balanced budget, and how the government can pay off our IOUs and deficit. This does not only apply to our national government but also our state and local governments.

Through their portion of taxes in the consumption of goods and services, local governments should pay for education, firefighters, and police along with other civic improvements and infrastructure. This local-based structure would then allow education vouchers to be introduced, along with a pay-for-results outlook, thus bringing reform to public education. The correct management of our tax system could solve so many of our other problems.

Income Taxes

Obviously I believe that income taxes in general are counterproductive, but since we have them, they should lead to better, not bigger, government. I am in favor of government playing its role as arbiter of the law, regulating financial issues, environmental oversight, and looking after defense and homeland security and trade policies, as well as energy policies and infrastructure at the national level. In addition to those tasks, the government should support a cutting-edge platform for health care provisions led by the private sector, educational attainment goals, disease control, and national transportation infrastructure and development through public-private partnerships (often called P3s; we will discuss these more later on). And the government of course needs to be the steward of our foreign policy and deal fairly with our states. Those are serious responsibilities.

All of the aforementioned tasks are best served by three basic forms of taxation. First, the only items I believe that income tax should be allocated to address are those related to the workforce, such as health care, retirement, unemployment, and disability.

Sales Taxes

The second basic form of taxation I am in favor of is a tax based on our consumption. Consumption is what drives our nation and accounts for 73 percent of our GDP. A flat national sales tax or value-added tax on goods would be healthy for our citizens. So, in effect, tax the real horsepower of our economy and leave the remainder of the would-be tax money in the hands of the people for their own use in the economy.

The same can be said for special entertainment and retail districts, including the performing and visual arts. I am not opposed to the use of special improvement district taxes or special sales tax additions to pay for such unique quality-of-life centers, but again the taxes should be paid by the users of these services and those who live within the service area.

User Taxes

The last form of taxation I support is what I refer to as user taxes; I would include sin taxes in this category as well. The best way to pay for major asset investments and special costs associated with our personal behaviors are user taxes and sin taxes. Such taxes fairly apportion the costs of the assets and the maintenance of such assets into the realm of those who use the assets on a personal-choice basis. This form of taxation would also include transaction taxes, which would be imposed on the banking, finance, and stock exchange industries to provide insurance against their own mismanagement. This way there would be no more federal bailouts.

Property Taxes

The use of property taxes is just another form of taxation that has been held onto since the era of feudalism—even before that, in times when monarchs, dictators, and emperors ruled. Paying for local and state costs is best completed through sales taxes, not property taxes. All parties pay for their services if they live within a service area, and if the costs are too great for the population, perhaps the government is out of balance with the actual needs of the people and—rightfully—should be downsized. Some items in this category would also fall into user taxes, such as the monies used to pay for sewers, utilities, and even public parks and recreational centers.

The three types of taxation I support are not just more-equitable taxes—they are far more efficient and would generate much larger revenue sources for communities. This type of taxation, regulated for the most part on a local level, holds citizens accountable to make sure that the use of such taxes is appropriate for their desired expectations. This type of community-based taxation gives the voters more accountability concerning whom they elect to represent their interests locally, in the county, in the state, and even nationally.

In the end, the cost of governance should be around 20 to 30 percent of our total revenue, no more; otherwise the taxes are simply burdensome and lead to too big of a government for the wrong reasons. Overtaxing also begets too many temptations to meddle with civil and economic rights. One of the best ways to tax ourselves, if we must tax income beyond the cost of the labor safety net, is a flat tax of 12 percent of gross revenues. Every man, woman, and corporation owes this off the top of their revenue. The remainder is paid for by use and consumption taxes. This simple but highly lucrative tax system would make us the envy of the world and force government to rightsize according to the scale of the budget. Now, when we add in our sales taxes and user taxes, our cost of governance is in the 20 percent range overall. Our goal should be to keep it at that level as a national strategy. Putting more cash into everyone's pockets would make us highly successful in the economic development of our nation in this century.

Questions and Solutions

The next questions we must ask are how we want these taxes spent and how we can make our government accountable to us for carrying those desires out. These questions lead to further questions. How much do we pay? What do we expect to happen with those taxes, and how will we know that government has done all it could? The answers to these questions provide the main structural changes that we need to build and then enforce with our politicians today. My overall premise is that no matter how much someone makes in this country, at no time should the income tax be higher than his or her own portion of take-home earnings; to do so creates a disincentive to earn more, since in a sense that individual is making the government wealthier, not himself or herself. Our overall goal for the total portion of our income that should be absorbed by all forms of taxes should not exceed 30 percent of our total income. Of course, the more money we make, the less the percentage will be, but at no time will it be less than 20 percent if we are working. Here are some examples of structural changes in both taxes and economic development catalyst projects that would increase our economic vitality; increase jobs; and create a better overall quality of life for all Americans, not just the wealthy (these are listed in bullet form so we can visually see the variety of ways we can change the system to work better for us):

- Reduce income tax to 12 percent across the board (no deductions). These benefits are only for the provision of unemployment, disability, health care, and retirement. They are to be individually directed by the worker, and every worker would get his or her own voucher in order to take advantage of government-approved sources. These benefits would be portable and thus would belong to the worker as they are earned. These deductions would also apply to 1099 employment or personal productivity paid by the parent company.

• Eliminate corporate taxes on profits. It is just a moneymaking game to apply massive and deceptive accounting practices to reduce the tax consequences. Close the loopholes.

• Create a gross receipts tax on corporate revenues (3 to 5 percent) on all corporate revenues as the only corporate tax on products and services. Such a tax is clean and easy to determine. Deductions would apply as noted in this list.

• Create a portable set of workforce benefits individually directed, as mentioned earlier, with a personal responsibility voucher system.

• Eliminate the death tax. It is unfair and is double taxation.

• Freeze the tax on dividends at 12 percent (and allow deductions) for energy investments, economic development tax credits, low-income housing tax credits, and other investment tax credits.

• Eliminate property taxes, and pay for services from local sales tax. The current payment for taxes on property we own is an infringement on personal property rights and, as I mentioned earlier in this chapter, it is a holdover from the old feudal and Roman systems. Our payment for local services should come from our consumption of things, thereby empowering our individual choices in our expenditures. Where we spend our money should be tied to our domiciles of residence to some degree. For example, if I live in one place and shop in another, the money from my expenditures would be shared by both places.

- Increase local sales taxes proportionately to cover the costs of school, fire, police, and other administrative services not covered by user fees.

- Create an additional national sales tax, which would pay for the overall cost of governance in general, including the military. We are a nation of consumers, and consumerism is the greatest piece of our GDP, so this is the best way to create reasonable revenue instead of taking our money without choice in the form of income taxes as we do today. I believe a national consumption tax of up to 9 percent would accomplish this purpose, exempting groceries, health care, energy (because we would create a separate 9 percent carbon tax), pharmaceuticals, and real estate purchases.

- Have a one-page tax form (corporate, household, and individual). This would reduce the cost of accounting for the government, reduce the resources needed to collect and submit taxes, and shift our priorities to more productive uses of human ingenuity. Tie this tax form to a taxpayer ID card that could be used in all our transactions. This allows us a way to keep track of our payments and our benefits; it would also be an easy way to manage personal-choice vouchers.

- Require mandatory coverage of benefits that meet federal requirements for the workforce social contract for insurers.

- Eliminate social security and national health care entitlements except in the rare cases of those unable to provide for themselves, such as children, the homeless, and the severely disabled.

- Expand the practice of rapid depreciation on critical assets to rebuild our economy more quickly. Giving corporations the incentive to write off strategic investments in new equipment, machinery, technologies, and facilities would spur new jobs and capital investment that would make us more competitive.

- Fully allow the write-off of expenditures on energy efficiency that meet certain high levels of energy savings, writing off up to 100 percent on dividends/capital gains, energy taxes, and gross receipts. This would be one of the few deductions individuals (dividend income) and corporations would take on their taxes as part of the tax credit secondary market.

- Tax carbon at the consumer level . . . and at the source. This will force both consumers and producers to take energy use issues seriously and incentivize them to make investments to reduce their exposure to such costs. Our government, using a 9 percent carbon tax, would have the funds to create vouchers for rebates on energy-efficiency purchases by consumers. An example: anyone purchasing an automobile that exceeds the Corporate Average Fuel Economy (CAFE) standards set by the US government by more than 20 percent would receive a rebate of, say, 10 percent on the purchase. This rate would be progressively raised to 100 percent above US CAFE standards, so that the consumer would receive a 50 percent reduction in price, and so forth. This would not only spur consumers to purchase the most energy-efficient vehicles but would also encourage manufacturers to produce these vehicles, which would give us a wide variety of choices. The same system can be used for home and building heating, cooling, and lighting. Early adopters in the first year should be given a 10 percent bonus to spur popularity and move the energy-efficiency peg faster than expected. The key to making this system work is that these carbon tax funds need to be used only for these purposes, not other purposes. It's our money, so put it back in the hands of the people as long as we make good decisions about our use of energy.

• Fine companies with highly polluted production, products made with highly polluted production offshore, and energy-inefficient systems for carbon emissions. This creates a first-among-equals status for investments made domestically so they are not undermined by third-party imports that do not adhere to the same standards.

• Tax the consumption of water . . . at the source. Water is a finite resource and must be managed so that we do not run out of clean water. This tax will hurt, but it is for our own good.

• Legalize but regulate gaming, prostitution, drugs, and alcohol. Simply put, the regulation of licensure would be just as effective as the criminalization of such conduct.

• Tax the sin categories at the consumer level. Tax these for the cost of mitigation and license fees for oversight. This would single-handedly reduce crime and police costs.

• Tax financial transactions for oversight regulation, and disallow consulting within the agencies that provide the oversight. We have to tax the financial system to get unbiased oversight and then lock out the potential for conflict of interests. We do this by restricting the agencies providing the oversight from consulting with these same financial companies.

- Invest in a robust mobile transportation infrastructure for highways, intermodal transport, high-speed rail, airport security, and air control. Increase port security, and require inspection of 100 percent of all imports. Pass such costs on to the importing party and the traveler. We have to have zero tolerance for hazardous and dangerous materials being illegally shipped into the United States.

- Require mandatory competition and provisions for bundled workforce benefit plans for health, disability, unemployment, and retirement insurance. This would come as a requirement for being in the money management business within the insurance industry.

- Create a secondary market for tax credits created for economic development projects that can be used to reduce dividend taxes. Monetize the attraction of capital for economic development through the sale of tax credits, and give such investors a deduction on their federal dividend taxes. This creates much-needed public capital for investment into economic development projects. Such projects should have a matching one-to-one requirement from a suitable private sector partner and a repayment provision for the public sector funds.

- Create a national education voucher system as part of the sales tax that a person pays to the state, local, and federal governments. This voucher can be used only on education throughout the lifetime of the citizen. Require that all schools accept these vouchers as a form of payment for annual tuition. Give special bonuses from the voucher system to high-value educational and technical training in the science, medicine, math, and technology fields of study.

- Pay the full-time military like the professionals that they are, and make their retirement income-tax free, with the exception of their health care costs if they opt for health care.

- Stop all farm subsidies, and provide government loans to small, family farmers based on clean crop production, sensible crop rotation, and the growth and maintenance of a healthy crop and herd yield.

- Increase the gas-guzzler tax on inefficient, low-fuel economy vehicles, airplanes, ships, heavy equipment, tractors, and trains. Every fossil fuel–based vehicle can be improved in energy efficiency, and, as such, strict standards for improvement must be implemented.

These steps have been carefully constructed to increase portable and disposable income while allowing for reinvestment in critically needed areas, areas of cutting-edge economic benefits. These steps are troublesome to those who want to continue poor practices but rewarding to those who want to work and invest in new, energy-efficient technologies.

These steps require a structural change in how we pay for benefits like health care, retirement, disability, unemployment, and other values that Americans believe are part of the pursuit of health, happiness, and prosperity.

These investments would position America to first and foremost have a capitalism-based response to the social contract we have with our citizens; secondarily, it would provide a fiscally prudent and aggressive approach to reinvigorating our national economy to compete globally. As you can see, my taxing system is based on personal choices that allow us as individuals to appropriately address our tax burden as we consume things, which increases the revenue stream for the government but gives us as consumers a role to play in minimizing our tax burden responsibly.

The Point

At some point we have to address our underlying inability to manage cash flow as a nation. We must stem the snowball effect within government programs or else we will have to sacrifice more of our individual freedoms and economic opportunities. Additionally, looking away while more government freebies are handed out right under our noses will hinder us from becoming wealthy and prosperous individually. If we provide welfare for the less fortunate with the toils of those who are more productive, better educated, or more successful at innovation and managing risks, it will simply cause this latter portion of society to seek better climes outside the US that cater to their desire for less government but more economic prosperity.

The common basis that seems to cause us to take no action is the myth that by making these changes we as a society would somehow be worse off than letting the current scenario run its course. Nothing could be further from the truth . . . protecting our liberties and rightsizing our government costs and our individual economic freedoms will be a profound benefit to all of us, though perhaps not for a couple of years. These changes may be inconvenient in the short term, but they are prudent and highly profitable in the long term. They need not be done in draconian style or without concern for individual hardships, but the emphasis of government intervention needs to be in favor of the citizens, not the corporations.

By sending this message, we encourage business oversight and changes to business practices that are not, in the end, profitable to the economy. Changing the way our government handles taxes, in the ways I have suggested, will stabilize our economy and bring economic peace to our citizens, restoring their prosperity. Isn't that the purpose of government?

Here are some questions that pertain to taxes and our general financial state:

1. Generally speaking, what does the public think should be done about the choices their leaders make concerning taxes, insurance, retirement, and so forth?

We want to know that our interests are being considered and that our interests are being weighted more heavily than the government's desire to profit from the taxes we pay. We are tired of our bought-and-paid-for Congress selling us out and constantly misleading us concerning what is real and what is being postured to manipulate public opinion for the benefit of our rock-star, power-hungry politicians who are living completely out of touch with us, their constituents. This means that those who work for government and are elected to represent us in government must live as we do, with the same benefits and costs. With regard to those who serve on an elected basis, the service should be a sacrifice, not a manner whereby they can gain wealth, power, and privilege.

2. What might the tax solutions offer as possible additional windfalls?

Creating the world's best tax and business climate for investors would reinvigorate the American economy and rebuild economic opportunities for all income levels in our nation. Our goal would be nothing less than to be the best in the world within all categories, including quality of life, life expectancy, energy efficiency, income, return on investment and banking, and workforce productivity. With a secure business, social, and political climate open to all those who will live by our rule of law, we will have a republic based on the best interests of our citizens as well as humanity.

3. What should be the driving economic philosophy as we restructure the tax system?

For this answer we turn to a quotation from Churchill:

> *We contend that for a nation to try to tax itself into prosperity is like a man standing in a bucket and trying to lift himself up by the handle.*
> *—Winston Churchill*[1]

---

[1] Churchill, *Winston S. Churchill*, 95.

Enjoying the Fruit of Our Labors

We have to enable productive Americans to keep more of their pay. The cost of government should not exceed 20–30 percent of their total income. If government cannot pay for our expectations from these revenues, then we must cut down on services until the ideals and economic realities are in balance. Keeping the vast majority of the fruit of our labors is essential to a successful, industrious America. Furthermore, giving our workforce self-directed benefits for all their needs concerning vacations, health care, disability provisions, unemployment help, education, and retirement is essential to consumer confidence and overall quality of life. Creating a distinctively American public-private collaboration on this with a market-driven yet affordable set of programs would re-create wealth in America for all income brackets. Programs depending on income taxes would be based on a flat tax so that all will pay their fair share and reap the rewards without restriction of their labor according to the same level of their contributions. We owe nobody a free ride. Our retirement and benefits will be based upon the amount of income that we have been productively able to create by our own works.

In the next chapter we will discuss, among other things, how the changes suggested in this chapter, along with other restructuring needs in the banking and insurance sectors, will bolster our economy and allow capitalism to remain the primary means of growth in America.

CHAPTER FOUR

Fiscal Responsibility: Restructuring Banking Regulations, Mortgage Practices, and Insurance Policies

It is the highest impertinence and presumption, therefore, in kings and ministers to pretend to watch over the economy of private people, and to restrain . . . They are themselves always, and without any exception, the greatest spendthrifts in the society.

—Adam Smith[1]

Since the spring of 2008, evidence of the fragility and interdependence of the world's economies has been revealed in the form of the ugly, deep, and painful fiscal wounds suffered by individuals and countries everywhere. As economies contracted inwardly and then reeled from massive blows, financial triage became the default strategy among governments of the world. With blazing headlines proclaiming the ever more urgent and apparently desperate CPR measures undertaken, we were informed that the life-saving, ongoing emergency cash injections were the only possible follow-up treatment to the economic crisis. This near-universal socioeconomic collapse has hopefully driven home a message: the failure of not addressing banking regulations, taxation, retirement, and health care issues will rain more blows on our heads if the current business-as-usual attitude continues to prevail. Many fail to

---

[1] As quoted in Crapo, "Budget & Fiscal Responsibility," September 16, 2011.

recognize just how close to the edge of insolvency our country is today. This chapter addresses how governments, both federal and local, can be more fiscally responsible by not exceeding their budgets and handling banking regulations, mortgages, and insurance differently.

Becoming Fiscally Mature

Our future depends—as a nation and as individuals—on learning to live within our means. Preparing for the future will also require that we take a new approach as to how we provide a social contract for our workforce that is fair and equitable to them, while at the same time being fiscally responsible as we do business as a nation. Rest assured, however, that living within our means does not, by definition, in any way doom us to a bleak and barren landscape. The media continues to build bleak pictures of either/or scenarios that do not provide for a uniquely American approach to creating hybrid solutions to our broken-down government vehicle.

The size and cost of government and the lack of oversight of government spending are all impediments to living within our means. Our government is a runaway train with regard to record deficit levels, trade imbalances, and public indebtedness. Simply put, we can't afford what the government believes it should be doing for us, and even if it does provide a service, its efficiency and ability to meet our expectations can be improved. This isn't totally the government's fault. We spend more as a nation, as consumers and as households, than we can afford; we have no realistic means to pay for our desired quality of life. Even more frustrating is the media trying to convince us that our lifestyle is as it should be; we are the greatest and therefore we deserve the greatest. Most of us are now beginning to see how invalid these media-driven, sensationalist tactics are. Thus we must adopt a humbler attitude when it comes to our personal finances. When we are living within our means at home, we will see how important it is to live within our means politically and economically. Only then will we stop paying the government exorbitant amounts of money for programs with subpar results.

Reflections on the Perfect Storm of 2008

In my opinion, you are either a capitalist or you are not. There is no capitalism-socialism hybrid, and there is certainly no capitalism-communism hybrid. We are a republic founded on capitalism, which is the driver of economic opportunity. Capitalism is also linked to individual civil liberties and inalienable rights granted to us by our laws. If this makes sense to you, then the toxic asset bailout and American Recovery Act of 2008–2009 should turn your stomach. I want to emphasize these points regarding what happened: we bailed out the wrong citizens; we owed badly run corporations no relief whatsoever. We should have given our citizens a realistic game plan to overcome the economic pain they experienced because they were duped by poorly managed corporations. Thus, beefing up our guarantee on deposits is fine, but bailing out toxic mortgages at the expense of consumers was wrong, at least in the way it was handled.

If, for instance, GM is destined to fail for its legacy costs, poor production of cars, and lack of leadership in hybrid energy platform technologies, then let it fail. Yes, people will be out of work, but the assets worth salvaging will be purchased by stronger automobile makers and people will be rehired. Those who lost their pensions already had a federal guarantee in place for up to 60 percent of their pensions, so to handle that we should have made those benefits tax-free. Then we would have been almost back to where we were in the first place, and the outcome would have been much more capitalistic. We cannot subsidize poor performance and dying concepts or products. Would I have been in favor of lending GM money to improve its equipment and technology to produce hybrid cars, trucks, and vehicles? Sure, that makes more sense. Simultaneously I would have halved the pension costs to current employees by making GM convert the pensions to 401(k) accounts over a period, and I would have made those funds tax-free by using current Roth 401(k) accounts. Then we would have had a solution that would have helped GM and improved the plight of the employees at the same time.

Financial Markets and Banking

The oversight of the financial and regulatory agencies involved in our central banking, investment products, stock markets, bond sales, and other forms of commercial paper and commerce transactions were at the heart of the global meltdown. This failing deeply displaced the age-old belief that the markets know what is best and will always act in methods that dictate fair practices and equitable solutions. Those beliefs have been broken into a million pieces on the rocks of reality. The truth is that regulatory oversight, done by biased agencies that derive their revenues from the companies they watch, is simply a bad idea. The regulatory oversight and enforcement of rules within the financial, environmental, and energy industries needs to be autonomous and paid for on a fee basis. We see this conflict of interest over and over again as those who are being observed, monitored, and regulated are getting paid for advice from those doing the oversight. This huge conflict of interest is not in *our* best interest.

The best method to provide funds for regulation and oversight is to require that all transactions carry a regulatory oversight tax to pay for unbiased, professional government staffers. These staffers would provide clear direction on meeting the expectations for proper conduct and transparency regarding financial transactions, as well as risk disclosure and fair communication on the valuation of products. The decoupling of the regulatory agencies from conducting their own consulting on financial matters would begin to bolster transparency and confidence in the financial markets once again.

With regard to the mortgages of American taxpayers and the banking fiasco, I would have recommended the following. These suggestions can still be put into effect so that this problem doesn't happen again.

First, any bank executives taking funds for TARP (Toxic Asset Relief Program) have to conduct themselves in the following manner:

- Mortgages must be refinanced to the current market value, and all funds that are given to the lender for the difference between the value and the loan amount must be repaid to the government at a cost of 1 percent over 20 years or written off at the discretion of the lender.

- If the current homeowner cannot afford to refinance the mortgage, then the bank can foreclose and sell the property for the same amount and finance the gap in the same manner as in the first suggestion.

- Small business loans can be refinanced for 15 additional years, and the defaults can be covered under the original Small Business Association guidelines for loss of repayment, which would be lowered to approximately 70 percent of the unpaid balance. Use of these funds requires repayment on the same basis as the first suggestion.

- Mortgages can be written off under bankruptcies and according to the level of the current valuation of the home. The difference can be loaned to the banks under the same terms as in the first suggestion.

- Banks can invest in projects that create jobs and new equipment with existing companies as a priority. These new loans should have a 100 percent guarantee for the first five years and then the same 70 percent for the remainder of the loan balance, under the same terms as in the first suggestion.

- Any bank or insurance company taking loans from the government may not pay any executive bonuses or increase salaries more than the cost of living annually until the government funds have been repaid.

The difference in this approach is that the consumer confidence is bolstered; thus spending, which drives most of the local and state taxes, would be more stable. By the government showing its capacity to reasonably rescue the consumer, people would have more confidence in this recovery and the government. In contrast, what happened exacerbated the people's belief that the government is only interested in saving corporations. By using the methodology I have set forth, well-managed corporations would survive and thrive and those not capable of meeting such conditions would die . . . in capitalism this is how we get economic progress. The inevitable food chain of economic chaos is a cleansing force in true capitalism. This would also have given the government more incentive to fix the social benefits and costs of entitlements as yet another fundamental structural change to make our workers more competitive. If we had used this approach, we would already be well on our way to mending our economic structural deficiencies today.

Insurance Reform

Just as banks have the capacity to help people survive financially by helping them save and earn interest and by loaning money, good insurance practices can also help us ride rocky financial waves. Designing a system of reasonable costs for health and other insurance products is a major matter, but the biggest issue facing America today is getting more than 60 million uninsured working Americans covered for major medical coverage. Cost is secondary if a person has no medical coverage for treatment and prescriptions. The biggest problem is that with 25 percent of our population obese, members of the working population cannot qualify for coverage if displaced or unemployed, especially if they are forced to work as independent contractors, as many of us are now required to do in the globalized, outsourced work environment. Rather than mandate government-sponsored health care, we should require that the insurance companies cannot decline applicants for medical coverage and that coverage cannot exceed a certain percentage of a worker's income, such as 6 percent. This same percentage should then be part of the employment tax system, deducted from all work-related transactions, and also be portable to the employee or independent contractor. This arrangement would then create some creativity within the insurance industry, encouraging insurance companies to find out how to make the numbers work to their advantage, spurring competition and thus choice in the markets. In addition to this requirement, we would add three new insurance products for the unemployment, disability, and retirement categories. Each would be not only separable by the employee but also capable of being bundled if so desired. As a result, the private sector would have an entirely new set of products with huge revenue potential; as part of the reward for coverage, we would give them complete participation. In addition, we would have shifted the vast majority of the entitlement costs over to the individual with free choice.

So then the tax deductions of the employee or independent contractor would be scaled to include the three additional requirements and managed by the private sector with oversight from the US government. The surety of the products by the US government would guarantee just as in banking deposit insurance. Of course, the guarantee comes at the price of a transaction tax to the insurance company. Then, with a sliding scale from 5 to 10 percent on retirement; an additional deduction of about 3 percent for disability and unemployment/retraining; and another small percentage for health care, holidays, and sick time, such as 4 or 5 percent, all workers have paid their individual costs on par with their actual incomes. This is capitalism; it does not try to make someone who has made $20,000 his or her entire life capable of retiring at the same level as someone who has made much more; consequently, those in lower tax brackets will have to be prudent and realistic in their expectations. In the same vein, those who have saved the maximum amount of money possible and have made good use of their wages will retire quite comfortably. So if an employee voluntarily maxes out the brackets, he or she can create a voucher for more than the 12 percent minimum and max out his or her benefits to the ceiling of 10 percent retirement, 3 percent disability and unemployment, and 5 percent health care, thus having a new personal productivity tax of 18 percent. When we add in the long-term health tax of 3 percent mentioned in the next paragraph, it makes the combined personal productivity tax 21 percent.

There should be an additional tax for long-term health care on the wages earned, such as an additional 3 percent that is saved for post-retirement health care coverage. By creating this voucher system, we would generate market competition and long-term economic stability. Then our wages would be taxed at about 15 percent of our earnings, and the benefits would be portable. The competition for different products would keep the industries competitively priced and affordable. Placing caps on fees and costs related to income will spur proper management of insurance risks and penalize speculative investing by the core insurance companies. Now, with these costs and our national, state, and local sales taxes, people would be paying the actual costs of government and their expectations. Even better, this very capitalistic-based philosophy would be uniquely American.

Reforming both our bank and insurance practices is a cornerstone of our future economic stability, especially when trying to restore consumer confidence. The final chapter in Section One is on education, which also needs to be addressed at the national level. Making changes in our education policies will result in our citizens being taught to not just be investors but to be intelligent investors who can use their knowledge of both domestic and foreign matters to be successful in the capitalistic climate we are trying to foster.

CHAPTER FIVE

Education

We learned that successful schools weren't the product of tens of billions in federal spending. They were characterized by parental involvement, local control, an emphasis on basic academics, and dollars actually spent in the classroom.

—*Peter Hoekstra[1]*

Unemployment is aggressively culling our best and brightest in the workforce today. Our stalled economic recovery and joblessness grow at an anemic rate that makes us look sickly. That America is still a superpower is now in question. Worse yet, when we track the total number of unemployed people—currently about 10 percent of our population—when we consider how many of those people have ceased being eligible for unemployment benefits, and when we add to that all those who are now underemployed because of this economic transition, the total amounts to nearly 20 percent of our workforce . . . and that number is growing. If this does not shock and concern us, then we lead a cushiony life and need to acquire some empathy. This reality is not only here today; it is here to stay for a long while. Digging ourselves out of this pit is not going to be easy, cheap, or without pain.

Continuing Education for Our Workforce

When we face such huge economic hurdles as we (and the rest of the world) do today, it is essential to have a realistic plan to turn the game

---

[1] Hoekstra, "Bringing Education Reform Back Home," March 8, 2011.

around, change the stakes, and ensure a different outcome than the hand being dealt to us today (I live in Las Vegas, Nevada, so of course I had to use a poker analogy at some point in this book).

We have been hearing for years from the business community here in the United States that the quality of workforce applicants is significantly subpar. More to the point, the attitude of many of our workforce participants is that they do not have the time or the inclination for continuing education and thus workforce skills improvement. Furthermore, the onslaught of technology advancements has outpaced the acumen of the aging workforce such that we now have a state of almost complete functional illiteracy with regard to employers' needs. The advent of new programs such as the ACT WorkKeys program—which tracks workforce requirements, identifies steps to grade proficiency, and brings needed remediation to the workforce—has been met with mostly dysfunctional governmental participation. We have standardized tests for those leaving schools but nothing that measures their preparedness for the workforce.

Why, we may ask, do we need to also test workforce readiness? Many people, especially those in the business community, point out that members of the public educational system do not desire further scrutiny; they are tired of being grilled on how proficient they are in achieving government-specified outcomes. Less arbitrary accountability, more time to teach, they say. These educators perpetually complain that they aren't paid enough now, and adding extra responsibilities to their underpaid roles without additional compensation would only make things worse. Members of the business community, in turn, argue that lousy teaching is costing businesses a fortune because their workers lack basic educational skills like reading, writing, and math. Teachers must teach these skills just to make students marginally qualified to learn actual job skills needed today, business people say. How can a worker write a proposal for a client if the worker can't put together a functional sentence? How can architects put together massive structures if they mess up on simple math equations (not to mention the complex ones)? Additional costs to train workers, they argue, make it nearly impossible to pay a wage that meets the expectation of the workforce. All this is happening, of course, in a time when economic chaos has created an unfavorable climate for consumer confidence, which further erodes the economy. Thus, the failure of our governmental programs to help the now-unemployed with the necessary skills training and provide them with an economic safety net is amplified. We can witness this now as we watch the daily news.

A well-trained, highly competitive workforce, ready to successfully confront and cope with the fast-moving challenges of the twenty-first century, can evolve and thrive only if we have a modern, comprehensive education system to support the workforce. In practical terms, this means we need not only accountability and transparency on the part of decision-makers who supervise primary through postgraduate education, but it also means these decision-makers need more realistic, adaptive, and flexible attitudes in accepting rapid changes.

When we have to solve modern-day problems, we have to examine solutions that have not been tried as well as solutions that have worked in the past. Combining modern-day examples with historical examples can and must create new hybrids able to generate a paradigm shift away from what is not working today.

Military Training

I have given great thought to this part of my platform (which I know is radical to many) on how to improve the plight of our nation and restore power and pride to our citizens. I have looked at the public models of citizen soldiers, and I doubt in these days and times that we need a standing army of 100 million to 150 million folks. Such wars are just not very likely in the future. I am reminded of the concept of mandatory service that the Swiss use in their armed forces; this is a great model to build upon for our own uses.

Adapting this model also means that I believe that military reserve training for our youth (ages eighteen to twenty-four) is a positive requirement. It would instill the ability to fight if called upon. After that six-year period of training, we could give rewards for military service when citizens sign up on a part-time basis for twenty years, like they do in Switzerland. Participation would be an honor, not a requirement. Participants would be paid a market-based per diem for their service, and employers would be required to pay for any time of service at 70 percent of the normal wage level. Every person would be required to give thirty days per year of active service. All members of this force would participate in a physical fitness regime or lose their pay status until they achieved physical fitness proficiency. This system would go a long way in battling the bulge in America's waistline. We all know that child obesity is exponentially on the rise. We have to stress health, wise eating choices, and proper exercise during youth. We must make youth accountable for achieving goals like they do in school for academics.

If we compare this requirement to the GI Bill of Rights, which gives educational stipends to soldiers, this mandatory military service requirement would be a great resource for our citizens to earn money for their continuing education while learning a civic skill. Taking the idea further, if the reserve training is beneficial for those who are eighteen to twenty-four years old, why not allow the training to be open to those up to age 50? We would have the brightest population on the planet (not to mention a fantastic reserve force), and that would be a good thing.

Paying for Education

Along with the changes that Richard Florida and I are suggesting (See Chapter 3) is the need to democratize the cost of education through the creation of a national education fund. This fund would be accessible to every member of our society who incurs, or will incur, education expenses throughout his or her lifetime. I am not a proponent of just giving this fund money away willy-nilly. I am in favor of a voucher program based on a national consumption tax. This tax would dedicate a portion of an individual's income to education. I believe 1 percent is fair; employers and 1099 contractors should pay this money into a fund similar to a 401(k), which would benefit individuals' personal accounts.

When an individual entered college or a trade school, his or her fund would contain next to nothing, but over the individual's lifetime of employment, the fund would be repaid and hopefully would continue to be used to improve skills and thus wage or productivity earnings. In addition, there should be a local 1 percent sales tax apportioned and tracked per household that could be used for local K–12 education. It could be used for primary education at the local level (city and county), and it could be used for workforce training at the state level; at the federal level, a certain percentage of the tax could be used for college-level courses. This 2 percent solution could provide a market-based fix to overhaul education and make the outcomes much better across the board. Education would no longer be based on property taxes, thus freeing up choice in the ranks of the common folks, just like the elite wealthy in many cases.

When we look at what defined the greatest stage of growth in our country, it was the decision to implement a national public education system. This system allowed us to create a much better educated pool of voters, workers, and entrepreneurs. Almost everyone recognizes that America was formed upon the building block of the finest educational system in the world historically. Even today our university degree programs are still the most sought-after in the world. Our foreign exchange student population is an economic windfall for our economy. However, we have failed to keep our educational system in tune with reality. We are letting it fall into disrepair, which causes the private school systems to become more elitist (the rich buy their education à la carte) and yet less capable of producing the oil of the American economy: a knowledgeable workforce. The costs to go to a private school are wildly out of pace for the average American, and the cost of even a public university education and graduate-level education can put students in debt for almost their entire working careers or at least two-thirds of their careers.

The increasingly exorbitant and prohibitive cost of higher education is not merely a national security issue—which it most assuredly is—but is also a national disgrace. How many scientists, engineers, and doctors, for example, have been lost to us because of sky-high, un-affordable price tags? People should not be sentenced to a lifetime of debt in order to receive an advanced education. Throw open the doors to education, and keep them wide open—bountiful rewards will more than justify the means.

When we reflect upon the requirements for a successful economy, we will no doubt include a superior and functional educational system for everyone.

Strategies to Improve Education in America

So how do we go about making structural changes to our education policies that will rebuild the American Dream and create a workable solution for the dysfunctional educational system of today? First, we outline the core expectations of both political parties and agree on an achievable plan of action with measurable outcomes and performance-based accountability and success fees. Education is just like business; in fact, it is a business and should be one of our core business endeavors. Making it better will only make it more sought-after and more copycat-ted by our competitors. This plan of attack meets the theme of this book, because I believe our solutions must be uniquely American and reflect a currency of reality that will cause economic abundance for our citizens in the global marketplace.

Let's examine a possible set of strategies that is primarily effective and secondarily done within a cost-effective framework. Yes, these strategies require that all sides make huge functional changes, and yes, these strategies will require abandoning our parochial attitudes and sunk-cost legacies that America can no longer afford in the present; otherwise we will be in a perpetual state of decline as far as the eye can see into the future.

Accountability

We must create better testing guidelines and requirements annually; at the very minimum, both private and public schools should include

SAT/ACT/WorkKeys examinations. These measurements are essential to building a solid core of both university-bound and technical school–bound students. These examinations need to be standardized on a national scale and not subject to local modifications to game the system. Any students who do not pass the examinations should be given a remedial course until they are proficient. Local, state, and federal governments must penalize schools with failure rates exceeding 3 percent and average proficiency rates below 80 percent. Once this foundation is in place, we can then evaluate the management of resources, teacher talent and proficiency, and the administration of educational attainment standards.

Performance-Based Pay

There is no doubt that we get what we pay for, and in the case of education it cuts both ways. We get lousy results on a national and international scale as compared to other educational systems around the world. According to the Organisation for Economic Co-operation and Development (OECD),[1] the United States currently ranks about twentieth in overall educational outcomes but spends the second highest amount per capita in the world, at about $11,200 per pupil, just behind Switzerland. Thus the argument of getting good results for our bucks is horribly incorrect. While not a simple solution, we must have a harmonious agreement in which we will indeed pay for excellent results.[2]

To introduce performance-based pay to the educational system, I suggest teacher merit and performance evaluations by parents, students, and peers. By using four categories ("Exceeds Expectations," "Meets Expectations," "Marginal Performance," "Below Expected Performance") and averaging the evaluation results, the teacher would receive a weighted score that would be reflected in his or her paycheck. Teacher

---

[1] OECD, *Establishing a Framework for Evaluation and Teacher Incentives*, 94.

[2] See Gratz, "The Peril and Promise of Performance Pay: Making Education Compensation Work," 232.

pay should also be linked directly to national free market valuations, with cost-of-living adjustments based on the local economic costs. Pay should be attractive enough to entice the highest-quality college graduates in science, technology, English, and math (STEM) sectors. Merit pay for teachers who exceed expectations should be linked to their students' test scores; that is, merit pay would be granted based on how many percentage points their students achieve above the national average. Teachers who received an average ranking of "Marginal Performance" or "Below Expected Performance" would not be given merit pay. Teachers who received an average of "Meets Expectations" would receive a bonus of 50 percent of the percentage of students whose scores met expectations, and teachers who received an average of "Exceed Expectations" would receive a bonus of 125 percent of the percentage of students whose scores met expectations. An example would be if 80 percent of the students meet expectations, the teacher would receive a bonus of 50 percent of the student percentage, equaling a 40 percent bonus above his or her base pay scale. Of course, the base pay would be adjusted to reflect this performance metric, but even so, this new performance-based system would increase good teachers' salaries by more than 20 percent in most cases, and these teachers would deserve it. If, for example, 20 percent of the teacher's students rate that they have exceeded expectations in their per capita scores, then the teacher would be eligible for an additional 60 percent bonus. All these bonuses would be divided into a blended average, so the teacher in the example would receive an overall performance bonus of 50 percent. Of course, the other end of the spectrum cuts against them. If 20 percent of students are failing to meet expectations, it carries a double whammy penalty of 100 percent of the teacher's awarded performance bonus. Since 100 percent of 20 percent is 20 percent, the teacher would see his or her 50 percent bonus reduced by 20 percent due to the rate of failure within the classroom. The same would be true of administrators. The administrators would be allowed to receive a similar merit pay based on the cumulative scores of their teachers versus the expectations set by the US government.

Success Fees

Entrepreneurial attainment and economic growth are directly linked. This link can in turn be linked to new patents, business start-ups, and success in new investments. While we reward sports athletes with mega contracts, there is no commensurate reward system for the next great scientific discoveries. You can blame Hollywood, the media, human nature, or whatever you would like. The straightforward response is that scientific discovery can be fun, glitzy, and gratifying if portrayed correctly and rewarded on a similar scale as in our current athletic system. Those who obtain a patent should receive a reward stipend generated by the fees for application.

Breakthrough patents in areas of critical needs, such as health care, bioengineering, pharmaceuticals, genetics, crime solving, computer and software technologies, robotics, advanced manufacturing, renewable energies, clean energy and smart grid technologies, advanced manufacturing and power plants, building efficiency, and designs for affordable conservation of resources, should receive massive patent award recognition, again paid from a portion of the patent fees and the national sales tax I have suggested.[1] Make our scientists our new rock stars so that brains become a ticket to wealth just like athletic sports have done to inspire so many in the ranks of humanity.

And speaking of sports, some schools are spending so much on their athletes and athletic equipment that the students' education is being thrown off balance. All sporting events at schools should require an economic methodology to pay for the cost of the facilities and teams, such as a ticket tax, a transportation tax, and participation fees. We should not subsidize athletes. Athletes who do not maintain a C average in school should not be allowed to participate. Grade proficiency should equal participation approval.

---

[1] See also Bok, *Universities and the Future of America*, 28.

Measurable Outcomes

The outcomes we need to establish are largely based on world comparisons. Our goal is to become number one in educational outcomes such as the following:

- STEM scores,
- College and university acceptance,
- K–12 graduation rate (and in full compliance with testing requirements),
- Effectiveness of educational services as they relate to costs per pupil (i.e., are we getting what we are paying for).

More Money Doesn't Equal Success

Everything in the current arguments always relates back to the availability of money. But it still does not account for our poor scoring versus the rest of the world, since we still have high costs in education. So more money does not, in the current situation, guarantee a better success rate. Structural changes that may appear to cost more might in fact be the needed fuel to create better outcomes, even though naysayers might claim the changes would destroy the public school system. Examples of how to rectify this are to create a national, state, and local sales tax voucher system that produces educational vouchers that which can be used to pay the schools we choose. Although these vouchers might not cover the costs for attending the best private schools and parents may need to pay the difference, individuals and households must make such investment decisions. In addition, since teachers would be paid a portion of their pay based upon their students' scores, the same system would apply to those who work in private schools. Then parents and nonparents would not be subsidizing the system by way of property taxes. Since some people would still pay sales tax and not use their vouchers for lifetime education, college/university tuition, technical school tuition, or K–12 tuition, there would be enough excess money to provide for a better and more accountable pay system.

Paying for STEM Needs

Rewarding students who score well in the STEM areas with additional voucher tuition (paid for from our excess sales tax) should be a priority. Such rewards should be commensurate with the additional costs for an advanced education at America's best colleges and universities. These excellent students would receive vouchers that would be 200 percent of their face value; the vouchers would remain so as long as the students' grade point average (GPA) were 3.0 or above. Students who achieved a 3.5 GPA would receive an additional 50 percent, and for students who maintained a 3.75 GPA or better in the STEM areas we would pay an additional 100 percent on their educational vouchers. Doing this would ensure a great education and access to the best universities for all students. In addition, if college students signed a four-year teaching contract with the K–12 public education system, they would receive a four-year 50 percent voucher for school expenses related to their time in college; they could turn in this voucher after college to help them adjust to the working world. Furthermore, if a student received, say, a $50,000 educational voucher for school, then the remainder of his or her educational costs would be paid off from future earnings from the national sales tax voucher for continuing education.

Those who oppose this strategy might argue that students who have little or no sales tax cannot pay for the cost of education without paying into the national sales tax system. Good point; it is a future-based system. What that means is that a portion of a national sales tax would be allocated to our educational costs and continuous education concepts. Each member of a family would have a national sales tax ID. The expenditures of each person and household can be used (up to 75 percent of the allocation) on a voucher for educational purposes. This would allow folks to save and pay for college or technical school during their lifetimes. This voucher system would also be much more efficient than student loans, which leave us in debt forever. Also, immediate family members could apply their own allocations to help pay for their children or their grandchildren. I would advocate that the remaining allocation (perhaps 25 percent) be used on each individual's need for improvement and to keep his or her skills current or add new skill sets during his or her life. After a person retired, he or she could pass on the remaining allocation to their children or grandchildren. It would be a new type of inheritance, in a sense.

This voucher system would work similarly for local K–12 education, since a part of the local sales tax could be allocated to pay for the school of choice for one's children, whether it be a private or public school. Of course, the allocation may not be enough to pay the full cost of a private education and there may still be gaps, but it would make for a more competitive system. The same type of process would only apply to local sales tax where a person lives, so grandparents, unless they live in the same city, would not be able to transfer their allocation to their grandchildren. This would make education more accountable and give us better discretion over where our kids go to school and the quality of education we afford them.

Since there would be many who would not use the system at all, there would be plenty of excess money for rewards for exemplary performance. The point is that the system should be based on the market, sensitive to performance, and incentivized toward results. Within one generation, this would lift the United States to the position of having the world's predominant educational system. It would transform our workplaces and protect our civil liberties with regard to taxing personal property, which taxation I oppose. The money spent on education would therefore be helping us, not hurting us. Again, if we combined the sales tax with productivity taxes paid by the employer (1 percent), we would have a hybrid solution with ample funding to meet the objective. Since the employers benefit from the workers being better prepared, they should carry part of the yoke for making this drastic improvement in their workforce needs.

Retraining the Workforce

Our educational problem today is not going to be solved by our students entering the workforce but by addressing our legion of existing workers (many of whom are functionally illiterate when it comes to technology) and their need for new and retooled workforce skills. We need to dedicate 100 percent of these workers' educational sales tax vouchers toward providing them with the marketable skills they need for reemployment at or above their current pay levels.[1] Restoring economic stability to households through better jobs, not worse jobs, must be linked to part of the educational mission. As such, every teacher, administrator, professor, and adjunct faculty member needs to play a role in this lifetime educational process; their pay should be partially elevated for successfully assisting in workforce retraining, remediating educational shortcomings, and increasing their technology acumen. Teachers who participate would receive a per-student stipend for teaching continuing-education students; the stipend would be tied to the insurance voucher system for unemployment retraining, which would also be paid by the educational tuition vouchers assigned. Participation in the retraining would be mandatory in order to receive an unemployment pay voucher for 80 percent of the teacher's previous pay while he or she is in the defined program. Since this pay would be tax-free because it is an insurance payment, the employee should have relatively little interruption in his or her household earnings while unemployed. Verification of applications for employment once the retraining is completed would then be used so the employee could receive continued payments until he or she is hired at a level of pay within 90 percent of his or her last wage. Retraining and the WorkKeys testing would be mandatory to determine current skills and shortfalls; retraining would commence, giving the teacher or worker the necessary skills to be reemployed and meet current job demands.

Without these changes, big government and the even bigger administration of the current business-as-usual system will only further waste

---

[1] See Cisneros, *Interwoven Destinies*, 129.

money we do not have to spend. We have to empower individuals to raise their own self-confidence, to show them that they can and will be highly effective and thus rewarded for their pursuit of new and enhanced skills. Education is the answer once again to gain access to economic success. We have shifted into a knowledge-based economy; even our service and manufacturing jobs are knowledge based. Just as energy touches everything, so does education. It is the jet fuel of our economy. Making these fundamental changes would raise the bar globally and create the most robust and highly capable workforce on the planet.[1] This workforce is what high-quality employers seek, and if we build it they will come, and they will find solutions to their needs here—solutions made in America, by Americans who are better off in all aspects of life because of the education they have received.

---

[1] See Garmise, *People and the Competitive Advantage of Place,* 142.

Rethinking and Fortifying Our International Policies

O ne of my promises to myself when I started to write books was that as my eyes were opened to other or better possibilities I would evaluate new information and seek to determine the value of new experiences and expand my own knowledge. Thus I have reserved the right and privilege to change my positions without being accused of changing my moral and ethical views. This is the process that makes humanity better; we should not be afraid to admit we don't always base our beliefs on the absolute truth, just the truth as we understand it at the time and within our own perceptions of justification as they fit our own moral compasses.

Sometimes our religious convictions, especially those that pertain to "the other"—the outsider, the sinner, the foreigner—have led us to commit atrocities in God's name as we try to force His will—or what we think is God's will—on other people. Some of us have xenophobia—that is, a fear of people from other countries, their ways, their beliefs. As we reach out in political, economic, and neighborly ways, we will strengthen our ties to nations that would otherwise hate us as we would hate them. This section looks hard at not just the dangers from extremist factions but also our stereotypes. Addressing these issues can allow us to understand the benefits of globalization.

CHAPTER SIX

Homeland Security and Foreign Policy

Winning the long war against terrorism requires homeland security policies that will help to keep America safe, free, and prosperous—and do all three equally well.

— *Jay Carafano*[1]

Today many of the people taking to the streets of the world harbor intense anger toward the Western world—and, admittedly, sometimes for good reasons. The United States stands on top of that heap of great Western powers and has become the most hated nation on the planet. Extremist clerics of Islam incite hatred and call for a jihad against the satanic powers of the West and their oppressive Uncle Sam–led coalitions. The great Western powers (Europe, United States, Canada, Australia, Israel) are all targets of extremist hatred. This hatred of Western lifestyles is taught at a very young age. We allegedly have radical religious leaders of Islam who are preaching that the expansion of Sharia laws and the taking of all previous Muslim lands is a holy mission. This includes the destruction of others who would stand in their way. Thus far, diplomacy has failed to contain the radical elements of Islam, and radical Islam has become more emboldened and widespread since the 9/11 attacks. The United States and its allies have had to spend an enormous amount of time, money, and resources,

---

[1] Carafano, "How to Fix the 100 Hours Homeland Security Bill," February 1, 2007.

including our entire military manpower, to contain the current terror-ism movement within areas we have dubbed as our combat operations areas. The United States has also acted as a focal point for terrorists, in many cases, so their efforts are not as dispersed to the mainstream or at least aren't given the necessary resources to be carried out effectively in other theaters of possible operations.

The enormous reservoir of goodwill and compassion for the Unit-ed States around the world after the 9/11 World Trade Center attacks has been depleted and squandered during the ensuing years as alle-gations, and often proof of those allegations, came to light, revealing prisoner abuse and torture, secret prisons, rampant killing of civilian noncombatants by military personnel and civilian contractors (dare we say "mercenaries"?), and extralegal actions domestically and abroad—all committed in the name of national security and necessary military operations concerning Iraq and Afghanistan. Now, with the advent of the Obama administration in Washington, as we begin to aspire to a path to restore our national sense of moral purpose and honor and to reclaim our center of moral gravity, we also must continue to repair our standing internationally, regaining our lost prestige among the world's nations. Only then can we demand and enter into truly last-ing and successful fair-trade treaties and collaborative security agree-ments. We cannot live in a vacuum, and isolationism will only hurt us economically.

As we examine the ability for the United States to address global threats today, we see that the threats are religious-based terrorism; eco-nomic geopolitics; and politically driven, ideology-based threats. There is simply no easy way to handle the multiple threats from within and without our borders in an easy, cost-effective manner. Over the last de-cade, no country has learned better than the United States about the actual cost of freedom, our civil liberties, and the protection of our way of life. We have sent our young and old soldiers, our active soldiers, our reserve soldiers, and our homeland National Guard units abroad to address what we have been told are actual and direct threats to our national security. The expansion of Muslim radicals only grows as we attack them directly with our security forces. We have, at considerable cost, kept more terrorism at bay through the forfeiture of our privacy, a significant civil liberty we took for granted (ask any frequent flyer and he or she will tell you that there have been better days). However, this intrusion on our privacy seems to have assisted in stopping terrorism acts within our borders thus far. But these two measures—mobilized men and women and superprecautions at home—have come at a cost to our moral conscious as to who we are as a people and what we stand for. Today, post-9/11, we discuss the use of our forces wherever we deem necessary to contain terrorism and keep our global dominance in trade, mostly to keep oil flowing in our direction.

The United States also faces cyberterrorism and the economic chaos that would ensue with the loss of electronic network security. If members of a remote terrorist group or just a motivated set of hackers wants to cause economic chaos, they can do so from the comfort of their chairs. How are our leaders going to handle these new threats from an international standpoint?

When we look at the motivation of how all this political, ideology-based jockeying for power was intensified to the level of terrorism, we can see that it all really started when the United States decided to combat the onslaught of communism, which threatened our own ideology of civil liberties and capitalism. We fought first in Europe and then in Asia. The US decided that after World War II we had to break the tradition of our previous foreign policy of keeping to ourselves; we had to be more assertive. It could be argued that by doing so we made ourselves the political, religious, and ideological target for all groups different from our own. Is isolationism the answer for our problems, then? Obviously not. But, the die has been cast; we are in turbulent times, with horrific events happening almost daily around the globe.

So, you may ask, what should our foreign policy be—a policy that would in fact work? I do not believe any of us know for sure, but what I do know is that our current path, driven by excessive use of military force, has slowed but not contained or stemmed the growth of threats against us as a people. In this book, I am surely not going to claim to be a foreign policy expert; my own level of experience is limited to my travels in Asia, Western Europe, and Greece. I have never dared thus far to venture to the Holy Land and to the Middle East because of the urging of my wife, who believes I would run my mouth off and put myself in grave danger.

However, I have made some observations. I believe a good path for us through these murky international waters includes tweaking our foreign policy so that it is neither hawkish nor dovish in philosophy. If I were in charge of US foreign policy, it might look something like this: we would admit that radical elements of Islam are our enemy by their own declaration, so we are at war with them. Thus Congress would declare war. We would further state that those who use US funds to promote terrorism, as well as any country that harbors such terrorists, are our declared enemy. We would have zero tolerance for it. If countries that are predominantly Islamic want to live in harmony with the United States and any other nation that joins our coalition, then those countries must police themselves and stop such radical elements before they can gain power, acquire economic strength, and act on their radical beliefs in a manner that harms us. Failure to provide such a treaty of peace would result in a restriction of trade with the United States, the reduction of travel privileges for the country's citizens, and the use of punitive force by the US military.

For those who voluntarily join us in a peaceful treaty, we would share education and trade benefits; we would even provide an easier way for them to become citizens of our country. Such people would, of course, enjoy the protection of the greatest military power on the planet.

The pursuit of cyberterrorism has to be treated almost at the same level as the threat of religious terrorism. If a nation allowed cyberterrorism and did not at least try to police such actions expediently, then the United States would, as mentioned earlier, place restrictions on that country. Restoration of the privilege to travel, trade, and conduct global commerce with the United States would be restored once a government could provide assurance that it could meet the conditions. When people are allowed within their own systems to do harm to others and the nation's leaders take the path of plausible denial, it cannot be resolved by diplomacy; if we could, we would not have fought so many wars in the course of humanity. Humans respond to the need to protect their families from harm and provide shelter, with food and whatever creature comforts they can safely acquire. Humans with no regard for this normal desire need to be bothered until they are either exhausted or defeated.

The use of our military force should never be for economic advantages but for the protection of our people from those who would harm us within our own borders. This does require that our military, when such views are challenged, take the fight to their doorstep. But by declaring our zero tolerance for governments that fail to try to police themselves, we will have sent a clear message. At this point, our worldwide popularity can't get much worse, and while others may not agree with this maverick approach, it would restore respect for the United States and make countries harboring terrorists think twice.

A word on international treaties: some of the treaties enacted in the past and those proposed for the future give foreign organizations direct authority over the American people. There is an international effort, with the cooperation of many of our elected officials, to purposefully cause the United States to fall under the authority of foreign organizations and courts, all in the name of international globalization of markets and equitable human rights. We will have no or little voice in the election and appointment of any of these international groups.

The World Court, located in The Hague, Netherlands, has on several occasions attempted to force its rulings upon not only our Congress but also our state governments. Several US Supreme Court Justices believe this court has the authority to do so; unless our own Constitution limits such judicial powers, this authority could become a reality. As a result, a Constitutional amendment is necessary to prevent our government from delegating any authority to international groups or courts.

I believe the battle among the ideologies of communism, commulism (the communist version of capitalism), socialism, petrolism, and capitalism will be won in the same manner the Cold War was won—by demonstrating the power of our economic values; systems for capitalization; economic and civil liberties; and the pursuit of knowledge, happiness, and a world-class economic quality of life. This is best demonstrated by our uniquely American ability to present the American Dream as a beacon of hope to all those who feel oppressed.

In addition, the United States must create an impregnable security net around our borders and ports of entry so that all packages and people are monitored or inspected. While I do not believe the Great Wall of America, as it has been proposed, would actually work, it symbolically can be achieved by allowing those who want to come here the ability to do so legally and more easily. This does not mean we do not track them, regulate their activities, and require absolute adherence to our rule of law. It means we create technologically advanced means of tracking them with identification cards embedded with chips that can be traced by GPS. Failure to have the ID would be automatic grounds for detainment, review, and possible expulsion, as well as the loss of all economic property within the United States. Admittance to the United States would cost money at the point of entry; the same would go for the cost of importing goods to our country and the cost of their inspection. Such costs must be paid no matter the outcome of the goods purchased.

Freedom and safety come with a cost; just look around and see the poor soldiers coming home, dead or alive, and tell their parents that there is no cost for our safety and civil and economic freedoms. Yes, these measures will force the cost of international goods purchased by us as consumers to go up, but it will also drive the expansion of producing goods more often within our borders, making such consumer goods more affordable again.

The answer to alleviating the world's hatred toward us is to be the place everyone wants to live. Being a US citizen, or living like a US citizen does, should be the noblest pursuit among people of other nations, giving them a driving desire to enhance their own quality of life. The way to protect our own ideals is to make them valuable to others outside of our borders so that they either seek to emulate us or join us directly here in the United States.

CHAPTER SEVEN

Immigration

The only thing we have to fear is fear itself.
—Franklin Delano Roosevelt[1]

I mmigration is the lifeblood of the United States, predating the founding of our country. Without its constant replenishment and nourishment of our country's physical, intellectual, and moral well-being, we, as a people and a nation, are doomed to wither and die—a death sentence that cannot and must not be carried out. Using national security as a pretext for inflammatory anti-immigrant rhetoric lowers our standing among other nations, thus undercutting our claims of moral superiority and leadership, while at the same time potentially limiting, if not squandering entirely, a valuable resource, legal immigration—without which we cannot survive. Those who seek to incite fear of all immigrants, whether legal or undocumented, by waving aloft the banner of national security do a disservice not only to themselves and their fellow citizens but to their country as well. This is an issue that we can and must resolve through reason and careful decision-making.

The Statue of Liberty stands as a great reminder of just how important immigration is and has been throughout the history of our nation; almost since our inception we have tried to be a role model for others to aspire to match. Our nation has used this famous sonnet to identify powerfully with immigration as a driver of innovation, entrepreneurial spirit, and societal advancement through diversity:

---

[1] In Hardman, *Rendezvous with Destiny*, 39.

Not like the brazen giant of Greek fame,
With conquering limbs astride from land to land;
Here at our sea-washed, sunset gates shall stand
A mighty woman with a torch, whose flame
Is the imprisoned lightning, and her name
Mother of Exiles. From her beacon-hand
Glows world-wide welcome; her mild eyes command
The air-bridged harbor that twin cities frame.
"Keep, ancient lands, your storied pomp!" cries she
With silent lips. "Give me your tired, your poor,
Your huddled masses yearning to breathe free,
The wretched refuse of your teeming shore.
Send these, the homeless, tempest-tossed to me,
I lift my lamp beside the golden door!"

—Emma Lazarus[1]

Recently immigration has come under attack for many reasons, but most of them are related to the general public's lack of understanding of the situation, facilitated by media and special interests that sensationalize the issues out of context for their own benefit.

Let's take the most common complaints that tend to drive anti-immigration feelings and address them head on.

- Too many immigrants mean that the English language will be "demoted."

- Illegal immigration is costing us billions, taking jobs from Americans; illegal immigrants are using our system without paying for it.

- Illegal immigration is a hotbed for terrorist movements and thus a threat to our national security.

---

[1] As found on the website of Legal Language Services.

- The federal government is doing a lousy job of protecting our borders so states and even quasi-state militia groups are forming their own responses to this threat.

First, as a nation of immigrants, we are joined together culturally by the use of a common language, English. A common language was the ingredient in the "melting pot" that turned the United States into a global force that the world had never before witnessed. It is important to keep this cultural bond that allows us to communicate with one another.

Mainly because of illegal immigration, the federal government has enabled and many times encouraged the use of languages other than English. There are elected officials in Washington who believe we should become a dual-language nation.

Large cultural enclaves of individuals who do not speak English are developing in the United States, and their growth is encouraged by federal law. An amendment could make English our national language, preventing us from becoming a split nation, like Canada. Business activities should be conducted in English, and there should be no mandatory second language requirements in schools or within the government. Citizens must speak English, and if they don't, they must pay to learn it—otherwise they will have no voice in our system.

The movement of illegal immigration is a problem and should be addressed. Contrary to many folks' beliefs, I am not convinced that building a modern-day Maginot Line across our borders would halt such activity . . . such a fortification might make illegal border crossings much more difficult, but those who want to cross will find weaknesses as fast as we construct barriers. However, in the current economy, building a perceived impregnable barrier around us would be a great job creation project for our unemployed citizens who are in the construction business; in many cases the situation is similar to our highway projects of the 1950s and our WPA projects of the 1930s. I am not saying that this would be a smart investment when our nation is so severely in debt and on the brink of insolvency, nor that it would even work, but for the sake of debate I mention it.

In my opinion we can address illegal immigration issues in several ways. First, we could simply declare to Mexico and Canada that anyone who would like to visit or work in the United States is allowed to come as long as he or she requests a visitor's visa and/or a work permit at the border and adheres to our rules for visitors and visiting workers. In other words, make getting into our country similar to the process in the European Union—easy but requiring accountability. Then, we would have a much better idea of who is attempting to come and go within our borders. Second, I would require each person entering our country to pay a nominal entry payment if he or she is a visitor and a bit higher if he or she is a working visitor. These fees would probably be substantially lower than what individuals are paying coyotes to get them across the border illegally; in addition, the legal way would be far safer for the person wanting to come to the United States. The argument against this, of course, is that we could be flooded with terrorists or others wanting to do us harm. That may be the case, yet today they invisibly come across our borders anyway. This method would give us much greater management over the vast majority of folks entering our country. In addition, it would supply the US government with a payment for individuals' entrance and assure us of getting paid participation in the workforce. Under this system the visiting worker would not be entitled to US citizenship rights such as health care, retirement, disability, and unemployment benefits, which are only for those who fulfill the requirements and become citizens. A pool of funding would come from taxes on working visitors' wages in addition to their current income taxes; this additional tax would provide them with a visiting worker voucher for health care benefits.

In addition to this change in immigration would be a change in the EB-5 legal immigration system, which would further expand and allow wealthy immigrants from around the globe wishing to secure US citizenship to do so. The provision would be that they invest $500,000 into a qualified economic development project; in doing this, they could gain the right to apply and be vetted for consideration of US citizenship. The local government's economic development organization would be responsible for applying for such funds and thus monitoring the loan for eventual repayment. The organization would also be responsible for reporting all investments to the federal government annually, including job creation outcomes resulting from the investments.

The final step in making sure we control the flow of illegal funds and benefits to others outside of our country is that all payments (not including payments for services rendered outside the United States) made between a person here to a person outside the United States would be subject to a gross transaction tax of 5–20 percent, depending on the size of the transfer. The lower the amount, the higher the deduction for the gross transaction tax. This would allow us to capture money being made here and sent to benefit others in the family in another country.

Of course, the greatest complaint heard for the case against illegal immigrants is that they are not paying their fair share or that they are taking jobs from existing American workers. I do not believe this to actually be the case. They are fulfilling jobs that many Americans are not willing to do or cannot do because of the nature of the activity (e.g., hard manual labor). Even more, these immigrants are working at jobs that the average American does not feel pays an appropriate living wage according to the perception of his or her own self-worth and educational attainment. I think if Americans applied for many of these jobs, they would more than likely be hired since they usually speak the language and would not be kicked out by the government if caught. To that end, if an employer hires an illegal immigrant, the employer should be subject to massive fines and prison time for his or her decision. This should apply to anyone who is aware that the person is an illegal immigrant and does not take action to report it. There should also be a finder's fee, paid by 25 percent of the employer's fine, to anyone who blows the whistle on such illegal activity.

The greatest opposition, though, lies in the perception that illegal immigrants are using or gaming our system and not paying for it. First, the laughable part of this is that our own citizens do that as well: it's called welfare assistance. Today over 51 percent of our own citizens pay no tax or are in a negative tax status. Of course, the proposal of using regressive taxes and especially consumption taxes would greatly undercut this argument. Since most illegals work in the underground economy and operate on a cash basis, the most effective methodology to capture their fair share of taxes is through sales taxes, consumption taxes, and user taxes.[1]

The best approach to address those who are not capable of working or not willing to work but who want to consume services is my taxation proposal of a national flat tax on all sales and a value-added tax on goods and services. When coupled with a gross transaction tax to corporations, the US government would then have the means and the cash flow to deal with people who feel they are the exceptions to the rule, those not willing to be productive and lawful members of our society.

And finally, there is no need for individual citizens to take the law into their own hands and form militant groups. Such actions only amplify the problem and cause our people to commit grievous moral crimes. Let's not forget that foreigners and recent immigrants account for over 20 percent of our current patents in the United States today . . . cutting off all those bright people would only harm our overall economic viability as a nation.

---

[1] See Maxwell, *Texas Politics Today*, 343.

CHAPTER EIGHT

Petrolism

As the price of oil goes up, the pace of freedom goes down in what
I would call petrolist states . . . states that either are very weak
institutions or are already authoritarian states and are highly de-
pendent on oil for their GDP.

— *Thomas L. Friedman*[2]

Mass production and consumption of renewable energy sources are critical to our country's long-term future. However, we
won't be able to achieve widespread use of renewable energy
until we break the political choke hold of the fossil fuel lobby. A seemingly endless flow of money gushes from the fossil fuel lobby's powerful financial pipeline, drowning energy reform efforts. These forceful
lobbyists are all too eager to distract and subvert our local, state, and
federal decision-makers. Keeping our nation addicted to fossil fuels is
in the lobbyists' best interests; thus, their destructive agenda is to keep
Americans scared of energy alternatives. As Ron Polina said:

> In 1968, there were sixty-two lobbyists in Washington; to-
> day there are thirty-four thousand, outnumbering mem-
> bers of Congress and their staffers two to one. By 2008,
> these lobbyists were spending approximately $8.2 million
> for influence per day.

---

[2] Friedman, "The First Law of Petropolitics," 154.

Few, if any, of these lobbyists represent the majority of Americans in the middle class. So it's not surprising, given these statistics, that real median household income in America has stagnated for over a decade.[1]

The problem with our current system of formulating national energy policies is that we don't have an unbiased, transparent, nonpolitical body that has authority to investigate our energy situation, make policy recommendations, and adjust our energy practices to ensure we achieve energy independence during this century. Managing our energy use is no less important than managing our money and banking systems. We recognize the need for the Federal Reserve to manage our financial systems, and we must recognize that it is equally important to establish an organization that manages our energy and that plans for the future of energy. Yet, our nation is unlikely to recognize this need because most people are either in denial that we have a problem or are in a state of ignorance, the result of careful actions by fossil fuel companies.

Despite the denial and ignorance, in reality we reached peak oil—the point at which the demand became greater than the supply—around 2003. We will continue to find more oil, but it will not be enough to offset our current consumption, let alone future consumption, which is expected to double in the next thirty years. The laws of supply and demand are well known and so is the inevitable outcome if we don't reduce our consumption of oil and increase our use of alternative energy. Oil prices will increase exponentially as the gap between availability and demand widens each year. In addition, since energy touches everything we do, the increase in oil will increase the costs of everything else, including basic necessities, such as food.

The increase in costs will create political tensions even beyond the current levels because the vast majority of money funding terrorism is supplied by our own fossil fuel addiction. This continued addiction will lead to conflicts on a global scale as industrialized nations and

---

[1] Polina, *Selling Out a Superpower*, 46.

emerging-growth nations compete for much-needed energy. Indeed, if there is ever a third world war, it will not be fought over money or national debts; it will most likely be fought over energy assets, such as supply, production, and distribution infrastructure. Currently, the United States and China are the dominant competitors trying to secure the oil resources of Russia, Canada, the Middle East, Nigeria, Venezuela, and Brazil. Living green is not just a personal virtue, as many corporate messages would have us believe; more importantly, it's a national security imperative.

The biggest threat to America and its values today is therefore not communism, authoritarianism, or religious extremism. It's petrolism. *Petrolism* is the term for the corrupting, antidemocratic governing practices that result in artificially trying to maintain $60-a-barrel oil and using swings to more than $100-a-barrel oil when tensions are heightened to flex the political clout of those nations trading in this commodity. Petrolism is the politics of using oil income to buy off citizens with subsidies and government jobs, using oil and gas exports to intimidate or buy off one's enemies, and using oil profits to build up one's internal security forces and army to keep oneself ensconced in power, without any transparency or checks and balances.

We have thus been led into a world of foreign policy that is focused on petrolism and that uses the US military to carve out more than our fair share of energy from fossil fuels. This has set us on a path of military conflict with some of the most dangerous and nondemocratic nations on the planet, each of which is armed to the teeth with dangerous weapons that could snuff out humanity with the push of some buttons. The resulting nuclear scenario would play out on video screens in the deep bunkers of the elite, the few who believe a nuclear showdown would be survivable. Scary stuff to be sure, but it is not so far off from the capabilities of the world's most dangerous. What we do *not* want to do is create a world ready to snap over such tensions as fossil fuel energy demands, water scarcity, and food scarcity—or, God forbid, over debts owed and the people who are unable or unwilling to pay those debts.

When a nation's leaders can practice petrolism, they never have to tap their people's energy and creativity; they simply have to tap an oil well. And therefore politics in a petrolist state is not about building a society or an educational system that maximizes its people's ability to innovate, export, and compete. It is simply about who controls the oil tap.

—Thomas Friedman[1]

We must stop playing oil games. It's too slippery. Besides causing potential international security problems while vying for control over fossil fuels, our obsession with oil-produced energy causes environmental damage the world over.

Lesson Learned?

On the evening of April 20, 2010, at about 9:45 p.m. CST, an offshore oil rig named *Deepwater Horizon,* positioned in the Gulf of Mexico fifty-two miles off the coast of Venice, Louisiana, caught fire and exploded in a ball of flame, killing eleven of the crew—nine riggers and two engineers—and injuring seventeen others, four seriously. Its subsequent sinking two days later, on April 22nd, marked not merely the end of the rig's existence but also the beginning of a prolonged struggle to contain and stop the oil gushing from the damaged wellhead to the surface of the water. The resulting oil slick covered, by some estimates, some fifteen hundred square miles. Additionally, the debacle ignited the commencement of a BP public relations damage-control campaign to preserve, and, if possible, even enhance, the oil company's less-than-spotless worldwide reputation.

A quick review of BP's history can offer us insights into how BP evolved into the clumsy, seemingly clueless prehistoric corporate behemoth—a sort of latter-day Tyrannosaurus rex—that it remains to be

---

[1] As quoted in Strategy Unit, "Tom Friedman on 'Being Green Is the New Red White and Blue,'" January 8, 2006.

to this very day. In many respects, BP represents those companies that beset, painfully and at great cost, the entire global fossil fuel industry— while also affecting people's lives for better or worse in every part of the world. This incident will have a profound impact on environmental regulations and protection in the future. I do not believe that BP's failure to take significant precautions against such accidents should deter us from continuing the exploration of offshore oil in the United States. But because of BP's failure, companies that cut corners in the future shall— and should—be financially affected on their balance sheets for all costs of such incidents, including loss of economic vitality for the region and the cost of rebuilding the ecosystem in short order.

There cannot be an easy financial mitigation for energy companies, or bad behavior will be rewarded and companies will be encouraged to view cutting corners as a necessary risk worth taking in their undisclosed business practices. Although Dorceta Tayor, an environmental author, said, "Green Consumption has become a public signifier of status and environmental identity,"[2] these big oil companies must be held accountable no matter how many times they use the word *green* in their advertising.

The fact remains that BP, which has been the center of attention as of late due to the Gulf oil spill, has had a well-documented history of bad decisions. It is with this in mind that government must provide us with more protection from such abuses of wisdom as companies harvest fossil fuels.

Money Talks

As you read these words, hordes of ravenous locusts are busily eating Congress alive. These locusts—otherwise known as lobbyists—besiege Congress without surcease, and the figures prove it. More than 11,100 corporations, trade associations, unions, and other groups hired approximately 10,500 lobbyists since 2009 (with lobbyists outnumbering

---

[2] Tayor, *Environment and Social Justice*, 155.

members of Congress roughly twenty to one), and the trend continues to rise. Lobbying efforts have increased exponentially over the past decade, and this has happened mainly to keep the United States in the dark on energy policy creation that would be useful in making us more energy independent, increasing our efforts to be more energy efficient at all levels of society. These efforts have worked to stymie the expansion of affordable renewable energy, home- and consumer-based alternatives, and other measures that could begin to lead the United States toward a much more energy independent future.

Lobbying on behalf of all oil and gas interests in 2010, as reported by the Thompson Smitch Consulting Group and derived from the Senate Office of Public Records, totaled $74,902,352, and the lobbyists involved numbered a staggering 696. BP alone spent more than $3.5 million in the first quarter of 2010 and a total of almost $16 million in 2009. Since 1999, BP's federal government lobbying outlays have approached $61 million.

The following are the lobbying outlays by the seven biggest oil and gas spenders during the first quarter of 2010:[1]

- ConocoPhillips: $11,931,980,
- Chevron Corp: $7,010,000,
- Royal Dutch Shell: $6,370,000,
- Exxon Mobil: $5,910,000,
- Koch Industries: $3,900,000,
- American Petroleum Institute: $3,570,000,
- BP America: $3,320,000.

Lobbyists are given an enormous amount of money to persuade Congress to favor the oil companies. As Antonia Juhasz, an environmental and energy activist, said:

> Big Oil has simple needs. It wants to explore for, produce, refine, sell oil and gas wherever possible without restriction.

---

[1] OpenSecrets.org, "Lobbying: US Oil," August 27, 2011.

It wants laws that allow it to expand all operations. It wants to prevent laws that stand in its way and roll those back that already exist. Big oil wants friends in office and enemies out of office. It wants friendly regulators in government and unfriendly regulators out of government. Big oil does not want to pay taxes, fees, or fines. It does not want to be slowed down or financially burdened with bureaucracy, environmental laws, protection for public health or workers safety, or concerns for human rights.[2]

We must not let democracy fall prey to these juggernauts. Members of Congress must take the moral high ground no matter how much money is pushed at them.

The People Require a Stronger Voice

Despite a recent Supreme Court decision strengthening corporations' grip on our elected representatives in Washington, the country still belongs to its citizens rather than to lobbyists and to those who finance and conceal themselves behind lobbyists. More effective legislation is required both to prohibit lobbyists from rendering our elected representatives in Washington as well as on the state and local levels mere functionaries of those who can inundate, and thus corrupt, the electoral process with endless streams, rivers, and oceans of cash.

As you can see, we have a staunch adversary in decoupling energy politics; we need to create a robust American Energy Public Policy Board, charged with achieving energy independence for America in the next twenty-five years. This movement is our twenty-first-century equivalent of the 1960s US initiative to go to the moon, which launched NASA. Not only are these new goals achievable and in our best interest from a competitive and economic development standpoint, but working toward them will create millions of new jobs and

---

[2] Juhasz, *The Tyranny of Oil*, 209–210.

inward investment into our energy economy. This movement will affect everyone in America in a positive manner, and from there it will
also affect the entire world, allowing all of us to take better care of our
natural resources worldwide.

CHAPTER NINE

Globalization:
An Opportunity and a Threat

Growth in the global economy encourages the development of state-less elites whose allegiance is to global economic success and their own prosperity rather than the interests of the nation where they are headquartered.

—Larry Summers[1]

G lobalization is the much-publicized process by which regional and national economies are integrated into a larger, more diverse, and more competitive global economy. There are many myths and misunderstandings with regard to the pros and cons of this mostly American-created economic dragon of the twentieth and twenty-first centuries. The global economy drives, and is driven by, the greater mobility of capital, people, businesses, and information, and as such the reduction of borders is an inhibitor to such mobility. The reduction of borders is enabled by the widespread use of the Internet and other information- and communication-based technologies (ICT), which create linkages within economies worldwide. This technology is similar to the creation of the US interstate freeway system in the 1950s, which linked major markets to the rapid access of goods, people, and raw materials, thus spreading mobility within the United States. As markets enlarge, trade and competition grow, which bestows new wealth to some

---

[1] Summers, "Rethinking Globalization," May 12, 2008.

locations and the disruption or degradation of wealth to others. While globalization presents serious threats and unquestionably has created a more volatile, uncertain economy, it is also rife with significant and unprecedented economic opportunities.[1] The rest of this chapter contains information on the facts and the myths surrounding the globalization of the US economy.

Myth 1: The economic benefits of globalization are largely derived by the host country.

Fact 1: Globalization was largely the mastermind of US multinational companies; it is used as a means to create access to new markets and increase profits by lowering the cost of producing goods. As we will discuss later, the economic benefits are largely derived by the company shareholders, who in many cases live outside of the host country.

Globalization at its most basic level is the creation of a larger, more complex marketplace that stimulates economic activities that flow into and out of the national and local economies. This creates quite a paradigm in economic development because the interplay between competing local and national economies (with regard to business investment) has significant implications for promoting local economic prosperity. Those conditions are an increase in the number of competitors, access to a much larger market, and the introduction of globally standardized technologies, which together are substantively restructuring how business is organized.[2]

Myth 2: Other countries are better at producing high-quality workers than the United States.

Fact 2: The truth is that the United States still leads the world in the quality of education, educational outcomes across the board, and the ability to attract highly skilled students to our country for undergraduate

---

[1] Federal Reserve Board of San Francisco, *Globalization*, Number 2004-12.
[2] Garmise, *International Economic Development Council*, 5, 7–10, 14–17.

and graduate educations. Globalization is driven by the need for a highly skilled and talented workforce. This is highly dependent upon educational outcomes in the STEM core areas.

Our ability to attract students from abroad has become a double-edged sword, however; it has driven the cost of education up for US residents, who have to compete with foreigners willing to pay (and import cash) for their educations in the United States. It is for this reason that I believe we need to rethink our approach to education funding for the brightest, most talented members of our country. Instead of having them go into debt for their educations, we should allow American students who maintain a 3.0 GPA or better to have forgivable student loans in the fields of STEM. I would expand these "forgivable fields" to health care as well and education (teaching). This would be the best investment the United States could make to increase our global competitiveness.

The global economy creates more competition, but it has also created a larger market for goods and services and thus more investors looking for opportunities. There has been a substantial broadening of the consumer base globally as new developing nations want access to goods and services just as the dominant economies have learned to desire. In 2007, consumer spending in the seventeen countries with the largest emerging markets reached 65 percent of US consumer spending, up from 48 percent in 2000.[3] Consumer spending in these seventeen countries is expected to surpass US consumption by 2015 if this trend continues,[4] and we see no reason, even with the global meltdown, that this will not be the case.

Access to cash is the basis for how all these business opportunities get funded abroad. Likewise, attracting foreign cash to invest in the United States is a huge benefit for our own economy. Foreign direct investment (FDI) is growing substantially. Just as trade investments flow

---

[3] Hale, "Brave New Economy," A14.

[4] Garmise, *International Economic Development Council*, 7.

in two directions, so does FDI. While competition for FDI is increasing, so are overall FDI opportunities, and the United States remains a significant FDI recipient of such investments.[1], [2] In 2006, India, China, and the United States were the three largest recipients of FDI in terms of job creation, according to a report produced by IBM Global Services. While the United States is also the most important source of FDI investments, China and India are becoming visible sources as well. The United States also remains a significant recipient for R & D investment, with India emerging as a significant front-runner.[3] China has been stymied in the quagmire over intellectual property rights and the theft of such developments within the country.

Myth 3: FDI investment in the United States equates to selling ourselves and our assets off to foreigners and thus weakening our national security.

Fact 3: FDI increases the ability of the United States to create new businesses at home, to increase American jobs, and thus to create economic growth at home. In most cases, such assets cannot be removed and taken to some distant shore, so the economic prosperity resulting from the local tax base, sales tax growth, and income distribution is a greater benefit to the local economy than to the host ownership corporation. In terms of wealth, it is a win-win scenario. We should hope for and develop strategies to increase FDI within the United States.

This is why the EB-5 investor citizen program developed by the US Department of Immigration[4] has grown so much and become popular over the past decade. This program allows foreign investors who would like to become US citizens and can pass our citizenship requirements and background checks to become citizens, but only if they invest $1 million USD into a new enterprise and the investment is

---

[1] Economist.com, "Winners and Losers," February 28, 2008.

[2] See also Bureau of Economic Analysis, *Foreign Direct Investment*.

[3] IBM Global Services, *Global Location Trends*, 8.

[4] Immigration.com, "EB-5 Investment Green Card," March 20, 2009.

verified to have created ten new jobs in the United States. Now this is a win-win scenario, and if the members of Congress were smart, they would increase this program to widen our catch of global entrepreneurs and wealth.

Global trade is accelerating among all nations. According to World Bank statistics, the global volume of world trade in goods (agriculture, fuels, mining products, and manufacturers) has been growing at twice the growth of GDP since 2000.[5] In 2006, world GDP increased by 3.5 percent while global trade of these goods increased by 8 percent. For countries that are resource rich, such as Canada and Australia, this growth has insulated them somewhat during the recent economic meltdown.

Myth 4: The United States can no longer compete for manufacturing jobs abroad, so there is no hope for turning this around.

Fact 4: To maintain a sustainable and robust national economy, a country has to manufacture items, not just sell raw materials for short-term gain.

The opportunities for a rebirth in US manufacturing are abundant in the global corporation scenario, especially when we consider the demand for a highly talented workforce and increasing fuel costs for transporting items (and thus the need to be closer to markets), as well as the increased demand for border protection and homeland security. All this intensifies the need for 100 percent inspection of all items shipped into a market, which also raises the costs to the consumer.

Trade export and import figures are clear evidence of accelerating and expanding markets, but they can also be a misleading measure of the economic benefits of globalization. For example, 50 to 80 percent of Chinese exports include foreign inputs, according to a study backed by the US International Trade Commission.[6] A recent study

---

[5] World Bank, *Global Economic Prospects 2008.*

[6] Koopman, "How Much of Chinese Exports Is Really Made in China?" March 2008.

from the University of California illustrates this little-understood fact with regard to a most recent phenomenon, the iPod. The study determined the accrual of benefits from the US sale of Apple's iPod. Although the final product is manufactured in China, only $4 of each unit's sale stays in China. About $160 returns to the United States to the firms involved in iPod design, transport, and retail.[1] This denotes why the expansion of trade and FDI, the increase of our own R & D capacities, and our focus on renewed manufacturing can pay off in spades for the citizens of our country.

Larger markets and the increased personal use of information technologies have strengthened the power of consumer preferences in a global marketplace. This power is even playing out in the new push at the individual and corporate levels to be green sensitive and to leave a smaller carbon footprint. The push toward greener, more sustainable business products, services, and practices is a direct response to increasing consumer demand and consumers' awareness of their sensitivity toward the earth. Consumers, however, are diverse and thus quite segmented. A larger market of diverse consumers (individual and business) means more target or niche markets, which open a wider space for entrepreneurship and new companies to be born.

Myth 5: Immigrants are taking US jobs and are thus hurting our reemployment opportunities, exacerbating the already high unemployment rate.

Fact 5: Increasing immigration further to include an expansion of visa availability for budding entrepreneurs would further increase the competitiveness of the United States. Nearly 25 percent of the new US patents between 2000 and 2010 were awarded to immigrants to our country, according to the US Patent office.[2] Many of the largest companies launched as of late are also products of immigrants (Google, Intel,

---

[1] Wadhwa, *America's New Immigrant Entrepreneurs*, 7–8.
[2] National Science Foundation, *Science and Engineering Indicators*.

eBay, and Yahoo come to mind). The most devastating basis for high unemployment is the need for skills and to retrain an aged workforce to meet the demands of new business opportunities. It is for this reason I have championed the nationwide use of the ACT WorkKeys program,[3] as discussed in the chapter on education, for such assessments, in collaboration with the community college system for such retraining. Employers wanting to keep a skilled workforce can use a standardized program such as KeyTrain by ACT to address areas of deficiency in their workers. Many of our states see this as a threat to their own workforce systems, which are woefully inefficient, hard to regulate, and difficult to improve because they have no disciplined efficiency for the curriculum. Creating skilled workers will attract investment back into local economies. That is why I advocate for these programs at the local level, in spite of state educational bureaucracies.

At the heart of globalization are information and communication technologies that support the World Wide Web: e-mail, satellite-based communications, global positioning systems, and handheld devices. These technologies have linked people, data, and knowledge together in the blink of an eye, and they form the basis of global transactions for information and commerce. What is often overlooked is that they do not just provide technological capacity; they also provide a common technology standard for information exchange that cannot be stopped at a country border. Moreover, the standards were established before they could be regulated and consequently are becoming the basis of general business standards, enabling the emergence of the global corporation.[4] It is because of this fact that I strongly advocate the continued expansion of our national and local infrastructure with smart technologies so that the United States gets more than its fair share of capabilities and thus receives new jobs dependent upon this infrastructure. Thus our global reach technologically affects our status locally.

---

[3] ACT, "Workforce Development."

[4] Garmise, *International Economic Development Council*, 9.

The way business models have changed in response to globalization has significant implications for economic development practices
at the local level. Our local economic developers have taken much flak
for not having answers to the current economic downturn. Some of
that criticism is well deserved. The economic development industry remains a key buzzword for politicians today, but the lobbying efforts of
this industry have not had the ability to influence with any great success any of these possible changes.

Worse yet, the industry has been made to sing for its supper to
the politicians, so the recommendations—if any—are sometimes tied
to unreasonable time lines and milestones. The trial-by-fire attempts
regarding this subject have made economic developers in the post-
2008 meltdown skittish; they haven't made bold recommendations
for US economic policy. According to Samuel Palmisano, president
and CEO of IBM, the multinational corporation (MNC) has evolved
into the global corporation, and the differences between the two are
significant.[1]

First, multinational organizations arranged production in a market-
by-market framework. Each affiliate worked within the borders of the
country in which it was located. Businesses located their affiliates strategically to enter specific national markets. For example, Toyota built
manufacturing plants in the United States to sell its products to US consumers. Ford did the same thing in Asia.

As capital and trade flows liberalized in order to weave national
economies into a single global economy, the information technology
revolution provided the technological capacity and standardization that
now enables businesses to function within this new global market. Palmisano emphasizes that the convergence of these elements has caused a
fundamental shift in corporate culture and organization—from a focus
on products to an emphasis on the production process. Put another way,
the global company's emphasis is on "the integration of production

---

[1] Palmisano, "The Globally Integrated Enterprise," 127–136.

and value delivery worldwide," which has led to significant changes in where things are produced and who actually produces them.[2]

Communities tend to find the growth of global sourcing patterns threatening, as some activities do move many good US jobs overseas. The outsourcing market is indeed quite substantial—estimated to be around $930 billion in 2006—and is growing, with projections that it will increase more than 54 percent by 2011. Economic developers seem to be stuck in the pre-2008 commerce scenario; they have yet to begin to demonstrate through local and especially national leadership recommendations that they truly understand how to create sustainable solutions to rebuild our national, state, regional, and, most importantly, local economies. This pre-2008 mind-set simply does not work in the post-2008 capital markets, where investors are seeking ways to invest in business projects today.

The expansion of communication and information technologies has enabled global corporations to troll the world for talent, and the expansion of talent pools internationally paints an unclear picture for the future of the United States. On one hand, this has been a traditional competitive asset for the United States both in terms of the quality of its primary and secondary education systems and its ability to attract foreign students and skilled workers. While other countries have increased in attractiveness, the United States remains the most important destination of global migrants generally, attracting 20 percent of global flows. Moreover, the United States attracts 50 percent of all skilled migrants. The offshoring of high-skilled functions does not replace US jobs, as many have been led to believe by the media and labor unions. Unlike offshoring of lower-skilled work, which does lead to direct losses here and thus increases the need for retraining to avoid underemployment or unemployment, this new trend represents a global hunt for talent, leading to net job creation, business extensions of new opportunities and investments, and market expansion. Studies done also showed that

---

[2] Garmise, *International Economic Development Council,* 10.

overall, companies are moving away from purely labor cost–driven sourcing decisions to more strategic approaches like creating competitive advantage, increasing the speed to market, and accessing talent.[1]

Myth 6: The United States is losing the battle for economic growth to China.

Fact 6: The United States economy is still the largest in the world and represents nearly 28 percent of global GDP.[2] China recently surpassed Japan as the second largest economy, and China represents about 6 percent of the global GDP. The Chinese economy faces some severe challenges ahead as more Chinese raise their expectations to a more Westernized standard of living; this will increase the demand for the Chinese to invest in lifestyles and amenities to satisfy their population's expectations. This will begin to soften their ability to grow without restraint.

As baby boomers exit the economy and birth rates slow, the size of the labor force will decrease just as employers' appetite for talented workers increases. Thus, of the three forces that spurred the growth of the US labor force in the twentieth century, only immigration remains significant in the twenty-first century. But immigration, which defined our country in earlier centuries, faces extreme opposition from segments of the US population, especially the less educated and those who have stagnating skill sets—those most prone to be economically harmed in this global expansion. The intersection of our demographic shifts with the global restructuring of the economy has shined the spotlight on the importance of developing, attracting, and retaining talent, with an emphasis on appealing to young professionals in the twenty-five to thirty-four age range. The millennials, also called generation Y, represent the emerging workforce and are the most mobile, ethnically diverse, tech savvy, global, and education-oriented of any generation in our history.

---

[1] World Economic Forum, *Global Risks 2008*, 14–15.
[2] Data360, "Share of Global GDP by Country."

It is due to this demographic trend that many communities will potentially face huge waves of migration if they do not continue to focus on building high-quality amenities and keep lifestyle costs at a reasonable level, because these people expect such amenities.

For the average American worker, income has not grown even though US productivity has, with the gains going disproportionately to higher-skilled workers.[3] As I have discussed, I believe much of this can be attributed to our faulty workforce investment activities at the local level and the lack of a disciplined workforce assessment and retraining system that is consistent and applicable at the national level. While productivity gains lift average wages, they affect individuals, industries, and communities quite differently, especially as the majority of workers fall into the lower-skilled categories. Moreover, data suggests that about two-thirds of workers who lost their jobs in manufacturing and other import-competing sectors were reemployed with an average wage loss of 13 percent.[4] While globalization may in fact play only a part in the stagnation of wages and the destruction of jobs, especially in manufacturing, the strong, visible consequences of outsourcing in terms of worker dislocation and real wage stagnation has led to an increasingly more protectionist and xenophobic US public. The general public has not been able to fully understand the benefits of globalization, largely due to misinformation from the media. While protectionist and anti-immigration sentiment pose a greater threat to economic growth than do globalizing markets and immigration, they are a critical reminder that the issue of income needs to be an important economic growth concern.[5] It is important that we focus our efforts at the local level, therefore, and on creating living wage jobs, jobs that pay individuals dignified-enough wages that allow those individuals to participate in society and feel greater self-worth. We also must remember that incentives, when

---

[3] See Aldonas, *Succeeding in the Global Economy*.

[4] Marler, "Underemployment 19.8% in February, on Par with January," March 3, 2010.

[5] Garmise, *International Economic Development Council*, 16–17.

used for such job creation projects, should tie investments more closely to the value of the jobs being created, rather than just the number of the jobs being created. Quality outweighs quantity in this case. And globalization can assist us in creating these quality jobs, the world over.

CHAPTER TEN

Flash Points: 2012 and Beyond

All great events hang by a hair. The man of ability takes advantage of everything and neglects nothing that can give him a chance of success; whilst the less able man sometimes loses everything by neglecting a sing one of those chances.

—*Napoleon Bonaparte*[1]

Sticking our heads in the sand and hoping things will just get better without some action on our own parts is just insane. In fact, this type of action or lack of action is exactly what has pushed the United States to the tipping point today. Without facing our nation's problems head-on, we face a horribly painful ice age of insolvency as a nation. Looming like ominous giant mushroom clouds on the horizon are menacing problems we dare not ignore. Chief among these is the crippling burden posed by foreign ownership of our debt, which is the enormous gaming of our financial system. This is particularly apparent when we consider carry trade problems. Carry trade is a financial gimmick in which currency is sold at low interest rates and those funds are used to buy a different country's currency that yields a higher interest rate. These traders create volatility in the market since their trading decisions affect the perception of how much a country's

---

[1] From a letter to the Minister of Foreign Affairs, Passariano, in 1797, as quoted in Yorck von Wartenburg, *Napoleon as a General*, 269.

currency is worth. Carry trade, whether public or private, continues unabated despite the recent weakness in the dollar and led to modest 2008 and 2009 improvements in our balance-of-payments deficit. This is not a good thing, because it creates volatility and currency speculation in the national markets, which leads to artificial values and penalizes savers and consumers—all because of speculation. As of January 2009, China and Japan jointly owned an estimated 45 percent of all US Treasury securities, followed by petroleum exporters Canada, Venezuela, Mexico, and Saudi Arabia.[1] Like health care, immigration, and other critical issues, this river of red ink flowing to creditor nations should be viewed as a top-priority national security threat, requiring hands-on attention from the best-available minds. This threat is not as the media would have us believe; rather, our nation simply cannot continue to borrow on our future and hope to miraculously pay off such generous loan terms. The fact that nations have so much faith in the United States that they continue to lend us money even though in most circumstances it would seem unwise is an enormous testament to our good credit with other nations. The main issue for me is that we cannot continue to finance our false expectations for our sensational lifestyle expenditures and make no corrective adjustments to those lifestyles in light of our actual financial solvency. To default on our debts would send the world, not to mention our nation, into a financial tailspin. So let's take that option off the table.

To combat this situation, the United States needs to address its financial solvency and discourage our citizens and our government from living beyond our means and on credit. By restoring fiscal balance and black ink to our balance sheet, we can stave off this second global meltdown if we act fast.

> *Intellectuals are cynical and cynics have never built a cathedral.*
>
> —*Henry Kissinger*[2]

---

[1] Brunnermeir, "Carry Trade & Currency Crashes."

[2] As quoted in Frisch, *Novels, Plays, Essays*, 91.

Religious extremism remains an as-yet unresolved problem expressed most prominently today by radical terrorist cells in Iraq, Afghanistan, and elsewhere. However, the fact remains that no matter what the proclaimed or unproclaimed religious or secular affiliation may be, wherever it may be located, or whatever permutations or forms it may take, the defeat of terrorism can be achieved successfully only through a comprehensive, multilevel approach that includes battling illiteracy and poverty side by side with law-enforcement and military components. America has to once more win the hearts and souls of the oppressed by being that shining beacon that Jane Lazarus wrote about so beautifully. Being that melting pot of civil and economic freedom is our best offense and best defense simultaneously.

All this said, I see major potential for flash points concerning immigration, direct investment, trade, terrorism, and energy. Our woes with Mexico and the flow of illegal immigrants, as well as drug wars and bandito raiders in Mexico, has brought Mexico's tourism economy to its knees. The flow of illegal immigrants to the United States is only going to increase as Mexico's civil unrest boils, forcing people to look north to the still-blessed life of the US citizen.

When it comes to energy, we have many fronts that I believe will become quite explosive in the next few years. Nigeria will be a battleground for foreign policy; the United States will want to strategically project its position within Nigeria's economy over China. The Chinese are already beginning to build relations through investments in Nigeria's economy. The second major flash point is Iran. The United States is not going to just leave the Middle East, not with so much energy at stake. At some point, the United States will seek to engage Iran to diminish the influence of China there as well. Russia and her pipelines represent yet another energy threat for the United States. You might ask why we are talking like this. Because since the world's fossil fuels industry has more than likely reached and surpassed its Peak Oil point, nations such as the United States now must use their foreign policy and ultimately their military to project power in such regions.

The trade imbalances and tactics of China and others have the United States quite alarmed. I believe the implementation of 100 percent homeland security inspections of trade will cause much tension between the United States and China.

Then we must look at the growth of radical Islam and the terrorist elements promoting it. They are growing in places such as Afghanistan, Palestine, and Lebanon. To combat this terrorism the United States, Israel, and the European Union need to begin a coordinated antiterrorist crackdown.

The goals of using solar panels (which would come in a variety of shapes and sizes and be as ubiquitous as cell phones and windmills), wind turbines in varying sizes adorning the land, and waterscapes should be viewed within the context of worldwide problems relating to food security, diminishing supplies of water, and access to clean water. Energy is what this century is going to be about. The introduction of renewable energy, coupled with energy efficiency and conservation, could cut our energy demand level to half of what it is today. This would also mean that we address local building ordinances, energy efficiency, conservation upgrades to equipment and facilities, and gray water reuse in our domestic agendas.

If we consider the flash points mentioned, it should appear evident to us that China and the United States present the biggest threats to stable world peace. Both countries are on a collision course that many think is impractical to worry about. Not true. While I believe it is not in China's or the United States' best interests to address such issues in the form of a military showdown, it is still a remote possibility. The last thing we or anyone else would want is to fight a war over monetary concerns.

The best philosophy for dealing with these flash points is a complete structural change in our foreign and domestic economic policies, immigration policies, and energy policies; a sound focus on humanitarian aid; and the abandonment of reckless economic overspending and living beyond our means. Creating an easy immigration policy and very low costs for immigrating could restore public confidence in our own governance. Lastly, to avoid such flash points we have to remain healthy and wise as a nation. Our educational systems need to be fixed, and our taxation system needs to be the fairest and most attractive in the world. If other nations value our country, it will reduce the temptation to bait us into a real shooting war.

> *When you fully understand the situation, it is worse than you think.*
> —*Barry Commoner, American Author and Scientist*[1]

If we address these domestic issues and then couple them with our foreign policies, not the other way around, then our nation should fare well in this century. The key to restoring American respect is a consistent policy on dealing with global economic stability, creating a responsible climate change initiative, striking balanced and fair trade agreements, enforcing equitable taxation policies domestically, and implementing an aggressive policy of zero tolerance for terrorism against the United States. If we raise the bar for our behavior and unhook our political decisions from special interest–driven politics, it will bode well for the reestablishment and preservation of America as the ultimate location for the pursuit of happiness and wealth creation.

Public policy in support of freedom and civil liberties, along with economic security, the rule of law, and adherence to property rights on behalf of individuals should be our basis for how we measure those we deal with. If they are oppressive to such conditions, they should not be our allies, but that does not mean they are naturally our enemies. The global cop on the beat cannot be the United States any longer. Neither can our policy of interjecting in others' affairs be our initiative. Our example is to be that lighthouse of hope to all those who would seek to have a better life. Our goals are to spread democracy and freedom by example and good public relations throughout humanity, not to instill such thoughts by use of blunt force from our military.

---

[1] Rawson, *The Unofficial Rules of Life*, 129.

There will be many opportunities for flash points in this century, from China's version of communism and capitalism to Middle East–driven radical Islam. Then as oil becomes more and more scarce, we will have flash points in places such as Russia, Venezuela, Nigeria, Iran, Canada, and other oil-rich locations. Our position has to be made by setting the bar of exemplary behavior in our domestic and foreign policies. We are not currently setting a good example: the amount of debt per taxpayer in the United States today stands at about $125,000, and the total debt of our nation exceeds $13 trillion (that's $13,000,000,000,000) and will quickly rise to $15 trillion by 2012.

> *It is crucial that governments find the most effective means in their country settings for encouraging the adoption of sustainability tools and for furthering innovation.*
>
> —*David Annandale*[1]

Getting our house in order and committing to realistic structural changes are the only solutions for us as a nation. We have to come to grips with the reality that our lifestyles are not going to stay the same. We are going to shape a different world with our new and unique principles that have been learned and adapted to meet the demand that we act far more responsibly than previous generations; otherwise we will pay a severe consequence in the very near future.

---

[1] Annandale, *Making Profits, Protecting Our Planet*, 152.

Recovering and Jump-Starting Our Local Economies

E conomic development always starts at the local level and cre- ates a groundswell that lifts the entire economy. It is as much an art as it is a murky, imperfect science. Economic recovery is always greatly debated at the national level, but it is always determined by actions and investments made at the local level. How successful a community will be is determined by its will to determine its own future and not depend on the regional, state, or national governments. In most cases, successful communities build their own assets to address all the concerns that they feel are limiting or impeding their ability to succeed. The communities that are willing to invest in themselves and not look to others before taking action stand the best chance of being winners in this century. Such grassroots efforts will build the momentum that will eventually increase the prosperity of higher levels of governance. This phenomenon is the opposite of the trickle-down economic theory of old. It will be these pioneering, world-class, entrepreneurial communities around the world that will lift the global economy to a sustainable, re- sponsible, and healthy condition.

Tomorrow's opportunities and progress start with us individually. If we each act individually, the collective outcome will be amazing. This section focuses on what local leaders (and concerned citizens) can do to ensure that our local economies can both handle success and ride out troubled times. Additionally, in this section we will discuss how to bring additional revenue and innovative change to our local govern- ments to keep us afloat in changing times.

CHAPTER ELEVEN

Designing Hybrid Models That Orchestrate Economic Recovery

Our whole education system needs a drastic overhaul to make teaching styles less rote and more dynamic, to encourage more hands-on, interactive creativity. The centralized school system as we know it is, after all, another product of the Industrial Age. . . .

Entrepreneurship should become the fourth R, right alongside reading, writing, and arithmetic. Kids need to learn more than just the abstract principles of economics—they should be taught how to form businesses, create business plans, and market their ideas. Education can no longer be confined to traditional academic subjects; students must learn how to create something of their own. . . . We are wasting time and resources training young people for factory and administrative jobs that no longer exist; they have to learn how to innovate and create jobs of their own.

—Dr. Richard Florida[1]

Whether or not you believe our economy and American way of life need a reboot, restart, rebirth, recovery, or restructuring, if we do nothing different we as a nation will follow the same path as other great empires: into obscurity. Obviously people are beginning to realize that the return to what they perceive as normal within the economy is not very realistic. In fact, we are hearing about even greater financial woes with regard to economic instability. Folks

---

[1] Florida, "The Road Map to a High Speed Recovery," August 12, 2010.

are now beginning to realize that business as usual will only prolong our economic problems. In fact, the complete structural redevelopment of our local, state, and national economies is up for debate as a republic. People do not want to see our American values and quality of life continue on a downward spiral. We may be impatient and compulsive, but we are noted for our resolve to overcome what others seem to perceive as Herculean obstacles. Political stability, civil freedoms, and economic growth on the part of nations, regions, and communities are discussed within the context of their individual histories and routes mapped out in order to achieve these goals. The commonality of recognizing promising opportunities and then quickly adapting, refining, and customizing the tools to seize and capitalize on the opportunities remains a key factor in interpreting and defining successes large and small. There are vastly different views on the role of government in helping us to rebuild our way of life and to restore our ability to pursue economic opportunities and protect our uniquely American civil liberties. The debate over these topics ranges from socialism-based big government programs with very steep costs (affecting our corporate and individual taxes) to pure capitalism with little or no intervention by government for failed or failing companies and institutions. If we looked at what most Americans desire concerning this dichotomy, I believe we would see a hybrid of the two views, but with more a capitalistic view than a socialist one.

The process of organizing tools to address the restructuring of our economy and restoring our uniquely American capabilities of purchasing the American Dream should be tied to the concept of public-private partnerships (P3s). We do not want to become a nation of isolationists with nefarious trade barriers; Byzantine governmental programs; and pervasive, overly zealous governmental regulations. We do not want to discourage economic growth through repressive taxation and a brutal foreign policy with a gluttonous appetite for fossil fuels that comes at the expense of other nations and the planet's environmental stability overall. We want to continue to be the lighthouse to others, showing them how they can become the wealthiest and most successful business entrepreneurs on the planet; additionally, we want to show them that they can enjoy the fruits of their work with the highest level of quality of life, as well as a very competitive overhead cost of government (fair taxation) based upon realistic expectations of services delivered by our government.

In this chapter, I will focus on the hybrid potential of P3s to meet some of these expectations and goals. Throughout the chapter, I will give numerous examples of successful P3s in various industries that have restored the confidence of consumers, the workforce, and corporations, all of which have greatly helped their local economies. In addition, I will provide some important principles to help keep our P3s strong.

P3s Begin at Home

All economic development begins at the local level. Once we understand that, we can comprehend that solutions trickle up, not down; they trickle up to the bigger governmental family of our American society. Local solutions can and should be the example based on which the American economy will begin to rebuild itself. P3s almost always involve local collaboration and partnerships. Of course, the national regulatory and tax climate does have an impact, many times negatively, on the capacity of local economic development to attract and induce strategic investments into their economies.

Most folks agree that rebuilding confidence in our economy is partly based upon the belief that our workforce can be put back to work in a manner that is dignified, economically prudent for employers and employees, and robust enough to instill stability in the markets. There is a huge disconnect right now between the willingness of corporations to place investments in our economy and capital providers to fund entrepreneurial-based new growth. Quite literally, the capital markets of small businesses and medium-sized businesses, which create about 65 percent of our total employment, are desperate for capital to fund their desires to retool and to develop their businesses. In addition, the capital markets are totally untrustworthy by most folks' standards because of continued governmental support with incentive or stimulus funds that most feel have been abused and misspent.

When we consider these huge obstacles to growth, we begin to see why cooler minds need to prevail at the local level to start the collaboration with capital providers, to take advantage of economic opportunities, and to help our available workers move forward again on solid ground.

We must start with the mind-set that big government does not mean better government; in fact, big government is quite counterproductive to economic health. As Matthew Bishop, an editor for *The Economist*, said, "The reforms we need require better government rather than bigger government. The crisis was also the result of a general failure of leadership in the business world."[1] Our government has never been noted for efficiency, fairness, or good stewardship of our public funds. As much as government officials tout these concepts, nothing over the course of history has been further from the truth. Today we almost across the board feel our government has become far too wasteful, out of touch with us as taxpayers, and oppressively large and invasive into our own economic best interests, unless we are on entitlements.

To begin to create opportunities for public-private initiatives (which could focus on getting capital investments flowing and creating meaningful employment opportunities for the nearly 20 percent of individuals unemployed or underemployed), we must focus on neutralizing the fear of lost investments because of oppressive taxation. Building a shared risk-and-reward relationship for such projects is a good start. A healthy economy is beneficial to government and the workforce and thus will allow our American lifestyles to be rebuilt. This does not mean that corporations should be given taxpayer welfare for their own reduction of risk; they would simply reap all the rewards of success and suffer no casualties for poor management and strategically flawed investments. There needs to be a healthy balance of power between the risks

---

[1] Bishop, *The Road to Ruin*, 20.

and rewards, equally placed upon both the public sector and the private sector for P3s to work.

The formulation of P3s should be predicated upon the actual need for public sector involvement. If the investment does not require such involvement to reach sustainable profitability, then those investors should not receive such special favors. This means the investment has to meet the "if not but for" clause of local and state government. What this means is that without public sector financial consideration, a project would not be able to reach profitability: "if not but for collaboration with a portion of the public sector, this investment would have failed." This phrase would serve as the first test of whether a P3 should be used. Does it meet the "if not but for" clause for a call to action? This would mean that invoking this call to action should have a set of normal guidelines that are determined by each locality as to whether investors should form a P3 or not. We measure many of these conditions in terms of public impact and economic viability, and thus we look for direct and indirect positive economic outcomes for the use of such special public favors. The decision to initiate a P3 also should contain a fairly strong requirement for performance and oversight of such investments. Some examples of requirements and regulations could be as follows.

Job Creation

Local businesses are more in touch with their local residents than county, state, or federal politicians. They know that job creation is important for citizens in their locales. Therefore, the first priority for local P3s is to establish good-quality jobs for the dollars invested in or incentives granted to private enterprises. Consider how effective this partnership is in creating hundreds of jobs:

> I believe that public/private partnerships for business start-up, attraction, and recruitment are by far and away the most efficient and effective model for an economic development entity. This model best matches area resources

with business needs. One of the country's exemplary ED
[economic development] groups is the Indy Partnership.
Their support, including coordinating incentives, led to
the location of a 600-employee shared services center for
Ascension Health.

—Dennis Donovan, Site Location Consultant at
The Wadley Donovan Group[1]

The biggest failure of P3s is the fairly inflexible approach to job creation, sustainability, and continuity of employment once investments
are made. For example, if all agree that a new business requires one
hundred jobs today to conduct the operations and they expect to create additional jobs in the future, then the basis for the measurement
of the investment must be on jobs created today. If additional jobs
are created in the future, then the further consideration of additional
public sector funding or incentives can be considered. So what is the
determinant of how much should be given per job? It should be based
on several factors: the payroll total, including part-time employment,
and the average wages compared to the average per capita wage for
the area. The last factor to consider is the actual number of new jobs
created that exceeds the normal wages for the area by some major percentage—25 percent or more. Those jobs should be given additional
precedent for economic benefit.

Direct Investment in Facilities, Equipment, Fixtures, and Machinery

The metrics of the age-old determinant for the amount of capital invested should be linked to actual capital needs for real tangible products.
These types of investments allow for something tangible to purchased,
built, and used in the market that adds to the tax base and direct value
of the local area's assets in the economy now and in the future. Today
is no different than the past; an economy based in both facilities and
infrastructure is essential to economic vitality. Too many communities

---

[1] Dennis Donovan, e-mail message to author, June 28, 2011.

are hanging onto dinosaur buildings that have decayed far beyond their useful lives. Real estate, unless historically significant, is not something to be emotionally attached to; it is a resource for economic development.

Diversification of the Economy

While working to keep local businesses healthy cannot be overlooked, the addition of new, innovative industries that are forward thinking is critical to maintaining a balanced local economy. Creating new investments in key growth sectors is not only wise, it is required if an economy is going to be highly positioned for sustainable growth and thus capable of replacing old economy jobs and investments with those in new economy opportunities. As this is an important factor, some industries deserve more merit in this category than others. For example, retail creates more overall instant cash for governments than manufacturing and other sectors of the economy, but retail jobs typically pay less; thus, the overall indirect value to the local economy is better served by creating jobs within industries that pay much better wages, which will result in employees in those industries spending more of their higher income in the local economy.

Return on Investment to Taxpayers (Direct and Indirect)

So how much money is prudent to invest in P3s? The answer should be based upon two major factors. The first is direct economic impact, measured by tangible outcomes with real economic return on investment. Examples include loan funds, forgiveness of fees, equity contributions, payment of due diligence, business case evaluation, and promotion to the investor markets. Included in this could be improvements to the physical site, such as grading, roads, and horizontal and vertical infrastructure. For these types of investments, the private sector should be required to repay the public sector the same cost of capital according to their own expectations and as a priority before any profit distribution. The other factor is indirect benefits, and those are linked to business climate adjustments. Entrepreneurs need to understand the amount of deferred costs that the public sector is allowing to be absent from the business during some predetermined period. Such examples are ad valorem taxes, business operational taxes such as personal property taxes, inventory costs, and profits. These considerations are necessary for job creation and the additional (though delayed) tax base increase, in what we refer to as "found money" or performance-based funds—those funds that are created by the investment itself but not present in the economy already.

Clawbacks and Penalties for Failure

As in all things, some investments will thrive and survive and some will die on the vine. The calculation of failure and its impact on public sector partners is just as important as the expectation of the impact of the success of the project on the local economy and the local government. Risk and reward are essential to the building blocks of a successful P3 strategy. Naïve public sector partners and unrealistic and/or greedy private sector partners can destroy a desirable foundation for a successful P3. The creation of reasonable expectations that are attainable should be the foundation for establishing clawback terms and conditions that are reachable by the private sector. The term *clawback*, widely used in the economic development industry, refers to the payback of incentive money for failure to meet performance requirements. If a private client does not perform as promised, the government has the right to require that the paid incentives be returned to the government, usually with steep penalties, plus interest and the loss of additional incentives.[1] An example of a clawback is raising the cost of interest on the public sector investment if the job requirements are not met. However, it is more equitable and less punitive, in my opinion, to raise capital costs than to require penalty payments. The reason for this is that flexibility is essential in such matters. Flexibility is important because there may need to be changes made to the business to keep it profitable by reducing employment and/or investing in additional automation and

---

[1] See White, *Financing Economic Development*.

technology. Such investment flexibility is essential to the overall success of private investors.

Variations on a Theme I: Local Venture Capital Funds

Another P3 model that involves raising local capital is nearly forty-two years old. Back in the late 1960s, members of the South St. Paul, Minnesota, community (which was the eyesore of St. Paul first-ring suburbs due to the stockyard facility) banded together to create a public-private local venture capital fund called the South St. Paul Future Fund. Members of the community partnered with the city and local economic development agency through the Chamber of Commerce and used a professional staff to operate the fund and manage projects to be funded. The fund sold shares to families, business people, and corporations, limiting the number of shares sold to a few hundred. This fund was reinvested each time a project came to fruition, and the payoff eventually retired the investment with profit. The profits were always reinvested into new job creation projects, such as speculative buildings for business and historic redevelopment (eventually turning the former stockyard facility into a business and industry park). Today the fund is worth millions of dollars and has invested in a host of projects that have turned around the image of South St. Paul, keeping it progressive and attracting large numbers of jobs for the citizens. The fund is so popular and exclusive that each year it holds a gala, so that stockholders who want to sell their stock for face value can be paid out and individuals can bid to become new stockholders. The price is always much higher by bid than the face amount, and the net funds go into the fund. The stockholders are truly the who's who of the community, and it is considered an honor to be part of this elite community group.

Variations on a Theme II: The Automotive Industry

Another example of P3 projects that have stood the test of time are the automotive factories developed by BMW in South Carolina and the more recent plant developed by VW in Chattanooga, Tennessee. The early BMW deal was a groundbreaking example of positioning the New South as the tip of the spear for a slow trend of manufacturing rebirth for the United States.

> The 1992 BMW manufacturing project in South Carolina (Greenville), now almost 20 years on, is the best example I have seen of the public and private sectors working together for the economic development of a state, a region, and individual communities. I have never heard any serious criticism about the effect of this project on the entire community and region. I believe the same thing is happening, in Chattanooga, with the VW manufacturing project.
> —Russ Fronenberger, FDI Consultant[1]

Clearly the US automotive industry has been hard hit and has suffered tremendous job losses over the past two decades. This has happened in many cases due to apathy. Civic leaders refused to believe that their plants would close, unions did not collaborate with the automotive executives, and nobody made decisions in the best interest of job preservation and rebuilding the competitive nature of the plants and the industry.

My own hometown of Dayton, Ohio, saw all its GM plants (seven of them) close in the last decade; this was followed by the announcement that NCR's world headquarters and the majority of NCR's production facilities were moving out of town. The entire economy has been decimated due to this series of events. Yet the automotive industry's leadership seems stuck in neutral. The only way to compete with global pressures is to take the lead in investing or reinvesting, in most cases in our communities, states, and country. If we couple investments in key industries with new rules restricting the exportation of know-how to other nations, we can turn the corner and rekindle American ingenuity and manufacturing.

---

[1] Russ Fronenberger, e-mail to author, July 1, 2011.

A great example of a P3 in the automotive industry is when Chrysler decided to close its Jeep plant in Toledo, Ohio, in the early 1990s. According to Don Jakeway, then-director of the Ohio Department of Commerce, he and Governor Voinovich learned of this decision to close at a dinner in northwest Ohio. They had little time to prepare for intervention, but they worked at a rapid speed to organize a team of stakeholders so they could respond to the urgent threat of the loss of the Jeep plant. The call to action was immediately sounded, and the result was one of the most exciting responses I have ever seen. Stakeholders who came forward to be a part of "Team Jeep" were the governor and the governor's administration, the state legislature, mayors, city councils, county officials, organized labor, members of the Chamber of Commerce, economic development agencies of all kinds (public and private), the media, workers, and thousands of citizens. There was a unique atmosphere present as everyone worked together to deal with the situation. No panic, just an overwhelming consensus of support that needed to occur in order to come up with a true, long-term business plan on how to respond to Chrysler.

There was no mention of "us versus them," "winners or losers," "Republicans or Democrats," "labor or management," or who might be to blame for the situation. It was 100 percent mobilization of very talented people, creative ideas, innovative financial considerations, and a desire to present as many business options as possible to "Save Jeep" in northwest Ohio.

When it was all said and done, Chrysler officials received one of the most creative proposals ever seen and they therefore made one of the best business decisions they could make. They chose an older urban area over a greenfield site (raw land or previously undeveloped property that has brand-new construction). Technology and advanced manufacturing opportunities were used in a concentrated effort to build the new Jeep complex, with world-class infrastructure and transportation capabilities. Labor brought to the table short- and long-term proposals to financially invest in the future sustainability of all the facilities, and the various levels of government participated with a wide array of very important incentive considerations.

This $1.6 billion investment was one of the largest economic development deals in the country and led the way for several best practices in the field of economic development.

> The current international and national challenges of our economy could learn from this project; they would realize they need such partnerships in the future, especially in hard-hit regions of the US.
>
> —Don Jakeway, President/CEO of Brooks
> Development Authority[1]

Variations on a Theme III: Tourism-Based Local Economies

Even places like Las Vegas, which have been going through tremendous economic strains and have been struggling to keep the luxury of huge revenues from tourism, are turning to more traditional economic development to offset the downturn due to the tighter coffers of their traditional tourists. Recently, Scott Adams, the chief redevelopment officer for the city of Las Vegas, presented me with the following description of the latest Las Vegas initiatives:

> While the term "public-private partnership" is a well-worn term within the economic development profession, it still is very pertinent as it relates to significant undertakings by the public sector. Examples include project-oriented partnerships, whereby the public sector engages with a private party to secure development of a major project, ranging from real estate developments designed to catalyze an area of a city, such as within a downtown area or a neighborhood, to business projects whereby with strategic public injection the public sector convinces or induces

---

[1] Don Jakeway, e-mail to author, July 5, 2011.

a business to locate in a community. In every instance the partnership implies that each party gives something (incentives, infrastructure, etc.), in exchange for each getting something significant in return (greater profitability, jobs, taxes, etc.). The more skilled community and professional will measure the benefits and costs to both parties in such an endeavor.[2]

Adams went on to say that an example of this in Las Vegas is a recent agreement with a developer and Zappos.com. They were allowed space within the Las Vegas city hall building for their corporate headquarters. The local city government was selling the building at a discount as an incentive for these private companies, but the city government reaped the rewards of this partnership by receiving a steady stream of income from the sale as well as the creation of jobs; Zappos.com started with 1,200 employees and may potentially accommodate many thousands someday. "Both parties received a significant benefit in exchange for a mutual commitment by each," Adams said.

Despite the potential success, the use of P3s cannot offset a horribly inefficient business climate with oppressive taxes and unproductive and costly workforce conditions in an inferior or antiquated infrastructure. Until we address the structural changes that will reset our economy, making it one of the most cost-effective business climates with extremely high investment returns, we cannot build a sustainable position to attract consistent investments. In the interim, the use of P3s can be used by localities to balance investment fears and allow time for corrective action to make structural changes to our overall economy, especially with regard to taxation.

Special taxing districts are one of the major benefits that have been derived from the concept of P3s. These districts allow an investment company or a group of businesses to partner with their public cohorts and monetize their future tax streams to create additional investment

---

[2] Scott Adams, e-mail to author, June 30, 2011.

equity on the front end of projects. This buys down the up-front costs and thus increases the return on investment to the investors over time, all the while reducing the tax burden during the initial amortized period to allow for the stabilization of operations. These special districts have been heavily used in the development of tourism-oriented venues, such as ball parks, theme parks, permanent festival structures, specialty retail, restaurant and bar zones, and performing and visual arts districts.

Joy Wilkins, senior fellow at the University of Georgia's Fanning Institute, referred to Atlanta in her explanation of how taxes and P3s can work in harmony. The following is from an e-mail to me on July 1, 2011, used with permission:

> The idea for Atlanta to serve as the host city for the 1996 Centennial Olympic Games was the brainchild of William Porter Payne, a highly regarded business leader and philanthropist with a vision. Payne and then-City of Atlanta Mayor Andrew Young led a group of business and political leaders to turn this vision into a reality. They set out to demonstrate how Atlanta's hosting of the Olympics could provide economic impacts beyond the games. The Atlanta Olympic venues continue to be used today in a number of ways and include facilities such as Turner Field (home of the Atlanta Braves), the Georgia International Horse Park, and dormitories at Georgia Tech. These facilities and others developed for the Games represent more than $650 million in investment of mostly private dollars. In addition, Downtown Atlanta benefitted from such an inflow of public and private investment that the Games are credited with spurring what was dubbed a "downtown renaissance." A core part of this renaissance was the development of a $77 million, privately financed, twenty-one-acre park known as Centennial Olympic Park. Having been inspired by his visit to the 1992 Summer Olympic Games,

Payne saw how Barcelona provided an exciting twenty-four-hour pedestrian experience around the Games using public space and decided to put his philanthropic dollars to work in 1995 at creating a similar experience in Atlanta. Soon thereafter, efforts were underway to create the Centennial Olympic Park Area, Inc. (COPA), a non-profit organization "to attract, guide, and facilitate the development of the area surrounding Centennial Olympic Park," which, at the time, was largely characterized by dilapidated, underused real estate. COPA soon partnered with the Atlanta Development Authority (ADA), the city of Atlanta's economic development arm, to develop a tax allocation district (TAD) around the park, which would incentivize private investment through tax increment financing. Since COPA's efforts, the City of Atlanta and other Georgia communities have used TADs as a tool to make other large-scale economic development revitalization projects with private partners possible as well.

The success of this P3 in Atlanta shows the importance of relaxing taxation to extend the partnership's influence and profitability to both public and private parties.

Variations on a Theme IV: Infrastructure Projects

Partnerships have led to the completion of a variety of real estate projects: mixed-use developments, urban renewal through land and property assembly, public facilities like convention centers and airports, and public services such as affordable housing and military housing. As of late, many P3s have engaged in retail sales tax–oriented tourism projects to bring in much-needed sales tax revenue to relieve the local public sector of shrinking revenue sources. In addition, these revenues help stem the increasing demand for cash to attend to the expectations of local constituents for basic things such as roads;

infrastructure; and maintenance of public lands and parks, including sporting facilities.

The need to rebuild and revitalize older portions of our towns, cities, and urban areas, coupled with the public need to monetize and in many cases off-load untenable and underperforming or underused assets, has dramatically changed the rules of this game for economic development and the concept of P3s. In the past the general public and even many of our elected officials have relied upon the private sectors' capital to pay the high price of assembling and preparing appropriate sites for redevelopment and new catalyst projects to spur economic development. In these increasingly fiscally tight economic times, the general public can no longer rely upon their local governments to bear the full burden of paying the associated costs for public infrastructure development and facilities renovation or retooling. One of the most-often inefficient areas of concern and thus the best starting point for many reforms is to address the planning and zoning controls, which are often either inadequate or too inflexible to ensure appropriate control of outcome expectations or desired private sector return on investment expectations.

Successful P3s around the United States

States are beginning to address the failure of traditional economic development agencies to close deals due to the tight financial markets. Moreover, traditional lending venues and the reluctance of those who provide nontraditional lending are hesitant to engage in restarting investments for new job creations projects, in particular greenfield projects (brand-new construction on raw land or previously undeveloped property). Since this has been a difficult issue to overcome, states such as Virginia and Texas, two powerhouse giants in the creative economic development industry, have adapted by creating special legislation to help state and local governments pool resources and invest in P3s, legislation which allows them to create new jobs and invest in new brick-and-mortar projects. This legislation will hopefully spur other states to

respond in kind and get their acts together to help the financial investment markets flow again. Consider these P3 examples in Texas:

> Texans have long embraced the vitality and efficacy of
> public-private partnerships. Several well-known ex-
> amples include the Cowboys Stadium in Arlington, the
> Texas Brain and Spine Institute in Bryan, and the Ameri-
> can Airlines Center/Victory Park in Dallas, among others.
> However, the need for transparency and better contract
> efficiencies was recognized in the recent Texas 82nd Leg-
> islative session where CSSB 1048 was considered and
> passed to Governor Rick Perry for his signature. Taking
> measures to expedite and reduce the cost of public proj-
> ects is necessary for our high growth state. Project delays
> can increase costs, as land and building materials become
> more expensive. This legislation will establish a unified
> and straightforward process for governmental entities to
> follow when pursuing public-private partnerships within
> their respective jurisdictions. A newly created Partnership
> Advisory Commission will oversee the implementation of
> comprehensive agreements for public-private projects.
>
> —Dr. Karin Richmond, Economist

Barry Matherly, the executive director of the Lincoln County, North
Carolina, Economic Development Association, explains the importance
of this symbiotic relationship between public and private entities:

> The greatest need for public-private partnerships, especial-
> ly in rural and ex-urban communities, is in the develop-
> ment of business parks and sites. Even the best marketing
> organizations cannot be successful without ready-to-de-
> velop sites. Communities need a product to sell. And this
> need comes at a time when developing new business parks
> is very costly and risky for local governments. In partnering

with the private sector, communities can greatly reduce
their liability and costs while bringing new products on-
line to meet the needs of their recruiting targets.[1]

Matherly went on to explain a specific example of this in regard to
Lincoln County's own development of a new business and industry
park. He said that in 2002, the Lincoln Economic Development Association and private landowners came together to develop a 500-acre business park in order to attract new companies to the local community. The
landowners agreed to contribute their land, through options, for future
revenue as sites were sold. "If not but for" this patient capital, the project might have been impossible.

This development alone saved the community over $12 million in
land costs and allowed the public sector contributions to go directly into
public infrastructure, so that the property was what is referred to as
shovel ready, a site that is ready for permitting. The local community
also partnered with private developers to provide speculative building as a catalyst to attract some early adopters to their park. After eight
years, over 3.6 million square feet of buildings have been developed and
over 2,500 residents have jobs in what was once a cow pasture—and all
these rewards are due to a P3. Mark Barbash, an economic developer
and former director of the Ohio Department of Development, gives us a
good reminder of what the motivations of each party should be and how
those motivations can be used to start an effective P3:

> The challenge and the opportunity in developing effective
> public/private partnerships are in bringing together dif-
> ferent cultures, in enabling each to understand the mo-
> tivations of the other, and then seeing themselves in the
> opportunities for collaboration. While we always hope
> that each of the partners is coming to the table void of
> self-interest—or at least with an open mind—the reality

---

[1] Barry Matherly, e-mail to author, June 30, 2011.

is that enlightened self-interest is at the heart of a truly effective PPP. In the context of economic development, this can translate into new creative ideas that could not have been imagined individually. And to start effectively, a PPP needs two critical elements: The first is the proverbial early-adopter, a strong community leader who can serve as the honest broker among conflicting interests. And the second, at the right time, is the first project that can help break the ice."[2]

Barbash also cited the following example of a very effective P3: TechSolve in Cincinnati, Ohio. TechSolve is a consulting firm that helps businesses in the aerospace and aviation industries to solve complex manufacturing problems. Why does TechSolve work? First, it has strong leaders who know how to bring people together. Its long-term director, Gary Conley, has an economic development background that has assisted in bringing people together. Second, TechSolve has a diverse and active board of directors that represents business, government, and education. Represented on the board are key business stakeholders at the highest levels, including Boeing, GE, Milacron, and P&G. Third, TechSolve has a professional staff who are focused on results. And fourth, TechSolve understands its core capabilities and always seeks to identify new opportunities. Ohio's TechSolve, North Carolina's Lincoln Economic Development Association, Texas' Partnership Advisory Commission, Atlanta's COPA and ADA, and all the other good examples of P3s from around the United States show that it is possible to form a truly successful and worthwhile partnership.

P3s around the World

With declining levels of public resources that must fulfill social and physical needs, and with more pressure from the general public for greater accountability in financial investments, partnerships between

---

[2] Mark Barbash, e-mail to author, June 30, 2011.

public and private entities must become increasingly permanent and their comprehensive nature must create the capacity to undertake new catalyst projects. Europe has been lagging behind the United States in this regard and as such, Europe's economic recovery may be prolonged due to this lack of collaboration. As described in a recent Pricewater-houseCoopers (PwC) report:

> Although there are a number of EU [European Union] statements and reviews concerning PPPs [private-public partnerships], there is no discernible EU PPP policy. . . . Little actual progress concerning the development of PPPs has been made, and there is considerable uncertainty as to how PPPs interact with EU legislation and regulations.

Our northern neighbors in Canada have been much more aggressive in their pursuit of P3s, but they are much more driven by local innovation rather than national policy, as are their distant cousins down under in Australia.

> P3s have long been a key component to economic development in Canada—investing strategically in projects that provide some level of public benefit while creating jobs is the key to public acceptance and understanding.
> —Robert Fine, Director of Economic Development of the
> Greater Kelowna Area, British Columbia, Canada[1]

Fine goes on to describe another success story, which involves benefits not only for Canadian public and private groups but also for groups in the United States. This example shows that P3s can not only benefit the country in which they are formed but can also bestow financial boons on other countries.

> The City of Kelowna was in desperate need for a hockey arena/seated facility in order to achieve a number of key

---

[1] Robert Fine, e-mail to author, June 28, 2011.

economic objectives. To begin with, the continued growth and creation of a cultural district in downtown could use an arena to move more people into the downtown core and stimulate the food, restaurant, and accommodation sectors. Secondly, to be deemed an attractive community to younger people (being the oldest Census city in Canada) a downtown arena would provide a venue for key entertainment figures and events. Finally, the Kelowna Rockets, a Western Hockey League Team, did not believe it was reaching its full potential and believed it could become a significant contributor to the local economy.

The City of Kelowna entered into a public-private partnership with RG Properties in 1998 to build, operate, and maintain the facility. The partnership agreement was the first of its kind in a medium-sized B.C. community. This unique partnership led to changes in the Municipal Act (now known as the Local Government Act). In 2001, the City of Kelowna/Prospera partnership garnered the City an award from the Canadian Council of Public-Private Partnerships for innovation.

The building has been a huge success by many different measures. The Kelowna Rockets commissioned an impact assessment last year that demonstrates the following:

The indirect economic impact of the Kelowna Rockets on the City of Kelowna is more than $31 million.

The direct economic impact of the Rockets is more than $3.9 million new revenue into the local economy.

The economic impact of playoffs, pre-season, and special events is more than $5.3 million to the local economy.

The economic impact of the Rockets' social activities is more than $242,000.

The long-term impact of former players and local staff living in Kelowna is more than $7 million annually.

All this would not have happened without the facility. It
also became a new cultural hub with a range of artists per-
forming at the arena, including Avril Lavigne, Hilary Duff,
David Bowie, Cher, Bob Dylan, Sir Elton John, Backstreet
Boys, The Black Eyed Peas, Jay-Z, Cirque du Soleil, and
New Kids on the Block, among others.

The government of Australia approached the opportunity for P3s
very aggressively when the financial markets melted down in 2008
globally. The Council of Australia Governments endorsed the National
Public-Private Partnership Policy and Guidelines on November 29, 2008.
All Australian state and territory government agencies now apply the
National Policy and Guidelines. This gives Australian communities access to a well-designed national guideline that will assist them not only
in drawing in national funds to match local funds but also in attracting
private sector investors.[1]

My experience at a local community economic development level in Australia revolves around creating a level
of trust between government, private sector and not-for-
profit organizations as the key ingredient to developing
sustainable public-private partnerships. Without the appropriate data and levels of trust how can there be a positive partnership?
    —Simon Millcock, Economic Development Officer of
    Australia's Indian Ocean Territories and Director of Eco-
                nomic Development in Australia[2]

Millcock also cited the following example of a rural initiative that
happened in Australia:

---

[1] Commonwealth of Australia, "Public Private Partnerships," August 4, 2011.
[2] Simon Millcock, e-mail to author, July 1, 2011.

An example of a project I worked on in South Australia's Adelaide Plains was a clear example of how partnerships can work to gain the maximum effect with little need for local outlays. The two local councils commissioned a housing study due to the lack of housing development in a number of their towns since they had been unable to attract housing developers. The study identified a lack of community housing and noted that the state government had a program where they would provide up to 85 percent of the costs for community housing.

This resulted in the identification of two parcels of land owned by the [local] Councils who provided them for community housing. They partnered with a community housing management group from a neighboring region, local builders, and the local high school, who undertook the landscaping. This resulted in seven new homes being built for an outlay of zero dollars within six months, which in turn stimulated a growth in local housing over the next three years, managing to construct close to one hundred new homes and three hundred new allotments.

Another unique and exciting example of a P3 came from an industry near and dear to me in the land down under. I learned of this on my speaking tour in 2010 when I traveled around Australia. I felt that the unique rural nature of this place, combined with the speed of implementation and exponential outcomes, made it special. I noticed this spirit all around Australia when I was there, in world-class farmers' markets and in unique bed-and-breakfast facilities. Much can be learned from our friends down under and up above.

The Keys to Creating and Maintaining Healthy P3s

The model for great partnerships must be driven by replacing potential confrontation with collaboration to achieve shared goals and objectives.

These goals include monetary gain in the case of the private sector and direct and indirect economic impacts in the public sector. This process requires that those involved demonstrate ample levels of acumen and statesmanship with regard to applying their efforts and skills to weighing and assessing parameters, bringing into a balance public and private interests, and heading off or minimizing potential conflicts. Today, P3s are considered creative alliances formed between government entities and private developers or enterprises to achieve a common purpose that is beneficial to both parties. There have been some early adopters of these guidelines in the Erie, Pennsylvania region. These early adopters have had some significant successes due to their acquired knowledge of brokering public-private collaborations.

> Public/private partnerships are about money, roles, and vision. Most of the time, the focus is on the money, but the most successful partnerships have complementary, clearly defined, and well understood roles for all parties involved that start with a clear and understood vision of the issue(s) being addressed. Tactics will flow out of those three components and execution will proceed smoothly provided money remains available and the roles and vision remain well understood."
>
> —Jake Rouch, Vice President of Economic
> Development, Erie Regional Chamber[1]

There has been an increase in entities most likely to engage in such partnerships, including nongovernmental institutions; health care providers; educational institutions; nonprofit associations aimed at community and economic development initiatives; and intermediary groups, such as business improvement districts, community development lending agencies, and special financing organizations. These special financing organizations have particular economic development

---

[1] Jake Rouch, e-mail to author, June 30, 2011.

purposes, such as job creation and reinvigorating capital investment at their core. There has been much debate regarding these partnerships around the country, many of which are being cited as successfully implementing a wide range of pursuits, from single projects to long-term plans for land use and economic growth. Still, the concept of P3s is widely used in terminology but little understood by the general public. A better performance would reignite economic growth in America.

P3s are the investment methodology that is moving economic development projects forward in today's volatile finance markets. The biggest challenge for economic developers will be to make these type of partnerships scalable so that almost any business can find a process that will facilitate the same vein of cooperation as in the larger projects discussed. These larger projects have demonstrated that it is possible, even when the project is a traditional small business with only a few employees.

Ralph Basile, principal of Basile Baumann Prost Cole & Associates, recently created a scorecard for financing tools. When these tools are coupled with a well-done P3 initiative, catalyst funding is created, which can make local investments flow again. While the five financing sources (tax increment financing, tax abatements, brownfield funding, community development block grants, and new market tax credit funding[2]) are great examples, they simply are not enough, in my opinion; they are only the tip of the spear in building a financial model that will garner investment in tough or highly distressed markets. When we approach the development of a strong P3, it is important to have some measure of realistic expectations, what will be achieved and why, and who will perform to the standards, as well as how we will measure success. The following is a solid overview of how to begin to formulate our understanding of this reality.

---

[2] Basile, "Scorecard," 50–56.

At the Outset

1.   Appoint a single public sector spokesperson. This may be tough politically, but from the private sector perspective, it's maddening to negotiate with a table full of people.

2.   Review any changes in public policy objectives or tools. Is there still an appetite for tax incremental financing on the city's behalf, to still charge for parking, to keep funding a convention center?

3.   Set a firm timetable to renegotiate. For example, give a couple months to continue negotiating terms, but that's it.

Problem-Solving Phase

4.   Keep a sharp focus on real estate basics. Remember that market principles govern the private partner's participation in the game.

5.   Equitably value indirect public contributions to solving problems. If the city changes zoning or other regulations that create value to the developer, be sure to monetize and capture that value.

6.   Limit public sector profit expectations. It may make sense to restructure the deal with a smaller share of the profit going to the public entity, at least initially. This frees up operating capital for use by the developer.

7.   Consider establishing or enhancing public reserves or paybacks out of profits. A city can backstop coverage of selected project expenses while it is still in distress and get any payouts returned when the project starts performing or is improving in profitability.

Ongoing

8. Avoid even the perception of suspicious renegotiated terms. Transparency is vital.

9. Be patient. It took time to create the mess; it will take time to work it out.

10. Stay in the way. Require public approval of future structural changes in business deals—for example, re-financing. It doesn't cost the public entity anything and keeps its hand on the throttle.[1]

The Urban Land Institute published the following information related to this subject:[2]

- Prepare Properly for Public/Private Partnerships,
- Create a Shared Vision,
- Understand Your Partners and Key Players,
- Be Clear on the Risks and Rewards for All Parties,
- Establish a Clear and Rational Decision-Making Process,
- Make Sure All Parties Do Their Homework,
- Secure Consistent and Coordinated Leadership,
- Communicate Early and Often,
- Negotiate a Fair Deal Structure, and
- Build Trust as a Core Value.

Why Do P3s Make Sense Today?

In conclusion, we can no longer afford to place our trust in one or the other—in the public sector or the private sector—completely. We must come to expect and demand more transparency in such dealings to create economic development outcomes, but we must also accept that with such partnerships the private sector will demand special dividends

---

[1] Basile, "Scorecard," 50–56.

[2] Corrigan, *10 Principles for a Successful Public Private Partnership*, 8.

that will bolster the return on investment and provide for better preservation of capital and surety of sustainability. To this regard, both the public and private sectors need to learn to work together to reinstate confidence in the economy and achieve what I refer to as "deal equilibrium," where both sectors have risks and rewards in the proposed solution or opportunity.

P3s can share risk and thus rewards between the public entities and private sector investors. Both parties can benefit from the collaboration. The reason we don't hear much about P3s in the press is that they are often based on unrealistic expectations and the media tends to view them as corporate welfare or a strategy that is not necessary for economic growth. In this global economy, however, the use of P3s is indispensable and should be exponentially encouraged in order to fundamentally improve our economic development conditions. Today, investors have literally worldwide suitors for their cash. As such, business climates vary across the board. P3s can assist communities that need to address what might normally be a very high cost of doing business.

Running the gauntlet today in order to get projects financed is no easy task, and it demands that both the private sector and public sector sit down and work together. In the case of such projects, it is also acceptable to hold the private sector to standards like creating living wage jobs, working on innovating long-term and sustainable economic growth opportunities, and attracting new investments that will both diversify the local economy and appeal to and retain highly skilled workers in the area.

This includes the creation of the necessary amenities to make communities more livable and attractive to both singles and families. The initiative to create more energy efficiency and improve the early adaptation of renewable and affordable clean energy sources is a wide net that can take this concept of P3s down to the individual citizen and family. Truly systemic change has to be nurtured at the individual level, and using these principles of P3s at grassroots levels can help us as a nation address our fossil fuel addiction and reduce our carbon footprint to become a much more healthy participant in the earth system. In short, the possibilities for P3 to solve other local, state, national, and international problems are unlimited as we choose to work together for greater goals.

CHAPTER TWELVE

The Art of the Deal Today

Often the difference between a successful person and a failure is not
one has better abilities or ideas, but the courage that one has to bet
on one's ideas, to take a calculated risk—and to act.

—André Malraux[1]

I n this post-meltdown economy, the way to finance business expansion and start-ups has changed immensely. Today, previous experiences mean nothing as traditional banking dries up. Friends and family are uptight and too scared to invest, if they actually have jobs and any funds to invest. The rules are just out the window. Today, business investment has to rely on new hybrid sources of capital, which is most effective when linked to public partners investing in collaboration with the private debt and equity sources. This reliance on hybrid sources of capital illustrates what I call "The Art of the Deal Today."

The deals that receive funding are usually part of a well-orchestrated P3. So how are we to create solutions that capitalize on P3 projects in tough times?

First, we need strong leadership in the field of economic development. We need men and women who are willing to try new approaches. An economic developer is a prime mover, a facilitator of means-to-an-end projects or a facilitator of developing public purpose that will economically benefit the greatest number of constituents. As such, the developer is expected to be a liaison extraordinaire, a provocateur of the feasible, a

---

[1] As quoted in Kerry, *Tigers of the Tigris*, 107.

person of specific knowledge interwoven with a general understanding of enterprise; a persona who above all else is a person of action.

Second, we need cooperation in and with the public sector to elicit change across economic America. It is a fundamental consideration that government is a servant of the people fighting for the best interests of the people. The fiscal basis of governmental operations is founded on taxing its citizens with reasonable oversight and transparency in such operations. Citizens, through their representatives or by means of referendums, establish tax policies. The distribution of tax money is a solemn undertaking; ostensibly, tax policy and distribution of this revenue is purposefully designed to serve the public's best interests exclusively.

The important concept of the rising value of P3s, as discussed in the previous chapter, is the ability of public and private entities to work on jointly beneficial ideals that enrich the private sector investors based on market needs as well as on the general public's best interests or desired outcomes. A developer tries to create jobs, diversify the local economy, redevelop a previously fallow or unproductive asset within the community, enhance the tax base by creating new facilities and infrastructure, create access to patient capital, and more.

The financial meltdown and then the freezing of capital and lending from traditional sources has been the most critical issue stopping America's economic engine from running on all fifty cylinders again. So if we want to solve our local economic development problems or create solutions to opportunities, then capitalization that is both locally oriented and controlled or managed is essential. Simply put, unless we locally strive to thaw our local capital markets, economic development will continue to be stranded in our twenty-first-century economic ice age.

World-class communities embrace the concept of shared risk and reward and put some proverbial skin in the game up front. This is a major shift from the more traditional pay-as-you go strategy by simply reducing taxes through rebates or abatements. Now communities are becoming equity players, participating in the risk of concept development, giving due diligence, supporting the basis for business investments, and providing their share of the equity required to help investors fund business opportunities. Their rewards are both traditional in value, such as jobs, tax base, and economic diversity, and also nontraditional, like additional revenue or profits used to further fund capital requirements for yet other projects. It is this catalyst approach to economic development capitalization that will create the local growth that should lift Brand America back to sustainable economic growth and restore confidence in economic vitality.

Facilitating employment, broadening the scope of a soundly dependable and sustainable taxable base, and spreading the burden of taxation and thus reducing the burden on US constituents overall creates a favorable business investment climate that should promote economic prosperity if done with fiscally prudent, balanced governance. Government must, while striving to fulfill its noted obligations to the electorate, mitigate the risk of the people's capital and not act irresponsibly. Otherwise, government will have the reverse effect, actually increasing the burden on the general public and creating additional or nonfundable liabilities. Achieving the dynamics of economic development is the challenging task all towns, cities, counties, states, and even the national government face as we consider how to assist the recovery of mostly local economies around the world.

There has been a paradigm shift in the United States over the last couple of years toward bigger government as a solution for economic development or economic recovery. The involvement of the federal government in such concepts is not something that should be done without considerable discourse. Setting precedents for putting taxpayer money at risk is a dangerous and slippery slope.

There is no doubt that government can and should play a role in the recovery process—in particular, in creating the right business climate for market makers and investments. In the end, it is always the local economic decisions that have the economic initiative and that create opportunity; it is usually the higher levels of public policy regarding business climate that require local level adjustments in order to maintain some modicum of reality for continued or renewed economic growth. These various levels of government are not efficient in their dealings with each other, and thus great disparity exists within the overall marketplace from city to city, state to state, and country to country.

This disparity calls into question the manner in which and under what conditions should taxpayer money be placed at risk and why and how would the money reduce liabilities and provide surety for such actions. Determining the risks and rewards of such considerations is a heady matter. Raising government involvement is not a panacea for success in such endeavors and could just turn into a boondoggle that consumes taxpayer money unnecessarily if not approached with the right mind-set. Running these gauntlets to achieve our goal requires a savvy approach, and beginning such endeavors should only be done under the right market-based conditions.

This book was written with the purpose of designing a real-world operational plan of action—a combatant's guide on how to analyze and decipher possibilities, establish project specific criteria, create an operational gauntlet, and use the power of persuasion in the interest of consensus. The following section lays out a plan for using a market-based approach to engage in balanced P3s in order to capitalize on economic development investments in this new era.

Step 1: The Gauntlet

Today the competition for capital is intense, and it places even more pressure on governmental and quasi-governmental entities to engage in catalyst-type projects to ignite or renew their local economies. The temptation to meddle and tinker with ideas of how to best incentivize the private sector to invest in economic development projects is as old as capitalism itself. Today people seem to think that each crisis we face is unique and the first of its kind; nothing is further from the truth. We have numerous lessons throughout history about governments responding to crises of all types, including economic bubbles, which are themselves as old as capitalism. Just think how silly the first bubble would seem today—the Dutch tulip bulb bubble of 1636–1637. Nonetheless, the mixing of public and private sector capital to achieve acceptable outcomes from the perspectives of various levels of government is an inevitable engagement.

Since the use of public capital is a serious matter, we must take a hard look at how best to engage such capital so that the gauntlet can be navigated with a high degree of scrutiny and transparency. In all cases there needs to be a practical approach that develops the use of criteria that can assist in avoiding transactions that would otherwise put public capital into nonrecoverable investments. Bad investments would erode the public trust that is given to governmental agencies as the representatives of the public's financial interests. Thus, running the gauntlet is as much a science as it is an art of skilled but learned practices that improve the odds of such investments being successful. Therefore, it is sufficient to say that calculating the risks is important, but averting risk is nearly impossible.

Step 2: The Audit of Public Purpose Leadership

One of the first criteria when considering the entire climate for creating P3s is the capacity of the general public to be engaged in such activities in the first place. Most private sector firms miss the mark totally on this issue until it is too late and they have inadvertently placed too much financial trust in their public sector partners, with the result that they cannot effectuate the financial outcomes that they had hoped for. The biggest cause for such misplaced trust is the complete breakdown of doing as much due diligence on the public side of the ledger as public sector partners require of private sector partners. While it may appear that we are discussing a financial review, we are not; that will come in the next chapter. When private sector firms seek to adjoin with public sector partners, it is essential to their success that they understand the actual connections to the public leadership with regard to the structure of the political jurisdiction they are considering, as well as the actual experience and acumen of the elected and appointed staff they will be partnering with.

There are varying forms of administrative management styles in economic development and other public sector agencies that are engaged in capitalization—the capitalization of business investments to create jobs, to increase the tax base of the jurisdiction, and usually to diversify the local economy. The enabling laws behind each agency differ widely and give a variety of powers (and limitations of powers) as to how the agencies must conduct themselves in any area of activities. If there is a question about whether the agency actually has the power to conduct the business transaction, there is even a process for determining that. Doing an audit of the powers and thus setting the parameters and limitations of the public partner is essential prior to getting into a P3.

In addition to the actual boundaries of public sector involvement in P3 capitalization projects, there is also the need to audit and understand the motivation of the leaders for doing so. What are their histories of success or failure? Do they have any experience in these types of matters? What is the political motivation for the elected leaders to consider such projects? How could the motivation change over the time line for good or bad and under what foreseeable pressures from the public? These are the types of questions we should ask ourselves of our public sector partners prior to committing to a major investment that depends on the surety of the answers to these questions. We must be sure that all parties will remain with the project until it is brought to a successful outcome. Nothing can blow a project onto the deathly waves of a stormy economic sea like a change in the political mood, which causes partners to disavow their involvement prior to sustainable operational achievement—or worse yet, to refuse to complete the original terms of the transaction because of a change in the perceptions of their constituents. Even public sector agencies get buyer's remorse and rethink their involvement in risky projects, such as when they perceive poor general public acceptance of the projects.

We will be discussing these issues and the steps that can be taken to protect both the public and private sector from engaging in a project that lacks enough political will or legal allowance to reach critical mass. Understanding the realistic constraints of each partner is critical in achieving a successful partnership.

Step 3: Public Solvency (Capacity for Risk and Reward)

In today's highly leveraged and debt-burdened society, government is no different from the citizens it is meant to serve; it has financial problems with cash flow, debt service, and in many cases the additional demand for services with insufficient resources to pay for its legacy costs.

One of the most common mistakes in considering how to create and then participate in a P3 endeavor is misunderstanding the financial capacity of the public sector, and vice versa for the private sector partners.

Just because an elected body of government officials agree to a set of financial terms and conditions and bind themselves to pay for their portion does not mean that they ultimately have the cash flow to do so. This can be especially true in these times, when cities derive a huge amount of the projected income from things such as sales tax, licenses, permits, and property taxes. As times get economically challenging, these revenues may decline significantly. Evidence of basing the public sector fortunes on these projected incomes and thus on a house of cards is all around us in the news today.

Government does possess the unique ability to create forced financial solutions—called new or increased taxes—to handle such matters, but doing so sets off a huge chain reaction of other potentially harmful side effects. It is for this reason that governments usually, if they are prudent, take the raising of taxes as a very grave choice and in most cases a last option for solving their financial matters.

Establishing a well-oiled and sustainable P3 that has adequate financial wherewithal to survive economic downturns (and flourish and reduce obligations when operating properly during normal or good times) takes good strategic planning. There is no cookie-cutter approach to designing such a partnership infrastructure on the public side, but understanding the tools available to the public sector is a good first step.

In this next step, we will discuss how to review and understand the financial capabilities of the public sector partner. Additionally, we will discuss how to think outside of the box to leverage tools and create some new ones, in some cases, to assist in securing the capital to invest in catalyst projects.

Step 4: Developing the Right Collaborative Mind-Set

Once we have in our minds the proper political disposition and motivation, we then can understand how the public sector jurisdiction is organized and what the lawful constraints are for operations and decision-making. Once we also know the public sector's financial capacity and approach to solving public investments, we are better suited to approach the task of designing the P3.

The private sector, rather than approaching the partnership as a corporate welfare opportunity, has its own set of challenges: it must prepare its own mind-set to think of the partnership as a unique opportunity for a joint venture. Treating the public sector partner as just that—a full-fledged, invested partner and an equity player in the deal—is the first requirement for a proper private sector mind-set.

We must then decide whether our project actually needs the public sector's involvement. The well-being of our nation rests on being able to say "no" when projects are not in the best interest of the nation. Involving the public sector in any endeavor that is not necessary is foolish, cumbersome, and bad for our underlying business climate as a nation. We do not want to knowingly undermine our country by being a part of the problem; rather, these types of opportunities should be approached as creating solutions to our nation's current problems, solutions that will raise our economic state of competitiveness, increase jobs and the tax base, and diversify the economy because of our joint efforts.

Therefore, taking on a P3 means that we, as US citizens, must think about the greater good and not just our own best interests. We would not like our own tax dollars, which we worked so hard to earn, to be squandered or foolishly invested and lost, thus raising our tax bills even higher the next year.

The use of public funds requires a higher bar or level of performance and surety than the private sector has for investment considerations. It also requires absolute transparency, accountability, and understanding of the "if not but for" clause of calling the public sector into action in projects.

A healthy and functional mind-set also involves several layers of predesigned protocols that should be adhered to in order to traverse these unique waters of economic opportunity and peril.

Step 5: Validation of Concepts

Once a project has passed the initial merits of "this sounds like a good idea" and "it seems to fit the desired outcomes of all parties," we step into the higher tier: proof of concept and validation of market reality. This is the stage where the stakes get exponentially higher and when miscommunication happens. It is essential in this stage that we always consider the mind-set of our partners and how due diligence information may affect their actions and opinions positively, negatively, unrealistically, or prematurely. It is good to remember that a course of deliberation, fact-testing existing experiences, and the practical knowledge of others who have navigated these waters before will help us ride any bumpy waves.

In the proof-of-concept stage, the public sector needs to have adequate assurance that the due diligence studies are being conducted by unbiased and expert resources. These experts should not be attempting to extend their work efforts for additional employment. The best approach is to make sure there is a proactive statement about the outcome; the statement must give a clear "no-go," "yes," or even a conditional "yes or maybe" as part of the requirements. Due diligence includes looking at the project from worst-case scenarios, best-case scenarios, and likely outcomes based on historical assumptions and hybrid "what if?" considerations. The proof-of-concept stage should include the application of market conditions and financial realities; for such considerations there should be a carefully vetted modeling approach, again conducted by an unbiased outside source to ensure the best knowledge and oversight for such findings.

Since the public sector is involved in this process, the outcomes should not be skewed with that prospect. In other words, the "what if they weren't involved" consideration should be the best course of deduction.

There are many pitfalls in this stage. First and foremost is the rush to verify our prejudice on the matter. The public sector is no different, especially in an election year. The politicos, in many cases, will want to disseminate the good news or potential good news too prematurely.

Remember, one expert opinion does not make it right . . . getting other perspectives is essential to designing and implementing a good project; reaching sustainable operations is an entirely different matter. Interviewing and understanding failures is just as important as understanding and learning about successes.

In the next step, we will discuss the best approach to validating the proof of concept from a market perspective and how to become comfortable with the costs associated with succeeding.

Step 6: Designing the Instruments of a P3

The choice of using a public sector or quasi-public sector partner has many pitfalls, but it also has many opportunities and benefits. The creation of unique financial tools is something that can be achieved by way of legal design when using a public partner. This can be done as part of a local decision already allowable under state charter, with the creation of special state legislation to enable such special circumstances, or with the exclusive design of a exclusionary business case in order to get market penetration and sustained market share. In other words, a public sector partnership can, for all intents and purposes, create a monopoly for some justified reasoning if the public sector so desires. The public sector is not necessarily held to the same rules for competition that are enforced in the private sector. This does not mean that I am advocating

such or that the public sector would agree to conduct its affairs according to the private sector competition rules, but it does mean that when a
public sector actor chooses one private sector business to associate with,
that business can, if it does its job right, stay in business a long time.

The creation of hybrid instruments, backed by the perceived value
of the good faith of the public sector, does create some unique opportunities for attracting funding for projects. Just the addition of a public
sector partner will in many cases increase confidence that the project
will be successful and thus pay back the investors. The addition of a
public sector partner can also result more favorable interest rates and
tax treatment for the project if there are public-designed incentives for
investors to participate in.

Some of the primary considerations in designing hybrid instruments are the following: how much should the public sector participate;
how will it be justified; what is the exit strategy, if any is allowed; and at
what point does the exit strategy occur?

In many cases the project leaders have not thought about the actual
vehicle for how folks will invest their money. Is it a corporation? Partnership? Is it a public company (traded via an SEC sanctioned entity), or
is it a private company? If it is private, does it have a private placement
memorandum to accept funds, and if so, what are the limitations on
investors? Finally, is the capital team experienced at using these tools,
with a track record of success within this spectrum? The answers to all
of these questions are part of the decision concerning what type of vehicle needs to be built to accept funds on behalf of the project.

In the next step, we will consider the criteria for building hybrid
instruments and how they can be used to successfully position a project
to attract private sector investment.

Step 7: Attracting Private Sector Participation

There is no better validation of a concept than the willingness of the private sector to pony up and financially support the project, with or without public sector participation. If the venture makes economic sense,

then the risk will be mitigated by the desire for making the venture profitable. The vast majority of projects fit into this category already. Private groups and investors believe in a concept and put their funds at risk to prove it and bring it to market . . . thus we have capitalism.

The new models of public participation in private risk projects are not new at all; they have been around since the inception of capitalism. China, Japan, the Netherlands, Denmark, Sweden, Singapore, Hong Kong, Switzerland—all have models that involve similar concepts for varying degrees of investments into industries deemed worthwhile and able to spawn new private sector industries.

The attraction of the private sector and its acceptance of the appropriate degree of risk are the best arbiters of validation of concept and market realities. Finding the appropriate private sector partners with the necessary solvency and financial expertise and depth is critical to the success of well-designed P3s.

In the next step, we will discuss what type of private sector partners to focus our efforts upon and what criteria might be used to peak their interest in our projects.

Step 8: Risk and Reward Balance of Power

The desire for reward, glory, power, and profits are all similar attributes of the human spirit. They are also present in public sector, private sector, and nonprofit activities—they are just expressed differently, sometimes quite differently.

Profits in the private sector are a good thing. Profit means the investment has funds to either reinvest in the further growth of the business and the expansion of the market or pass on as dividends to the shareholders (the risk takers). Profits in the public sector can (and normally are) looked at with a different mind-set. They are unused funds collected from the public, a carry forward. How often do we see the government say, "Oops, we collected too much and here is your rebate"? Not very often. In fact, the public sector may take a traditional mind-set of practicing the age-old "use it or lose it" approach. In other words, if we don't spend all we have, even the spending is not necessary, our funds will be cut back next year. So governments tend to spend all the budgeted funds mostly as they had predicted. But some governments allocates profits for special projects, like catalyst projects and P3 investments.

The nonprofit sector simply refers to profits as surplus funds and doesn't necessarily have the same philosophy or mind-set as governments, except in some cases when the source of the funds originated as public taxpayer money from tax collections. This approach to profits is essential in understanding the risk/reward mentality of dealing with nonprivate sector sources of funding.

Public sector investors tolerate more risk than private sector investors because public sector investors are less prone to see risk as a loss of their hard-earned money. That does not mean they do not take such considerations lightly; they look hard at whether these types of investments should be made. Nevertheless, their criteria for acceptable levels of risk are far different from those of the private sector and even those of the nonprofit sector.

The reward in the private sector is something we all recognize easily: profits, riches, increased economic status, and desired lifestyle attainment. These are identified in our American credo as the pursuit of happiness, otherwise known as the attainment of the proverbial American Dream.

The reward in the nonprofit sector is usually linked to sustaining the agency's mission; accomplishing a defined set of tasks to achieve the agency's goals; and fulfilling the purpose of the organizational focus in the world, in the community, and with the constituents the agency seeks to serve.

The sense of reward in the public sector is an extension of the ethos practiced in the nonprofit sector but to a much more refined level. It is normally linked to creating jobs or the preserving jobs today; to increasing or restoring the tax base to healthy, sustainable levels; and to diversify the local economy. The last goal is undertaken with the assumption that diversification makes the local economy less prone to small economic downturns that wreak too much havoc and chaos within the community and thus drive down the overall quality of life through the loss of economic opportunity.

In the next step we will discuss is how to design the rewards that provide economic justification for a public-sector partner. We will furthermore discuss what attracts a public sector partner such that the partner takes risks in a P3 catalyst project investment opportunity. Why should the partner choose to participate, and how should we design our rewards to merit the public sector's involvement? We must ask the following essential questions: how do we create an equitable balance of power and juggle private sector needs and expectations with private sector requirements, desired outcomes, and reality-based expectations?

Step 9: Answering the "If Not But for" Question Honestly

Perhaps one of the most misunderstood concepts today in governmental engagement in traditional private sector affairs (whether in banking, finance and equity markets, manufacturing, energy, infrastructure, or other economic development activities) is the basis for involving the government in the first place. I introduced the "If not but for" clause in Chapter 11, and its importance as it pertains to P3s cannot be understated. Let's take a closer look at what this clause means and what it signifies for us.

In the olden days (1990s and earlier), we used to practice the "if not but for" concept. The meaning conveyed the consideration of involving public sector funds in a private sector transaction so that the private sector would be the primary risk taker in the venture. The theory goes like this: those making the decision should be able to say, at the end of the venture, "If not but for the involvement of the government in this project (that involvement being creating or investing funds or providing a business climate stimulus), the project would not get funded by the private sector and thus would not come to fruition." However, inventing cause and justification is human nature, and we have often taken great pains to create false impressions that the ventures were needful. Entire consulting practices have been birthed to create these impressions, and legions of lobbying special interest groups sing the song of justification in every hall of governments around the world.

In the end, it is my opinion that such rampant abuse of this clause only lends credence to the need to adequately address the clause in the new P3s that will be birthed in this century. Paying honest attention to whether or when government involvement is necessary will help our markets, because many people think that government is becoming too involved in private matters; this opinion erodes their confidence that the markets can once again adequately perform with the right balance of oversight, regulation, and accountability.

In some circles within the economic development arena, there is a call to create a more robust set of standards addressing the "if not but for" clause by having it directly inserted into public investment agreements and defining the reasons for the venture and the potential benefits in very transparent and clear terms for the sake of the general public. Doing this would help the decision-making process and prevent those making such decisions from denying knowledge of the facts if they tried to take advantage of the system.

Given what many feel will be a rebound effect from the current big-government reaction to the economic meltdown of 2008, it is recommended that prudent practitioners of P3s begin to design for these considerations. These practitioners can meet the criteria voluntarily as a show of forward thinking and a well-balanced mind-set as they engage the public sector in transactions.

In the last step, we will consider how to design and create a well-thought-out "if not but for" clause with documented criteria recommendations on how to justify such investments. In addition, we will discuss holding all parties accountable for meeting their stated objectives with milestones and reasonable and transparent outcomes that can be measured and reported to the general public. Building a working relationship of trust and transparency with the general public should be seen as a positive outcome of designing these tools; restoring public confidence in governance could be a well-deserved though intangible windfall from properly designed "if not but for" clauses in projects.

Step 10: Fair and Equitable Exit Strategies

Just as investors seek a recognized methodology for how to reap their rewards, liquidate their investments, and decide how much risk to maintain in an investment (and for how long), so should the public sector.

P3s are not designed to last forever, in most cases. They are conceived to address the private sector's inability to take on a risk or a special project given the current conditions and economic uncertainties pertaining to the project investment opportunities. So in many cases, these P3s are referred to as catalyst projects, which spur action in the form of joint investment, involvement, and mitigation of up-front and ongoing operational risks. These investments should not be undertaken if the validity of the operation runs aground when the public sector investment runs out. If such investments cannot achieve critical mass in a reasonable time frame and thus become unsustainable, perhaps the investment was never founded on real market realities and probably should not have been undertaken in the first place.

A true catalyst project deserves a design that has a very well-defined exit strategy that rewards the risk takers—in this case, the public sector—for their involvement. I would argue that just avoiding risk for the private sector and paying back the original sum of public money is insufficient reasoning to garner the use of public funds or special favors that translate into increased profits for the private sector.

Therefore, designing an adequate reward and an exit strategy to fund the reward is essential in the initial stages of the P3. Many communities have very lofty goals for their quality of life: amenities, education, economic development infrastructure, performing and visual arts, tourism, and recreational opportunities. These communities can be considered as possible benefactors of P3s.

If We Build It, Will They Come?

This is not a Hollywood movie, but the risk and the potential for reward could be well characterized by an action movie's plot. If we choose to step out and do something unique that engages in a much higher degree of risk and shifts existing operational paradigms within our communities, it does not come without true risk of failure and the realistic loss of reward. The answer to the question "If we build this, will they come?" only materializes when we take that leap of faith into the unknown void of probable and potential outcomes and ride the currents to the inevitable outcome.

In this book, I attempt to follow the decision-making process that investors, entrepreneurs, and public servants may want to consider as they undertake projects. How can we best judge whether we should be involved in a project? And if it is a good project, then what should the potential terms and conditions be? How best do we serve our purpose, and then how and when do we get out of harm's way and let the market carry the project forward? These questions and many others will be addressed in succeeding chapters as we figure out how to conduct ourselves successfully in designing a worthwhile project, a project in line with "The Art of the Deal Today."

CHAPTER THIRTEEN

Jump-Starting
the Financial Markets

And I sincerely believe, with you, that banking establishments are more dangerous than standing armies; and that the principle of spending money to be paid by posterity, under the name of funding, is but swindling futurity on a large scale.

— Thomas Jefferson, Excerpt from a Letter Written to John Taylor, May 28, 1816[1]

Since the global meltdown of 2008, we have sat on the sidelines while the capital markets investors, who ultimately receive the majority of all global financial incentives, wait idly by and hover in their vaults counting money. Most investors are actually beginning to consider America a risky investment, not from investment risk but because of the uncertainty of how they will be taxed on their investments. Our economic landscape is a charred field of debris, replete with economic calamities and casualties from a global contagion. What is the cause of this destruction? The overexuberance for hyperprofit (easy money), greedy money engineering with no real tangible products, and pyramid-schemed financial bundling of toxic assets. All this has been done with the hubris of intended economic advancement for the sake of commissions and profiteering. The aftermath is a financial market that has massive amounts of government involvement without any catalyst

---

[1] Ford, *The Writings of Thomas Jefferson*, 11:533.

or directive to begin lending money to those trying to invest. These men and women need to invest in new equipment, to expand or update processes to remain competitive, or just to rebalance their companies' debt after the meltdown. The recipients of the last two decades of wealth distribution (the whales) are staying on dry land and taking a wait-and-see attitude about investing their dollars in new projects. Greenfield projects are virtually nonexistent. Worse yet, the only apparent movement on the field of this grim economic landscape is that of the vulture capitalists, who are busy trying to purchase distressed assets at rock-bottom prices. The recent passage of a US regulatory act regarding the financial industries does not go far enough to restart the economic engines of financing economic development in our country; the same fate is playing out around the world in other markets.

The Great Economic Transition

The Great Recession has led to what I call the Great Economic Transition. During this transition, people are asking, "How do we get out of this?" and "How much government do we really want?" In addition, we are wondering about what we are really expecting government to do and how the government can collect money from us to support the fundamentals without restricting our access to individual economic advancement. These questions must be addressed for recovery to be sustainable.

We have to look past media sensationalism and news funded by special interests to overcome the myths about our future economic success—that is, there is much misinformation being spewed by the media, so much so that most of us do not know what to believe any longer. We must tackle the issues of how we govern, how we tax ourselves in a form that is reasonable and fair, and what we expect the government to do with the taxes we pay. Our decisions on these issues will affect environmental policies, energy policies, economic development, education, individual welfare, and our ability to have meaningful lives. Discussing these great challenges does not make us any less patriotic and does not mean we are anticapitalistic or against the values of our nation. Progress requires that we revisit norms, adapt to change, and balance accountability with realistic capabilities. Many times, Americans have been made to believe that if the idea did not originate in America, it can't possibly work or be worth considering as a best practice. We remain arrogantly ignorant to opportunities we could adopt and adapt to create our desired outcome.

The Lost Generation

Many are contending that we have our own lost generation, those who are unemployed and underemployed because of our nation's decisions. They are hardworking, honest, and trying to find jobs. They are productive members of society, or were until we made some bad economic decisions. Hindsight will show that the first decade of the twenty-first century was a step backward for the American middle class in terms of wealth and quality of life. Today most communities fail to realize that they cannot hope to create net job growth; they can only slow the evaporation of their jobs so that the reality of innovation, automation, and process efficiencies does not wipe out all of the productive members of society in one generation. As Dean Barber, a site location consultant, says, "Like the trenches of World War I, we are seeing the human casualties that are the result of huge structural changes that we are having a tough time understanding and accepting. And one of them is this: Fewer people will be needed to do the work."[1]

Manufacturing has become more productive, and, in fact, the United States is the most productive country in the world in terms of manufacturing efficiency; however, that also means fewer warm bodies are required to do the work.

This is the real story of the lost generation: too many people willing and able to work, but without the skills now necessary to possibly put them back to work. As a result, they will be relegated to menial jobs, if

---

[1] Barber, "A New Lost Generation," September 25, 2011.

they can find any jobs at all. The jobs of their youth and those of their parents are gone forever.

In September 2011, the Census Bureau released its annual report, which stated that the ranks of America's poor swelled to almost one in six people last year, setting all-time records and continuing to bolster joblessness, which hovers at well above 9 percent for a second year in a row. The number of uninsured edged up to nearly 50 million, the biggest number in more than two decades.

The overall US poverty rate climbed to 15.1 percent, or 46.2 million, up from 14.3 percent in 2009. It is the largest number on record dating back to when the Census Bureau began tracking poverty in 1959. Obviously business as usual cannot continue if we want to survive as a world superpower and as a place where people want to live—more importantly, as a place where they can afford to live and make a decent living.

So what is the problem? Government is promising to be the end-all for all our needs, but that promise has proven to be just another bit of political doublespeak; the most recent government stimulus packages have fallen on the shore and produced nothing but fatter and richer bankers. There has been no new job growth as our elected leaders promised us. So as Paul Jacob sees it:

> There's way too much pressure on politicians to "do something." Most of the things they can do are bad. "Do something" too easily translates to "do anything," and odds are that "anything" will end up as catastrophe.
>
> There's a division of labor in doing things: Investors, capitalists, and entrepreneurs create businesses which employ people; legislators and government executives have the more humble task of setting up and refining the ground rules allowing others to do the great works. Politicians don't create jobs as such.[1]

---

[1] Jacobs, Common Sense Newsletter, September 26, 2011.

The crux of the matter is that to get America back on track we have to systematically change our expectations, how we pay for government, how much we want government to do for us or be involved in our daily lives, and how much we are willing to give of our annual revenue for these expectations. These days I see little evidence that government-based job creation stimulus or bailouts have had any real impact on making our lives much better during the past few decades. We must encourage those the government seeks to punish with targeted millionaire taxes to invest their funds in job creation projects rather than tax shelters. Additionally, we must address how to keep the cost of government within a range that makes all our programs possible and simultaneously creates the best business climate for investment, job creation, and an enjoyable economic quality of life on the planet.

Start Your Engines

According to many leading economic experts, even under the best conditions the United States will not return to normal levels of unemployment until after 2020, which is consistent with my statements that this is neither a depression or recession but rather a prolonged period of economic transition. It is a time when our elected political leaders and business leaders have failed to make critical decisions that would have been in the best interest of sustainable economic growth and health for America. This lack of action and overreliance on the market economy mind-set failed to prepare our workforce for the current scenario, and many of my own generation may never fully recover from the economic devastation to personal savings, retirement, the stability of affordable health care, and a happy and productive lifestyle (also known as the American Dream, but for us older folks).

The McKinsey Global Institute, one of the leading problem-solving institutions of our day, reported on a range of solutions. These solutions were based on lessons learned from the economic crash both in United States and worldwide. The McKinsey report outlined the following problems and solutions that need our attention in order to get us back on track:

- Companies recovering from the economic crisis are increasingly "jobless" because they are rearranging the structure of their companies, they are not matching up workers and jobs correctly, and they are not starting new companies.

- In order to regain full employment, the United States needs to create 21 million new jobs by 2020.

- US companies need to recognize that technology is changing the nature of how people work: "jobs are being disaggregated into tasks, work is becoming virtual, and firms are relying on flexible labor (temporary, contract workers). These trends offer new opportunities for creating jobs in the United States, a trend that some companies do not fully appreciate."

- To revive the flow part of the ebb-and-flow nature of job creation, we must help the US workforce develop needed skills, attract foreign investment and related exports, revive start-up businesses, and cut the red tape that hinders business expansion and new investments.[1]

In light of these findings from McKinsey, I have several specific recommendations that I believe would best jump-start our economy and get it running smoothly again:

P3s

I cannot emphasize enough the value of these partnerships. In order for local economies and thus local companies to begin to grow and to attract new inward investments, it is important that the concept of new P3s take root and produce some financial seeds. Receiving funds from interested local investors in concert with a struggling public sector partner can be a realistic way to invest in opportunities that could create jobs,

---

[1] McKinsey, "An Economy That Works," June 2011.

stimulate facility and equipment investments, and diversify local economies while serving a much-needed financial niche simultaneously. This cycle produces profits with a purpose. Community-minded individuals have the opportunity to help bolster the local economy and make a reasonable profit while doing so. In fact, this concept of creating investment funds that are specifically tied to P3s that are economic-development-oriented could become a nationally traded stock. This stock could amass a huge fund that would help communities access enough capital to take on major economic development catalyst projects. These new hybrids would not solve all problems, but they could be useful tools and provide some spark for the banks to get back to banking (instead of just collecting peoples' money and charging fees for banking services). There has to be adequate available capital for a real economic recovery to take root and stop the false starts that are largely stock market gyrations. One of my grave concerns regarding this issue is a deepening feeling that in America we are no longer dreaming big and taking on massive-scale projects, largely due to our lack of focus and resolve to create sources of funding for such major economic advancements.

Create Local Investment Capital

In fact, in order to open capital markets I believe we have to address the structural need for capital to be strategically invested in job creation (to build consumer and workforce confidence); in facilities; in machinery and equipment (to rebuild our tax bases at the local levels); and in intellectual capital, which would create new products and services (wherewith we could build our innovation base for new economic growth in new markets). Each of these endeavors is aimed at diversifying not only our local communities but also our nation as a whole.

As concerned citizens of this country, one of the most beneficial things we can begin to do is build our understanding of the types of structural changes that will make not only our nation more competitive but create more wealth for us as participants in this economy.

Investment Tax Credits

Another structural change needed concerns investment tax credits. As long as our corporate and individual tax rates remain oppressively high and our nation continues to tax us on wealth creation, not consumption, there will need to be major incentives to expedite investments in our economy. I am not saying that by restructuring the taxation policy we would do away with incentive contests between states and communities, but it would reduce the drastic need for them to equalize the business climate. In fact, cities and states will always war over better economic advantages unless it is forbidden by law. I am not in favor of that because it would have a counterproductive effect on the competitive nature of our economy. But seeing that this oppressive tax climate still exists, I will leave this argument for another day and focus on using tax credits.

The premise of the tax credit is that the corporation would receive a tax reduction on its federal and sometimes state income tax bills. The vast majority of corporate credits are still state-type programs. The company, in theory, would use the tax credits to defray the payment of the same economic value as the credits' value against income taxes. Most companies would much rather have up-front cash to reduce the actual out-of-pocket expenses for the project. This could be accomplished using the same tax credit model that exists today. If the state and federal governments would allow the credits to be monetized and sold on a secondary market, the credits could be assigned to those who would like to reduce their tax bills.

For example, if I owed $100,000 in federal income taxes, I would purchase $100,000 worth of tax credits for, say, $75,000 and thus reduce my tax bill by 25 percent, all the while creating a $75,000 equity injection into the company for its project. This is very similar to other existing tax credit programs today, specifically the Low-Income Housing Tax Credit programs. By creating these gap funds, companies would be able to introduce huge amounts of equity into projects and thus reduce the cost of capital, reduce the debt service, and increase the return on investment and thus the attractiveness of the investments to the investors.

Job Creation Grants

Almost every project can be measured to identify the number of jobs that would be created directly (i.e., those employed by the firm) and indirectly (jobs created by others that would be necessary to support the jobs created by the firm). These job creation numbers have an economic value to the state. For example, if the average wage is $15 per hour, then the discretionary income spent in the state would have some normal percentage value of these wages in proportionate sales taxes and other taxes. The value of the payroll would have a measurable economic value. In this case, instead of giving a workforce tax credit for each new job, it would be better to provide an actual cash grant for each direct job created—say, 10 percent of the expected expenditures per year over a five-year period, valued in expected receipts in sales tax and then net present value at a reasonable cost of capital, such as 6 percent. This gives the employer real cash to use to defray the cost of the project expansion. The state can borrow the funds at much lower than the 6 percent rate and use the spread for additional collateral coverage for business failures that do not produce a return on investment. This would require that the state have strict job creation requirements and repayment clauses if the wage levels are not maintained over that five-year period. This would also provide a huge economic stimulus aimed directly at job creation, which would bolster confidence in the economy.

Government Guarantees on High-Value Loans

In order to get banks to lend again to small businesses, primarily businesses that do not have access to the Wall Street capital markets, we need banks to lend money for business expansion, consolidation, and acquisition. These types of investments create about 65 percent of all jobs in America today. The current small business loan program has many problems. It is not sensitive to the new knowledge-based economy and is still highly focused on the traditional manufacturing and agricultural economies of the past two centuries. This is not to say that manufacturing and agriculture are not important, but the loan guidelines in many cases exclude the use of loans for intangible costs associated with intellectual property development. In addition, some of our private, small-bond programs do not allow investments into intellectual, capital-intensive knowledge projects. Such antiquated approaches are stifling investments that would be put into the most cutting-edge aspects of the global economy. Tourism, knowledge-based projects, renewable energy, and clean technology projects would be some of our hottest growth sectors for new jobs, and yet these projects are overlooked and ineligible for many of the best government-sponsored loan and bond programs. Opening up the criteria would allow capital to flow to companies that would create good-paying jobs.

Wall Street Transaction Taxes

Since much of the banking and trading schemes caused the actual meltdown, it is only fair that we place the burden on them to cover their own losses by funding their regulatory oversight from their own capital activity. This would reduce the burden on the taxpayers. These fees would also create a new regulatory process for accountability. This change in and of itself would create jobs in the financial markets that are not driven by the amount of investments made, but it would ensure that proper oversight is enforced. These jobs would not be built upon the greed of the system but on making sure of the boundaries and protocols are adhered to. In addition, those who monitor such transactions should be restricted from selling services to those companies as a separate activity.

Bank-Assets Taxes

By taxing the banks for their holdings that are not invested in small, local businesses, we would incentivize banks to lend and not squander their holdings. Of course, banks would still need to adhere to some level of reserves and lending practices. But incentives to invest in small, local businesses could further promote the creation of local jobs in direct proportion to the wealth in the local market.

Conversion of Toxic Assets into a Global Pool

Banks claim that their hands are full as they dispose of their toxic assets. This is a barrier to investment in new job creation projects. Perhaps there is some truth to this, so let's offer a remedy. Since there are many foreign and domestic investors that would like to purchase banks' toxic assets, let's bundle them up over a short period of time—say, the next 24 months—and sell them in the world capital markets with a guaranteed return on investment to investors, perhaps a tax-exempt 6 percent interest rate. Then the United States could off-load the debts to the same folks who purchase our treasuries today, thus reducing the demand on the United States to swallow toxic assets and freeing the banks up to lend money again. The banks would be responsible for paying the 6 percent dividend as part of the deal to help relieve themselves of the toxic assets. The US would provide the investors with a federal guarantee on the rate of return, and bada bing, bada boom, we have greased the cogs of the biggest capital engine on the planet.

Foreign Direct Investment (FDI)—Tax-Exempt Investment Credits

Whether most Americans realize it or not, we depend upon a huge inflow of capital investments from the rest of the world to make our economic engine hum. The irrational logic that is fanned by the media and some sensationalist journalists and politicians about America being for sale is ridiculous. Of course we are for sale—that is what makes our economy robust. Instead of believing the idiotic bantering of antiforeign investment, consider this: without foreign investors purchasing our debt (with Treasury notes, which are just promissory notes), we as taxpayers would have to pay the costs of our lifestyles today. That would raise our costs today by about 30 percent. Today we spend about $1.42 for every dollar we earn; we live beyond our means, plain and simple. In order to entice investments and thus create some jobs, we need more people to invest in us. While my forthcoming suggestion is not the answer to our debt-consumed attitude, it is the right choice for us to create jobs. By creating a 100 percent tax-abatement policy of investing in America, we could allow foreign investors to invest in our country with an invisible stimulus from "found money." Creating tax-exempt investments would bolster investment in our country and create some much-needed jobs. In addition, if we wanted to be even more targeted, we could direct such investments into manufacturing, renewable energy, infrastructure, software, and health care, thus addressing the areas of our economy with the largest need for investment and doing the greatest good for rebuilding America's competitive stature.

Matching Federal Guarantees for EB-5 Immigration Investment

The current immigration program allows people with money to immigrate to America and become citizens over time by agreeing to invest $500,000 into passive American investment projects that create jobs. I commend this program, but it is not marketed enough within our country to those folks who sorely need the capital now. In other words, if an entrepreneur has a project that will create jobs and he or she needs cash, this program is a gold mine. Basically, for every job entrepreneurs create, they can attract $50,000 to $100,000. So if our project creates 100 jobs, we could attract $5,000,000 to $10,000,000 in funds. The requirements for the foreign investors are also lucrative: their funds are treated as investments, but they are passive investors with no controlling interests in the deals. Where I believe the program needs modification is in two areas:

First, the US government should pool the money and then place a federal guarantee on it so the money is not perceived as at-risk. Then we should insure the money with the private sector and use the market to offset the risk. In addition, the money should be competed for by businesses, and the businesses with the most competitive proposals would be awarded points. This would maximize the value of the projects and create the highest-quality jobs.

A major portion of the project funds should be allocated to different-ly sized businesses to ensure that we have some economic diversity; for example, allocate 10 percent to microenterprises (businesses with less than $200,000 in annual sales) and that would create or retain just one job, so microenterprises need no more than $100,000 in funds. I would then allocate 50 percent of the remaining funds to small businesses that have sales less than $10,000,000 per year, have a capital need of less than $3,000,000, and would create or retain forty or more jobs. The remaining 40 percent of total funds should be directed at community catalyst projects where there is a P3, with the public sector investing its own cash and/or business development incentives. The investments I've outlined should be strictly for new jobs that are at or above the average wage in the area. This would create a huge boon for the capital markets.

Second, we could use the current broker dealer networks on Wall Street to develop investors abroad and walk them through the application and transfer-of-funds processes, thereby keeping our most elite members of the financial community employed and actually doing something useful and constructive.

Matching Funds by Local and State for SBIR Recipients

One of the most misunderstood, horribly managed, and nepotistic programs out there right now is our federal grants program. Despite its problems, it is highly effective in targeting useful research for innovation and inventions in our various federal agencies. This program is called the Small Business Innovation Research grants program (SBIR). The program normally funds lucky recipients in three stages. The first stage is product validation; the company or research team meets a key need the government deems critical or innovative. The funds at this stage range from $75,000 to $150,000 normally. The second stage is for proof of concept; the group must develop the prototype design and analyze the market to deduce the potential demand. The funds at this stages range from $150,000 to $250,000 normally. The third stage is market validation by trial and technology transfer. For this stage, awards grants normally range from $250,000 to $500,000. In this final stage, the team is expected to have developed a long-term capital source to commercialize the product or service. The concept behind the program is wonderful. Where it falls short is in requiring that the recipients use some third-party validation of concepts and work with universities to do additional research, as well as in providing enough funds for the recipients to dedicate 100 percent of their time to the project in the first year. By my estimation, that would require about 50 percent more funds than are currently being allocated in the first phase. Some states have created their own add-on features to this program and the features are quite unique, but none of the states have gone to the level of doing what I believe would be really effective. Kentucky, for example, decided at one point to match dollar for dollar the first-phase grants up to $75,000. That was intended to get more patent-based and knowledge-based research going in the state. I think it was a very effective decision. The grants can be paid for from application fees and vetting requirements for the program, as well as from a percentage of business licensure taxes. Arizona funds up to $5,000 for companies to receive assistance from a consultant who can take the idea and make it presentable in the SBIR grant application process; the consultant verifies that the project meets eligibility requirements, which increases the likelihood of the project being chosen for funding. These add-on programs from Kentucky and Arizona, if combined, would make a great entrepreneurial support program that would create new economy jobs in the United States and within an affordable format.

Five-Year Hiatus on Profits for Job-Creating Investments

In order to get capital flowing, we have to incentivize people to take action not just penalize people for not taking action. To jump-start this money flow, I think the federal government should allow individuals, banks, and investment groups a special provision of receiving 100 percent capital gains tax abatement on investments made in job creation projects over the next three years. The investments would receive a five-year hiatus on capital gains taxes, which would boost the return on investment instantly by at least 15 percent. The focus of the program should be on a required minimum number of jobs (such as 50 new direct-employment jobs) that must be guaranteed for at least a ten-year period from investment start to completion; otherwise, the tax would have to be paid. To make more targeted investments, we could give special consideration to the following types of investments:

- Light rail projects,
- Renewable energy production,
- Smart grid development and deployment,
- Airport and waterborne port improvements,
- City redevelopment projects in blighted areas,
- High-speed intercity rail projects,
- Highway and bridge improvements,
- Infrastructure (both dry and wet) improvements as well as replacements,
- Tourism destination development projects,
- Business incubation centers,
- Industrial and business park developments, and
- Clean energy retrofits and new, clean-energy production facilities (clean coal, nuclear, liquid natural gas, hydrogen fuel cells, etc.).

If we take this concept one step further, we could highly incentivize the amount of targeted funding to nonprofits during this same period. This three-year period could allow for a 150 percent tax credit on the investor's federal income tax for every dollar of donations made that are greater than $10,000. This would happen by granting a similar three-year status for gifts and donations that are targeted to specific nonprofit purposes, such as recreational facilities for the general public (parks, bikeways, walking trails, sports complexes, golf courses, museums, libraries, zoos, aquariums, performing and visual arts centers, etc.).

Now we have targeted the rebuilding of our cultural heritage at the same time as stimulating job creation. These projects are sorely short on capital all the time. The investments in these projects could be targeted to expand the projects' capabilities to meet intended outcomes per the general public's expectations.

These actions would be fairly painless—not completely, but they would be highly effective at not only getting capital flowing once again but also getting Americans back to work in a dignified manner, producing and building things that will make us more prosperous economically, socially, and culturally for the remainder of this century and possibly beyond. Nothing we do is going to be without some pain today. We simply cannot have a painless extraction from our current problems, but it would be categorically wrong to avoid a targeted and very focused approach that relieves actual working class Americans from some of their stress. There is no more sympathy to bail out the companies and institutions any longer; it is time for the American taxpayer to be the benefactor. Overall, all my approaches can be accomplished without raising taxes on ourselves and would even allow us to restructure and lower our taxes as I have recommended in earlier chapters. My philosophy is to use "found money" as the lubricant for catalyst capital—not financing projects with more taxes but through outside investment that is not at play today and therefore not a source of income. Therefore, there would be no real major loss of income.

These suggestions do require that our nation rethink how much we want government to pay for, and in my case, I want our money targeted to real action items that create competitive capacity, jobs, and innovation. These suggestions also require that we as taxpayers lower our expectations of entitlements and actually accept responsibility for our own workforce benefits through self-directed accounts. By using the private sector to assume risk and not providing the private sector with federal guarantees on risky ventures, we can shift much of our entitlement costs to an actual cost basis. This will also spur debate on what is really necessary versus what is too costly and what are unrealistic desires. The insurance and banking industries, in order to access the new flow of major funds, must provide universal access on a competitive and cost-effective basis. This will spark innovation and creativity inside the financial sector. The inflow of capital to our shores would be enormous, as would the fresh immigration of new entrepreneurs. It would be a huge boost to our level of overall desirability to the rest of the world. America would once again be the place to be to enjoy the fruits of the unique American Dream. By following this blueprint, we would be much better world citizens; we would be embracing our responsibility to the planet and simultaneously building the best business climate.

CHAPTER FOURTEEN

Thinking Outside the Box: Nine Steps to Reaching World-Class Community Status

All government—indeed, every human benefit and enjoyment, every virtue and every prudent act—is founded on compromise and barter.

—Edmund Burke, from His Second Speech on the
Reconciliation with America, 1775[1]

W ho says economic development is simply about being in the right place at the right opportune time? Well, whoever did was wrong. Economic development is a science that can be learned, applied, modified, and refined continually; it is also the art of developing human intuition and leadership skill sets. Critical thinking and decisive analysis are the key underpinnings of successful efforts to maintain the wealth and vitality of a community and to foster and expand vibrant local economies. For many of the participants, whether community leaders and decision-makers or community members who look to their leaders for guidance, understanding and successfully ne-gotiating the nine steps I will describe in this chapter requires thinking in a new way. Thus, past ways and habits that have become outmoded instruments of failure must be cast aside, like rusting farm implements unsuited to a new era, which should be regarded as museum pieces. No

---

[1] Griffith, *Historical Notes*, 185.

matter how difficult it may be to accept initially, those who can learn to appreciate the advantages of adaptability and the necessity of taking calculated risks stand a far greater chance of positioning themselves— and their communities—for a brighter future in the twenty-first century than those whose ideas and methodologies remain unalterably mired in the past.

The path to world-class status is not determined by a community's population, nor its natural resources or geographic location; the path is determined by the quality of the local leadership and the leaders' collective vision and capacity for critical thinking, decision-making, and forward investments. These investments must situate the community such that it may remain vital and competitive in the world economy. Many circumstances can form what many may claim to be obstacles so immense that they doom a community to failure. I would suggest that the only failure that will doom a community to failure is the members failing to believe in themselves, thus failing to invest in creating solutions to problems. It has always been my belief that all problems are blessings in disguise. Problems force folks to focus on action. Problems provide an opportunity for creating positive new ideas that can lead to unexpected windfalls. There is an old saying that in the midst of chaos there are always pearls of opportunity. Today, in the world we live in, there is plenty of chaos, economic uncertainty, and a genuine lack of consumer confidence and voter approval of political actions. All of these are valid issues and are also the underpinnings for public sentiment. Many communities listen to the grumblings of their constituents and decide that no action is better than the potential scorn that may come when they take positive steps toward a new opportunity that can change the local economic landscape. Failing to overcome public discontent dooms a community to mediocrity if it's lucky and a declining quality of life and eventual demise if it's not. I have spoken many times to community leaders, chamber of commerce audiences, and economic development groups, saying, "Life isn't easy, and it surely is not fair. If you fail to embrace your own potential, fail to invest in new solutions for sustained growth and an enhanced quality of life today, you will fail utterly and completely within time." I normally follow up that statement with my conclusion on avoiding traps for forward-oriented folks and leaders: "Successful people have to be willing to be a heel in order to become a hero . . . leading where others are afraid to speak up or take decisive action." What I mean by this is that those of us who blazed new trails and created wonderful and intelligent new solutions at some point had to take the risk and handle the scorn from all the nonbelievers. Humanity has a herd mentality, for the most part. If you wait for consensus, you will never take the challenge, conquer the fear to overcome the obstacles, and obtain the prize. We need fearless leaders. Once people see that the goal is obtainable, they tend to migrate to the cause at first in a trickle and then in a stampede. Once the prize is obtained, people seem to have a selective memory, forgetting their previous hesitations and trepidation and citing their eternal support for the cause, as well as claiming that they contributed to the victory. I know it is difficult to those of us tasked with actually leading the charge to take the hill of opportunity. It is tough not to be remembered for your efforts. Well, get over it; such is life—your reward will be the knowledge that you have helped to create a legacy of success that will empower your community and others who live there to have a great quality of life.

> *We must be ready to dare all for our country, for history does not long entrust the care of freedom to the weak or the timid. We must acquire proficiency in defense and display stamina in purpose. We must be willing, individually and as a Nation, to accept whatever sacrifices may be required of us. A people that values its privileges above its principles soon loses both.*
>
> *—Dwight D. Eisenhower*[1]

Now that I have presented the dark side of economic development, we can set a course of developing a world-class community mind-set,

---

[1] Yale Law School, "First Inaugural Address," given January 20, 1953.

so let's discuss the process for how we navigate these waters to land on that eventual golden shore. I have used the following nine steps for walking communities through this process. Each step is a practical, sequential process that not only helps leaders through this process but also builds public awareness and thus accountability and transparency in the leaders' efforts. The following can be used as a practical navigational instrument in taking a process-driven approach to becoming a world-class community.

Step 1: Building Awareness of the Reality of Today

Too many folks are stuck in the reality of previous accomplishments and glory from the past. We get emotional about historical real estate that is not appropriate for productive reuse. We want normalcy to return to how it was before the economic crisis . . . and that is simply not realistic. Change is inevitable, though progress is truly optional. In order to put our communities, companies, and our own lives back on track, we have to face the reality of what got us in this predicament and what the new expectations are for defining success in the future. This also means we have to realistically and critically review our barriers to meeting these new requirements for success and what improvements we need to make to reach sustainable growth and economic health.

Another reality is appropriately dealing with and overcoming corruption in government. Creating a world-class community or government of stature is dependent upon those we elect to lead the community or government. The leaders must think not only outside the box but also beyond their own needs for power and wealth to the needs of the constituents and constituents' posterity. The imbalance of public service today has been greatly tilted toward self-serving, wealthy egomaniacs who are willing to lap up the money of the special interests that throw favors and funds their way—and all at the direct expense of meaningful change that will directly benefit our nation, states, and communities. If we do not get this power imbalance under control, then reaching a renewed and sustainable economic prosperity for the productive members of society will not be attainable.

Those who have been once intoxicated with power, and have derived any kind of emolument from it, even though but for one year, never can willingly abandon it. They may be distressed in the midst of all their power; but they will never look to any thing but power for their relief.

—*Edmund Burke*[1]

Despite what Burke said, we must conquer our natural inclinations and rise above base desires in order to bring about meaningful change.

Step 2: Identifying the Risk and Rewards of Taking Action Today

There is a very big difference between gambling and taking a calculated risk. When we take a calculated risk, we assess the potential of the investment; we also look at the maximum risk or the risk most likely to occur and determine whether there are mitigation-based safeties or fail-safe precautions we can implement to curb the most severe of the downside risks. It does not mean that we downplay the negatives but that we simply state them as they are. There are few total failures in government-sponsored intervention actions, but there are still some that do occur. More than likely, even failure on a specific objective would still result in some progress that would have windfalls in other areas, which would hopefully create economic benefits. During this period, it is also important to identify potential windfalls and give them credible recognition in our considerations. On the flip side of the coin, we should not oversell the positive possible outcomes of undertaking world-class catalyst action steps in a community. Once we understand the potential risks and benefits, we should create a tally sheet for the considerations and assign a hierarchy rating to each so that the actions or projects with the most benefits and least risks are undertaken in the first stages; then we should work our way down according to the potential positive outcomes versus risks. Inevitably, we cannot take on every desired action or project immediately, but over time we can begin to knock them off our community bucket lists.

---

[1] Burke, *The Works of the Right Hon. Edmund Burke*, 478.

Step 3: Failsafe Analysis/Failure Is Not an Option

Every risk and reward as defined in Step 2 merits great consideration. The key element in most cases is the ability to create an understandable fallback position that can defend the ground gained and offset the risks undertaken. As we look at projects, some fail-safe options are more financially viable than others. Just as the risk-and-reward considerations should be ranked, so should the fail-safe strategies. Once we understand what we and our communities/organizations are capable of undertaking in the fail-safe mode, we can rank projects based on the likelihood of being implemented. The project most likely to be implemented gets a 10 rating, for example, and the project least likely to be implemented is assigned a 0. Then we could compare the rated projects to expectations and desires according to the risk-and-reward considerations and develop a matrix or table of action items ranging from immediate to long-term.

Step 4: SWOT Analysis of the Hand We Have Been Dealt

SWOT is the exercise of inventorying strengths, identifying weaknesses, stating opportunities, and giving credence to threats. This exercise is critical to gaining a perspective on the entire landscape of possible outcomes for our projects. Realists are winners as long as they address the obstacles and take action. Realists who wallow in doubt, allow fear to paralyze them, and fail to take action are losers. In this century, we will have some profound losers as well as some very distinctive winners who will rise to the awareness of the public. A SWOT is just a snapshot of where we are at this moment in time. But without a SWOT, we cannot create a foundation or threshold from which we can categorically measure improvements, design objectives to meet any threats, capitalize on opportunities, and measure the success of our milestones as they are achieved. If we blindly go down the road of change without a map of the landscape, then we will never know if we are making progress or just wasting time and resources, with no real advancement or progress.

Step 5: Building Community Buy-In

The biggest complaint that voters have with government—at all levels—is the lack of disclosure of the government's true intentions. Politicians and appointed staffers are afraid to disclose the objectives (if there actually are any) for fear of reprisal. Voters want to know what the government is doing, how it will make a difference in their lives, how objectives will be accomplished, and at what cost to them. Voters want transparency, not a gaming of the system that keeps things confidential via backroom leadership. Whether we believe in backroom leadership or not, we desire to hold our elected and appointed officials accountable. Rather than fight this process, it is important that world-class communities, leaders, organizations, and companies provide a real and meaningful platform from which they inform and engage the general public about their intentions, likely outcomes, the price of their endeavors, how that price will be paid, and what portion of that price will be paid by the public. We are not expected to be soothsayers, but we are expected to state our opinions and lead toward a distinctive plan of action that has the highest possibilities of success and positive outcomes. I highly support the use of town hall meetings, large-scale charrettes, and electronic and printed media to get this message out to the general public. At that point, nonparticipation is the culpability of the citizen, not the public sector.

Step 6: Identifying Where Likely Future Successes May Lie

It is critical that when we assess where we want to take our communities, organizations, companies, ourselves, and our families that we do so without encumbering the assessment with personal biases or unfounded beliefs that are not based upon facts or historical trends. Moving to where the puck is going to be, as the Great One (Wayne Gretzky) once said, is how to be where others have not anticipated going yet. It is a fine art of guessing and deducing likely outcomes. In defining how to become a world-class community, we have to take on projects that will boost us to that world-class level. So projects that boost our communities to that level are the only projects that should be in our view. This goes back to our principle that government should not be involved in all aspects of our lives and in every investment; government should be involved only when the lack of its patient capital would stymie catalyst projects (remember "if not but for"?). Since that is our litmus test, we now have to make sure that our projects are not possible of their own accord within our community or that they only require some business climate adjustments in the form of special incentives to cause them to take root. Such projects are what I refer to as the "Low-Hanging Fruit" of opportunity. They should be engaged and undertaken because they are quite possible to achieve and fairly cost-effective. In addition they are mostly projects based on performance or "found money." These types of projects are built on the deferment of future costs and therefore have little actual out-of-pocket impact. These projects should receive the highest ranking . . . but they should not be depended upon to offset the need for some projects that require a much greater up-front investment risk. Each type of consideration has to be ranked according to potential outcomes and the associated ability to handle the risks of slow growth or failure.

Step 7: Decide What Catalyst Project Would Best Deliver the Best Results (Warranted Investment Strategies with ROI/CBA)

Now we have to look at the financial validity of these projects and use an investor's eye to examine what is not only possible but what is most likely to receive private sector funding. This is where the value of the P3 is most critical. The private sector has to have credible and knowledgeable expertise involved in the project. Building the initial team that can carry this opportunity from inception to market is crucial in this process-driven methodology. We will find that many times the team members have to be replaced or exchanged as their value becomes invalid. The important aspect of this process is to make sure that our projects have a cause-related foundation (meaning they reflect a social value that resonates with our public sector investors and possibly the overall society); an example of this is renewable energy. Certainly we are not limiting such discussions to renewable energy; there are myriad projects that would fit this cause-related category. The other major aspect of this methodology is to build what I will call a model-driven investment strategy that strictly adheres to market assumptions and financial considerations that are industry standards. This model-driven approach is very much built upon the nuts and bolts of the practical and achievable scale of the financial investment. These types of approaches are based on the warranted investment; that is, how much a prudent investor should invest and what the anticipated return on investment is.

In business schools, colleges, and universities, we often hear professors discuss this warranted investment as a cost-benefit analysis. This analysis outlines what each party is placing at risk and how much each party stands to win or lose in this endeavor. If the scales are lopsided, then the balance of the deal's fairness has not been created to meet what I refer to as deal equilibrium. In cases of deal equilibrium, both sides feel they have extended to their maximum capacity and are still comfortable with that level of exposure. In building such a scenario, economic developers must often strike a balance of having both the community-minded, savvy financier and the risk-averse private sector investor. The best approach at achieving this balance is to use a specific, tangible outcome I refer to as an investor solicitation package. The investor solicitation package defines the market knowledge, costs, benefits, risks, and rewards, along with an actual model-driven evaluation of the public sector's pledged and current financial investment in the project. This approach will allow the private capital markets to determine what the internal rate of return would be for the investors as well as any specific terms and conditions that would come attached to the investors' money. This then provides the structure for the final composition of the P3.

Step 8: How to Pay for The Desired Outcome

The question of how to pay for a venture is what normally stops most economic development projects from going forward. Both the private sector and the public sector have unrealistic expectations of financial exposure, especially in the initial due-diligence gathering aspect of addressing catalyst projects. Again, in this post-2008 era, the stakes are much higher and expectations are much harder to meet. Getting a deal off the shelf and to the market has proven to be a huge burden. Our current Congress and president have thrown nearly $1 trillion at the situation, earmarking that sum as an economic stimulus, and yet the capital is still sitting on the sidelines. A huge reason for this stagnation is the simple fact that our tax policy on capital gains and dividends, along with the corporate income tax on profits, is predicted to rise perhaps exponentially; this projection has created a huge amount of market hesitation. Getting investors off the bench has not proven easy, and with the current situation, it is unlikely they will change their mind-set. I addressed this need for structural change in our taxation process earlier in this book.

For the purposes of this step, assuming the willingness of capital investors to invest, we have to look at what should entice them best to invest. The avoidance of guessing or taking too many calculated risks on market opportunities is a huge enticement to most investors. In cases where the public sector believes in the market and the ability to generate an acceptable return on investment for a private sector entity, the public sector should perform the due diligence to prove the point. There is no reason not to if the opportunity is legitimate. After all, if the public sector does not believe in the market enough to do so, then why should an outside investor be willing to do so? The critical point in this process is that the due diligence has to be conducted by unbiased third-party experts on the subject. These experts must be intimately aware of the local market and of the national and global market issues. The due diligence should not be limited to just one expert. I would recommend at least two independent professional opinions. Thus, the question of how we pay for the project comes in a two-part answer.

First, once the due diligence and initial design and concept validation are completed, I believe the public entity should seek out its first level of private sector involvement. At this early stage, the investment group members should be strictly chosen according to their know-how and wherewithal to be able to carry the project through to the end, including the acquisition of the project's debt and equity requirements. One of the best recommendations I have for communities is to treat this information and due diligence as intellectual capital. Because the information is intellectual capital, the private sector must be required to purchase the intellectual property, which can produce all or a major portion of the cost to prove all this and to repay the public sector for its initial risk of capital. The remainder of the public sector's funds can be paid for from the performance of the project. How? By granting land through a loan that would be forgivable as the public sector performs over time and by deferring (avoiding) taxes on transactions pertaining to real estate, personal property, permits, public infrastructure connections and hook-ups, road and signage costs, and other public sector costs that might normally be paid from the proceeds of the project. How do we come up with the required funds? We bond for them and require a letter of credit from the investors to guarantee performance, thus using this upside as our speculative risk in the project. Most communities, through collaboration and joint agreements with other governmental or quasi-governmental agencies, can usually come up with the capital to meet these types of costs over time. I would never advocate that the public sector take such a speculative financial position on a project that it would jeopardize the public sector's solvency or force the public sector to raise taxes on its residents if the project fails.

Step 9: How We Measure Success and Create Realistic Milestones

Every project has to have an agreed-upon set of standards to determine success; additionally, how can we know we are making progress on goals related to success? If we do not understand or cannot communicate to others what success looks like, how can others collaborate with us and help us achieve success? The establishment of realistic milestones that are achievable and affordable is essential to the core foundation of a world-class project; these milestones will create impetus for a community to reach such a status. Every decision in a community should be made in such a manner that the community should question, "Does this decision indirectly or directly support our goal of becoming a world-class community?" If not, then perhaps the community should not be engaged in the endeavor. This should always be the question raised when considering the objectives, milestones, and expectations for undertaking these paradigm-shifting investments.

Once we have considered these nine steps, we should ask ourselves why more communities aren't following these suggestions. It is a difficult question to answer simply. More effective economic development projects, as we have been discussing, require that our elected officials stop trying to be held up as economic soothsayers and sages. Their purpose is to evaluate situations, ask questions, and make critical decisions that are supported by real experts' opinions, and these decisions must be in the best interest of the constituents. Too many of our elected officials are too concerned about reelection, getting their claims in for responsibility, or building walls for plausible deniability rather than taking risks and sticking out their necks to facilitate real progress, something that would last far beyond their time served in public office. Certain honorable qualities in our elected leaders are essential to this world-class P3 process, the purpose of which is to make each community more cost-effective. This causes the community to be a more profitable place to invest and ensures that the community is a high-quality place to work, live, visit, and recreate.

Innovation

Your time is limited, so don't waste it living someone else's life.
Don't be trapped by dogma, which is living with the results of other
people's thinking. Don't let the noise of others' opinions drown out
your own inner voice. And most important, have the courage to
follow your heart and intuition. They somehow already know what
you truly want to become. Everything else is secondary.

—*Steve Jobs*[1]

The hallmarks of US capitalism—personal energy, a highly developed problem-solving aptitude, entrepreneurial enthusiasm, and persistence—characterize the freshness and unique innovation that time and again have led to success in just about every field of endeavor imaginable, including fields not yet defined but still on the drawing boards. While often envied and copied in many other countries, our system has been hard to duplicate because of the overall blend of qualities that have been slowly brewed to perfection within our social networks and economic infrastructure. Our track record of creating new and innovative products and solutions and bringing them to world markets might very well become the foundation for the next great economic boom in US history, if played out properly. Investments in green technology, clean industries, and a robust infrastructure promise to offer huge economic opportunities. But what if we allow the ubiquitous fossil fuel lobby—backed by petrolism's ever-ready financial muscle—to stall

---

[1] Scott, *I Don't Have Time*, 67.

or derail our efforts to promote alternative energies? What would the near- and long-term repercussions be to the United States compared to the rest of the world?

Innovation in America is a part of our credo, our ethos, our spirit. According to the United States Patent and Trademark Office, 7,861,317 patents have been issued from 1836 to 2011.[1] From air conditioning, the airplane, motion-picture animation, the adhesive bandage, the bread slicer, the laptop computer, the credit card, and e-mail to the electric washing machine, the digital wristwatch, the Zamboni, and the zipper, individuals in the United States have produced an incredible number of inventions that have hugely affected our quality of life today. And we haven't even mentioned how our philosophies, more effective methods and workflows, and informational discoveries—the less material-based inventions—have affected lives the world over.

The inventive spirit is part of our uniquely American identity. However, our position at the forefront of global dominance in innovation is shaky. This does not mean to say this situation is irreparable and that we are doomed to decline as the Roman Empire and others before us have done. Quite to the contrary—America is a land of great resilience and has, more often than not, responded to crises and challenges admirably. We are able to lift ourselves out of the ashes like a phoenix and re-create ourselves. We have done this over and over again in great times of chaos both in and outside of the United States. The ability to rebuild and renew ourselves under such conditions is at least in part attributable to that drive to innovate and to the entrepreneurial spirit of our citizens.

How do we nurture and strengthen this innovative spirit? First off, we should not pamper and spoil it within a socialist comfort zone. We must stay grounded in market-based economic realities. Here is a list of various ways to nurture innovation in our communities:

---

[1] United States Patent and Trademark Office, "Table of Issue Years and Patent Numbers," January 1, 2011.

- World-class educational opportunities for all citizens from birth to the grave and the promotion of continuing education.

- Private and public support of the R & D of new ideas.

- Private sector willingness to invest in seed, angel, and venture funding of new enterprises of all shapes and sizes.

- A business climate that is robust but cost-effective with regard to the amount of taxation applied to corporations and citizens.

- Availability of capital for main street businesses.

- A robust capital market for public and private offerings of debt- and equity-backed ventures. The market should have reasonable government oversight and regulation to protect financial investors against fraudulent and insolvent funding schemes.

- A regulated but equitable amount of governmental red tape for oversight of industry standards, practices, and safety issues concerning health and environmental resources.

- A fair social contract with our workforce that provides a self-directed, affordable, accessible, and universal safety net of health care, retirement, unemployment, and disability benefits to the productive members of our society.

- A highly mobile, hard-working, smart, and productive workforce that possesses a diversity of skills and rapid access to training to meet new skill requirements as business needs change according to the market and to technology advances and adaptations.

- Robust and competitive infrastructure for building and operating facilities that can produce products competitively in the world market and export them to other markets within a globally competitive, free-trade market-place. This means providing the latest and greatest physical infrastructure for energy, water, telecommunications, transportation, and other market factors to spur productivity. It would also increase energy conservation and environmental sensitivity, as well as provide cost-effective access to necessary resources and improve public safety and our overall quality of life.

All of these items are under assault today; that which would help us is being cast away. Just when the government has the opportunity to revisit and make structural changes to these areas, the government appears to be heading down the opposite path, believing that other factors are more important in rebuilding and restoring American greatness and leadership in the global economic markets.

If people really want to renew the American spirit of globally competitive leadership within the economy, we have to start by nurturing the things that fuel innovation. Only by repairing the pillars of the hall of innovation inside our great American republic will we have the power to set the bar even higher in this century for what can be achieved and what it means to be an American.

Building Utopgrilotis: Existing in Harmony with Our Environment

Since the time when we humans began to tell stories, we have created legends and lore of fabled places where people seek to find harmony and balance as a community. These places, such as Utopia, Shangri-la, Camelot, and Atlantis, have inspired books, movies, and our minds for a long time. Not only do the residents in these paradises have peace, but they also have symbiotic relationships with their environments. Essentially, we all desire to live in a community where there is cooperative and fair governance and great lifestyle amenities, but these things wouldn't mean as much if the natural resources in the area were being abused and the beauty of the area was marred with pollution and garbage. Environmental issues affect every level of society and every country in the world, so we must try to work together for the benefit of all.

Of course, these mythical lands are not real and no community can fully measure up to our idealistic expectations. But that does not mean we should not set the bar high for our expectations of where we live, work, and recreate.

The question thus remains, how do we build the best competitive business climate and highest quality of lifestyle communities that are also ecosensitive? How can our local communities become models for our nation and the world so that they too can overcome global environmental challenges? Fortunately, there are some examples of

forward-thinking community leadership efforts as local organizations venture out to vanquish universal challenges. While it will be
an uphill battle to work together to improve environmental conditions, the concepts presented in this section are worth considering as
examples of realistic strategies that can bring us one step closer to a
better life in a cleaner environment—one step closer to Utopgrilotis.

CHAPTER SIXTEEN

The Devil's Tipping Point: The Convergence of Humanity, the Environment, and Technology

Few men have virtue to withstand the highest bidder.

—*George Washington*[1]

Humanity is on the brink of a great invisible tipping point. Environmental issues will create a maelstrom of horrific problems that will befall humanity, the primary culprit of these series of storms. We have allowed the elite few to compromise what is in all of our best interests for a few pounds of gold or the promise of power and fame. Many of these problems are man-made, and many have been caused by human innovation and activity. If we continue to turn our backs on our global responsibility to read the signs of peril, this perfect storm will sweep across humanity over the next two decades with powerful waves of devastation, affecting the way we live, work, and recreate. The quality of life of not only Americans but of all humanity will be changed in some pretty terrifying ways. I am not a doom-and-gloom prophet, but the facts are powerfully in front of us. The first signs of the storm landed in 2008 with the global economic meltdown and now our anemic recovery. We have even decided that this time is not a

---

[1] Krieger, *Civilization's Quotations*, 16.

depression by media standards; it is instead the "Great Recession of 21st Century." As mentioned before, I prefer to be optimistic and refer to this time as the Great Economic Transition, when the waves of our poor fiscal, social, and environmental behaviors finally land on our beach of unrealistic lifestyles. With any luck, we will get the message and act before the really big waves hit.

The philosopher George Santayana is often quoted as saying, "Those who cannot remember the past are condemned to repeat it."[1] This quotation should lead to the question of how may we learn from the past in order to remain in harmony with nature, manage and apply technology appropriately, and yet encourage renewed respect and understanding of the positive and negative aspects of technological advancement? Surely, the answer to this question is rooted in creating technologies that breathe life into our planet while promoting and maintaining the essential dignity of human existence. Recognizing and acting upon our knowledge from past mistakes imposes the requirement, then, that we now behave intelligently and responsibly in mediating this delicate balance between, on the one hand, curbing humanity's seemingly insatiable and ever-present appetite to deplete resources and, on the other hand, harnessing the tremendous strength and power of technology for the greater good.

The Three Ps

To prepare for and attempt to mitigate the effects of this perfect storm heading our way, we must start with the three Ps. The three Ps can be defined as peak population, peak energy, and peak distribution of energy.

Peak Population

By peak population, I refer to the number of people who have reached retirement age and are now expecting to reap the benefits promised to them, benefits that supposedly protect the quality of their lives during

---

[1] Santayana, *The Genteel Tradition in American Philosophy*, 126.

the gray years. They begin to take out more from the system than they pay in, and we lose their productive capacities to pay toward the future costs of providing such benefits to others. The remaining workforce lacks sufficient contributions to pay for both their own future costs and the costs of those who are depending on those funds for their livelihood. This is in part due to the marked increase in the birth rate following World War II—the baby boomers. Population fluctuations like this can wreak havoc on our systems that can't handle these spikes.

Peak population also contributes to more basic human problems. We have not found a way to feed, cloth, and provide shelter for our burgeoning population; additionally, a growing appetite for energy is causing even greater geopolitical tensions as governments and businesses attempt to provide enough energy for their population centers. As we try to combat our addiction to fossil fuels, our use of alternative energy actually robs us of our food supply—corn-based ethanol, for example. This has had a profound and negative impact on food supplies because using alternative energy exponentially raises the cost of virtually all foods while having little if any real positive impact on our energy thirst. We have put off having a comprehensive energy policy, one that could implement the energy solutions that are already available to us. Our poor policies governing energy affect the basic necessities of life for Americans.

Peak Energy

The known amount of discovered and yet untapped oil field reserves is less than our demand for energy, and so we already know that we will be going into a deficit to find enough oil to replace the oil we are using. We are approaching the reality of peak energy, and it puts an enormous strain on our resources. Energy touches everything and thus affects the price of everything that we consume and use in our daily lives. Peak energy means we have found the greatest overall capacity for energy supplies and that as demand rises, we will find new supplies but not enough to make headway against the ever-declining, limited supply of energy supplies that are largely based on fossil fuels. Thus the price of energy will rise exponentially as we compete with both industrialized and emerging-growth nations to fuel our own country. The next world war could be fought over energy. We already see this being played out in our economic and military policies regarding Kuwait, Saudi Arabia, and Iraq; we are now viewing Iran and Nigeria as new sources of US diplomatic and possible military intervention hot spots.

Our infrastructure, as it stands, cannot shift and react to demand on a smart grid; our infrastructure isn't efficient and can't move power ubiquitously around our nation to where it is critically needed on a just-in-time basis. If combined with renewable energy solutions, a smart grid could reduce our energy demands between 30 and 50 percent over the next twenty years. Because of our lack of a coherent energy policy, we have not developed ways to conserve energy and implement clean technology to meet our current thirst.

Most folks don't realize that we have reached peak energy already and are rapidly going down the other side of the slope. What this means is that around 2003–2004, as some petroleum geologists estimate, we surpassed our ability to discover new energy reserves in the ground that would replace the amount of energy we were using. Energy will become more and more expensive and getting out what precious amounts we can find will be more and more dangerous. Just look at the Gulf of Mexico *Deepwater Horizon* catastrophe in 2010. The pressure on building a competitive economy will hugely evolve around how we address the energy needs of our century.

When we look at the pressures surrounding cyber crime, identity theft, and massive money gaming of the world's economic systems, we see that the technology available can do massive harm to humanity. This harm can come in the form of planting suitcase nuclear bombs or taking advantage of antiquated infrastructure and controls on our transportation systems, energy grids, and communication networks. We may experience a system-wide set of blackouts and give clever criminals access to communications and even our money. This could throw humanity into a real furor and cause huge civil unrest if radical terrorists can succeed in hacking and shutting down our technology-dependent world.

Thus, simply put, peak energy means we cannot refine or produce any more energy fast enough to keep up with demand, and it means trouble if we can't fix it.

Peak Distribution

Even if we could produce more energy, we could not distribute it to those demanding it because our capacity to do so is already at 100 percent. We would have to increase production capacity through clean coal, nuclear power, petroleum refineries, and natural gas terminals, along with a modern smart grid, to be able to distribute the energy fast enough to the market. The throughput of the infrastructure is currently not large enough to move enough energy to the point of demand.

These three Ps are the foundation for the other elements of our perfect storm.

How to Prepare for the Perfect Storm

To combat this perfect storm, we have to curb our energy demand, reduce our carbon footprint, and conserve water and other environmental resources. By doing these things, we will also curb the amount of funds available to radical terrorists by rechanneling fossil fuel funding. If we have an aggressive homeland security inspection program; if we focus our economic development efforts on new clean technology; if we invest in new, high mobility, mass transit systems; if we look into renewable energy platforms and advanced manufacturing here at home; and if we throw in a more competitive but fair taxation policy, the United States could lead the world in combating the approaching storm. Our ramparts should be built now, defenses that will withstand the storm surge and allow us to not only survive the storm, but also thrive during the storm and after it passes.

Even if the storm is less severe than we anticipate, the benefits of these actions are no less profound. Each step makes us more competitive for investments, less dependent upon fossil fuels, and more secure in our future from environmental, economic, and political threats. Simply put, there is no downside to this forward-thinking investment. By preparing to deal with Mother Nature, our thirst for a high quality of life and the security of our economic well-being will be quenched.

Let's Get Specific

What can we do to meet our increasing demand for energy? In his book *Why We Hate the Oil Companies*, John Hofmeister[1] suggests that we need to practice the "four mores" philosophy: more energy, more technology, more infrastructure, and more protection. Using this philosophy as the basis for America's energy platform and policies will put us on the right path.

More Energy

The easiest way to increase our energy supply is to build new nuclear power plants at the same locations as our current ones—most of our current nuclear plants are on tracts of land big enough to add another complete plant. Besides making use of available space, there is another benefit of building new plants next to existing plants: most communities in which nuclear power plants are already located understand the pros and cons of having nuclear power plants nearby and have accepted them. Building additional nuclear power plants on existing sites will remove the need to convince other communities of the benefits of building plants in their areas. This one initiative would increase our current electrical production by almost 40 percent instantly (well, over the next ten years—it would take that long to get the new plants in place).

Another step we need to take is to clean up coal-fired plants and modernize them with the latest clean-coal technologies. Since coal provides about 50 percent of our electrical capacity, improving coal plants will have a great positive effect on our environment. After implementing

---

[1] Hofmeister, *Why We Hate the Oil Companies*.

cleaner technologies, we should expand our use of coal for energy. The United States has a vast reserve of coal, and many estimate our supply will last for about four hundred more years.

More Technology

To increase the production and use of renewable energy, we need to implement energy policies that encourage investments in hybrid and clean-energy technologies for facilities, homes, automotive transportation, and other forms of transportation. For example, if facility and homeowners received 100 percent tax credits for the costs of installing clean-energy technologies, like smart energy devices, in their facilities and homes, many people would be motivated to invest in such improvements.[2] And these improvements have widespread application and the potential to bring great benefits. For example, more than 93 percent of all facilities and homes can—and should—use solar power for at least 50 percent (and in some cases up to 100 percent) of their total energy requirements. Of course, facilities that are energy heavy, such as production plants, have less ability to achieve this ratio of solar power use. But even if homeowners were the only ones who used more solar energy, we could reduce our demands for electrical power by 40 percent.

Currently, the major barrier to achieving this energy goal is the cost of purchasing solar energy technologies. As we are recovering from the recent recession, we have neither the money nor adequate resources to borrow the money needed to invest in such technologies. Clearly, to help our nation address our energy problems, the government needs to help individuals pay the costs of implementing forms of clean energy. This would especially help rural areas, where alternative energy can play a major role in creating clean power as part of the development strategy. As a side note, this type of government support would have another, much-needed result: the millions of people motivated to invest

---

[2] See National Academy of Engineering, *Real Prospects for Energy Efficiency in the United States*, 271.

in solar energy technologies would need professional help to install the technologies, thus creating the need for millions of new jobs in this area.

We can provide similar motivation for companies and individuals to invest in energy-efficient hybrid vehicles. For example, we could allow each taxpayer who buys a hybrid vehicle to take a depreciation deduction over the life of the vehicle, up to 25 percent of his or her tax bill until the cost of the investment is fully recovered.[1] The vast majority of Americans and American companies, whether or not they are strong advocates of alternate energy use, would take advantage of this opportunity to be reimbursed for purchasing new vehicles; as a result, the hybrid market would be secure and sustainable. The national average for vehicle fuel economy would skyrocket, and we would greatly reduce our gasoline consumption.

More Infrastructure

Even if we remove the barriers to retrofitting houses and facilities with solar technology and to purchasing hybrid vehicles, we still have other energy issues to address. Even if we had access to more clean energy and could refine it for distribution, our aged infrastructure could not tolerate the increased volume. To get cleaner energy sources to energy users, we need to expand our physical infrastructure to handle more energy from multiple sources, including from biomass, wind, the sun, hydrogen fuel cells, liquid natural gas, and water.[2] The need to build and maintain this robust infrastructure, which should be based on smart grid technology, would also generate a substantial number of jobs, again providing an added benefit to our nation: helping us recover from the recent economic crisis.

Building the most robust and up-to-date infrastructure to distribute energy from supplier sources to facilities and homes in America is a huge opportunity. This initiative would be the groundswell of a huge

---

[1] See Evenett, *Crisis Response and Openness*, 257.
[2] See Gevorkian, *Large-Scale Solar Power System Design*, 320.

American movement that would create millions of new jobs, a movement that would do something worthwhile: improve our competitiveness globally and improve our reliability at home. To accomplish this initiative, we need smart meters, smart switches, smart distribution grids, smart appliances, and a network that is capable of selling power back to the grid. This way we will have net metering and regulatory requirements that force the energy companies to buy back power at the rate that they sell it to the consumer (minus the legacy costs that have not yet fully depreciated). In other words, this project should be profitable enough to merit investments to achieve savings as the investors make the energy improvements. In order to spur investors, our entire system must have smart technology. Germany and other countries lead the world in requiring this technology, and as such, much of the solar movement has done quite well in Germany, as well as in some of other European locales, like Denmark and Holland.

More Protection

While improving energy options and conserving energy are important, having regulatory policies that enforce the need for such actions is just as important. In addition, we must make sure that all of us are sensitive to environmental and energy issues and that all of us are held accountable for being better consumers of energy resources, especially corporations that are responsible for extracting, refining, and distributing such resources.

Smart Recovery

David Goldstein, author of *Invisible Energy*, believes the best way to recover from the recession is to work toward energy efficiency:

> Energy efficiency is one of the strongest tools we have at
> our disposal to recover from the recession. It can address
> all of the major problems that led to the Great Recession
> and that continue to hold back recovery: from the fear of

inflation . . . to the trade deficit, high unemployment, and government deficits.[1]

Obtaining new and efficient sources of energy will therefore not only solve the energy problem but help us resolve our recession issues as well.

Here's another way to look at these long-term commitments that were made worse over the last generation. There are some 110 million homes for which people pay utility bills. Therefore, our nation is obligated over thirty years to spend some $8.5 trillion in consumer energy costs. And if half of our homes are located in widely dispersed urban developments, whose occupants have little responsibility for proper land use (the real fraction is probably even higher than half), we must add another $25 trillion (math enthusiasts will note that I assumed that the other half of homes are committed to "only" $150,000 in transportation).

This is $33 trillion in hidden obligations over thirty years, a problem made worse by observing that the figure will more than double if we extend our time horizon to sixty years. For comparison, this amount of money is of the same magnitude as future obligations for Social Security and Medicare, without the offsetting revenue sources that those programs have.

These national-level obligations are particularly troublesome in the context of an economy with a near-zero savings rate and a country that imports far more than it exports. Where are we going to get the money to pay our accumulating debts?

A plan for economic recovery must address all of these problems. It can do so by relying on vastly expanded energy efficiency policies as a cornerstone. Efficiency can cut the obligation of utility bills by half. If we borrow money for home efficiency investments, we can pay it back within five or ten years and then use the money saved for other purposes after that. This allows a recovery that is sustainable and creates local jobs in the meantime.

---

[1] Goldstein, *Invisible Energy*, Chapter 8.

There are well-developed and widely supported plans to do this, but they have been languishing in Congress for over a year. A similar plan for commercial buildings is in the Waxman Markey climate bill that passed the House around 2008. While Congress waits, the unemployment rate continues to rise, America's debt continues to increase, and oil prices have started to head back up.

The biggest challenge in adapting to new energy efficiencies is gaining access to the capital to implement them, which could be solved with government-backed loans on energy efficiency. These loans could be made available on a one-time basis per homeowner or facility owner; such a loan could be depreciable, in a rapid sense, against the tax bill up to the length required to fully repay the cost from tax savings. The repayment would occur over no less than five years but no more than ten years. The current federal program for PACE bonds (Property Assessed Clean Energy bonds—these allow energy consumers to apply their residential taxes to pay for clean energy and energy efficiency upgrades to their homes or facilities) to cities should be expanded and adapted to accomplish this goal of adapting to new energies by working with communities, corporations, and individuals.

To protect us and our planet from environmental devastation, as we have seen of late, it is paramount that we formulate a responsible national energy policy and start implementing it.

CHAPTER SEVENTEEN

Protecting Our Environment

Bigotry is the disease of ignorance, of morbid minds; enthusiasm of the free and buoyant. Education and free discussion are the antidotes of both. We are destined to be a barrier against the returns of ignorance and barbarism. What a stand will it secure as an alliance for the reason & freedom of the globe! I like the dreams of the future better than the history of the past.

—Thomas Jefferson, in a Letter to John Adams, 1816[1]

I f we fail to act today to protect our environment, we may very well be casting the die for the eventual destruction of our own kind. Humanity as we know it cannot win a war of wills against Mother Nature. Climate change and environmental shortages of scarce, but life-giving resources are going to be major driving factors of surviving and thriving in the economic chaos of today.

The potentially devastating consequences of climate change must not be underestimated—if left unchecked, rather than merely hearing about the gigantic hole in the ozone layer that now expands to South America, we will experience the problem firsthand as the hole expands over North America. Instead of standing by, ineffectual and passive, and then becoming progressively hysterical as we witness a doomsday scenario, we can and must act intelligently and decisively in concert with other nations to fight and counteract these environmental problems— carbon emissions; decreasing water supplies; the lack of clean water or

---

[1] Washington, *The Writings of Thomas Jefferson*, 27.

lack of access to clean water; scarce natural resources; and population problems, with some regions experiencing overpopulation while others are suffering population drain—all of these can and do bring harm to our planet.

This book is a call to action for structural changes that are necessary to protect our existence both as Americans and as citizens of humanity. On a less dramatic note, protecting our resources allows us to keep having a profitable economy and an enviable quality of life.

Most folks today are slowly but surely beginning to believe that our way of life is indeed threatened, that our elected leaders are disconnected from us as voters, and that the status quo and business-as-usual is simply not going to cut it; it is no longer an acceptable approach to our current problems. There are no greater grounds for debate and emotional arguments than when we discuss the environment, especially for business folks and those worried about the nuts and bolts of money and the economy. Tree huggers, as environmentalists are called, all too often take an approach that the business community finds totally unrealistic financially and thus absurd. Business people, on the other hand, take every suggested change in favor of the environment as a personal threat. Businesses justify their lack of environmental investment by using cost as an excuse. That is not a good measurement because if we were told that we must spend $20,000 today or we would starve, suffocate, get skin cancer, or have no money left to operate our households in thirty years, we would find a way to pay the $20,000. In fact, the argument could be made that by sticking our heads in the sand on the issues of climate change, renewable energy, clean water, carbon emissions, pollution problems, and finite resources, we are setting ourselves up to deal with some very harsh realities in our own lifetimes, not just our children's lifetimes.[1]

Though no scientific expert, I have observed some warning signs and I am of the firm opinion that the environment plays a significant

---

[1] See Glover, *Energy and Climate Wars*, 60.

role in our ability to restore the American Dream. We must thus pay for the structural changes we must implement to reach that dream safely. The major issues that need to be addressed are laid out in the rest of this chapter.

Environmental Collaboration on a Climate Change Treaty

The greatest way to have a positive impact concerning climate change is carbon reduction through the reduction of dirty energy. Even without discussing renewable energy, we have failed to realize that in the United States alone, the US Department of Energy has estimated that we could save 30 percent of our energy through existing off-the-shelf technologies available right now. The department estimates that the funds saved would equal $10 trillion over the next twenty years. Signing a compact with other nations to lead this same type of effort, which would be aimed at consumer products, business practices, and facility and vehicle efficiency upgrades, would be a smart move for the United States. A measure that could be set as a benchmark might be to endorse the requirement that all products must find a net average of 4 percent in new energy efficiencies per year within all industries. This would reduce energy by nearly 74 percent over the next thirty years. It would also spur continual improvements, research, development, and new product sales as consumers continue to find ways to save money through innovative product purchases and energy savings. Our entire global economy is built upon consumption, so our models must match our human nature.

Carbon Emissions Reduction

The biggest unknown is how much carbon the atmosphere can take before a cataclysmic series of events on the earth occurs—the rebellion of Mother Nature after too much abuse. Nobody really knows how much the atmosphere can take. The Intergovernmental Panel on Climate Change, a sanctioned task force of the United Nations, has estimated that the tipping point is somewhere near 450 parts per million (ppm). In 2007, NASA and other climate experts stated it could be closer to 350 ppm; in that same year, carbon emissions measured in the atmosphere was about 384 ppm, so in theory we could be well into Mother Nature's revolt.[1]

We should focus on cleaning up coal-fired energy plants with new zero-emission technologies that focus on clean coal. As I have mentioned before, we could double the nuclear reactors on sites that already have reactors. These two acts alone would address 90 percent of our electrical energy use and cause an enormous reduction in carbon emissions. In addition, we would solve other problems because in building and replacing old technologies with new, efficient ones we would create millions of much-needed construction jobs over the next decade. The energy savings from these efforts could also reduce energy costs by $4 trillion over the next twenty years. Reducing carbon could and should be quite profitable.

Carbon emissions are attributed mostly to vehicle emissions, as well as energy and production emissions. All of these could be addressed with clean energy technologies today if there was the economic will to do so. About 18 percent of US carbon emissions are related directly to the cars we drive. So encouraging cleaner vehicles, high-speed and light rails, bike paths, and pedestrian-friendly infrastructures could hugely reduce carbon emissions, not to speak of the windfall of helping Americans be more physically fit and thus addressing our exponentially expanding waistlines. It has been noted by many medical professionals that walking just 20 minutes per day could reduce heart disease and strokes in adults by up to 20 percent. This exercise would also burn an additional 1.5 pounds off our waistlines per month—about 17 pounds per year. This would in turn equate to lower health premiums, which would result in better health outcomes; better health equals more vigor and productivity and thus the domino effect of good decisions would continue.

---

[1] Spencer, "Global Issues of the Twenty-First Century," August 20, 2011.

Energy Conservation

Energy conservation should be the lynchpin in our next round of innovation and entrepreneurial investments. It represents the biggest economic opportunity of the twenty-first century. A *New York Times* article entitled "84 Ways You Can Help the Planet"[2] says that energy conservation of just 2 percent per year for the next thirty to forty years would result in about a 50 percent reduction of our greenhouse-gas emissions. The article continues to give excellent suggestions that would save trillions of dollars in the long run.

There are many hidden entrepreneurial opportunities within the field of energy conservation: building energy efficient appliances, taking waste or recyclable material and converting it to energy or new materials, and other products or services that help other people help the planet. The windfall of this type of investment in energy conservation is the annual creation of about 1.5 million net new jobs per year. This would be a huge economic mover in our stalled economy.

Europe now (since 2006) requires that a home be labeled when sold or resold according to its energy efficiency and the amount of energy use the new owner would likely consume over the life of a thirty-year mortgage. The more efficient the home design, products, and operation facilities, the lower the cost, and this cost is published on the buyer's closing papers and the sale flyers. The requirement was aimed at increasing consumers' awareness about how spending a few bucks more now could net them tremendous savings over the life of their investment. Purchasing a similar home that costs $10,000 more but that has a much more efficient design and operational products could save the buyer four to five times that extra amount over the thirty-year period.

Since energy has a direct impact on the consumers' discretionary income, this awareness could begin to positively influence buying trends and also indirectly incentivize improvements for homes that lag behind.

---

[2] O'Neill, "84 Ways You Can Help the Planet," November 18, 2007.

The same indirect pressure could be applied to commercial buildings. This strategy essentially follows the LEED (Leadership in Energy and Environmental Design) system; adopting LEED's environmental and sustainability standards would be very useful.

Energy Taxes

The convoluted manner in which we have devised a cap-and-trade energy plan (which contains proposed standards for addressing polluters) is just too absurd for the public to follow. In my opinion, it is simply another money-engineering scheme to look and sound responsible while creating loopholes for irresponsible people. Therefore, in the absence of an understandable road map to provide adequate incentives to address carbon emissions and our carbon footprint, I support a flat, clean, and understandable carbon energy tax. To me, cap and trade opens up too many opportunities to set up more corporate tomfoolery and Ponzi-type schemes; these energy plans are barely sanctioned and have fancy-sounding names. They remind me of the current hysteria in the capital markets about trading platforms . . . sound too good to be true, and usually they really are too good to be true.

I think we have to impose a flat carbon tax on the entire system so that all share the motivation for change and thus progress. That would include the importer, the consumer, the manufacturer, and of course the investors in pollution-contributing industries. By having an energy tax right at the source and for the end user as well, we motivate them to change high-consumption activities. Once the system carries the cost of doing business from the aspects of climate change and carbon emissions and pollution, investors will help fund clean technologies; this will create a groundswell of economic development outcomes, such as investment in new machinery, facilities, equipment, and intellectual properties, as well as job creation. Nothing would do more to spur alternative and renewable energy platforms and clean technology investments than a penalty on the old business-as-usual model.

Water Conservation and Clean Water

In addition to the man-made problems we face in energy and technology, we also face threats from the environment, such as the scarcity of clean water. We are using precious water at such a rate that many places will have a huge water deficit. All we have to do is visit the western United States and look at Lake Mead to see the impact of how our thirst for water has depleted one of our nation's largest water reserves in the Colorado River system. Our water system cannot keep up with the demand for agricultural water and the growing demand for water from the leisure and lifestyle markets in the area. Now, as another decade comes into view, we will face not only rolling brownouts across the United States but severe droughts and water shortages.

While we always discuss the need to reduce our appetite for fossil fuels, it is rarely mentioned that we must learn to curb our consumption of water at the same time. Water, like air, is a main staple for life. If we harm, reduce, or destroy the water supply, we are in effect killing our own future. Water conservation must be a component of our environmental movement. Requiring graywater applications for all homes and for irrigation purposes is a great start. Water is a national defense priority and as such, national laws must require graywater recapture and reuse, storm water reuse, waste water reuse, and lower rates of water consumption. If we throw in high-efficiency water appliances as well as part of our overall strategy for environmental protection, conservation, and efficiency, we will be on a good path to reducing the threat of running out of water.

Renewable Energy Platforms

Current studies show that a modest focus on renewable energy production systems such as wind, solar, biomass, hydrogen fuel cells, geothermal, and tidal currents could make up at least 9 percent of our total US energy by 2030. These could be the source of approximately 30 to 35 percent of worldwide energy by 2050. What is not reflected in this projection is that if we invest in these systems in conjunction with the

4 percent energy efficiency policy I have advocated, renewables could then handle about 60 to 65 percent of our total energy needs by 2050. This would mean huge savings in energy for everyone, and our goal of responsibly reducing carbon and addressing climate change would be well met. This also would allow us to continue to move away from energy dependence on fossil fuels and build a much more sustainable future. I might point out that this does not take into account what we don't know right now, which includes all the new advances that will far exceed our current knowledge of energy production and conservation today. These numbers are based on implementing known technologies of today. But we have to start somewhere.

Biomass: Responsible Production

There has been great debate over the uses of biofuels, such as algae, switch grass, and corn-based products. These blended, synthetic fuels, when combined with gasoline, electric, solar, and diesel, represent a huge percentage of energy savings. The National Resources Defense Council has suggested that we could save about forty billion gallons of traditional gasoline through these sources and that those savings would equate to a 75 percent reduction in carbon emissions by vehicles. This, combined with the lower operating costs of these energy platforms, is a positive economic outcome and also a positive climate change outcome; they are both achievable and affordable today. The biggest problem with the ethanol movement of the last few decades is that it had (and still has) a devastatingly negative effect on food costs for consumers. So using nonfood crops would be a dramatic improvement and apply the lessons learned from the corn-based energy difficulties of late.

Biopharming

Biopharming refers to the use of genetic engineering (and thus implanted codes in animals and plants) to produce highly successful yet cost-effective drugs to combat a number of human disease and ailments. The industry is estimated to bring in $16 billion per year. It has dramatic capabilities to give both small and large farms new economic opportunities through raising transgenic plants and animals. Additionally, plants can be coded to be more resistant to pests, thus reducing the need for fertilizer and pest control, which leads to reduced groundwater pollution in our systems. These issues will be on the forefront of economic investment opportunities in the coming years. As with any new change agent, there is opposition from people who have paranoid views or tend to resist change itself. There are also real negative consequences as well as advantages to this industry. I do think the pros, if regulated properly and given proper oversight, generally outweigh the cons.

Smart Homes and Facilities

Most people fail to realize that 39 percent of the total energy use in the United States is for buildings and homes, and of that, about 50 percent of those costs are just for lighting. Lighting accounts for 19 percent of the worldwide use of electricity. If we address lighting and then hot water, heating, and cooling, we can address a huge amount of our energy bills today. It is no wonder we have seen a massive move to new highly efficient lighting in commercial buildings and now in consumers' homes. Efficient lighting can reduce energy bills instantly by major chunks. So what can be done to make these changes happen more rapidly, and what can be done most easily? The following are today's off-the-shelf technologies that can be used to achieve at least a 50 percent reduction in our energy use within our households and facilities:

- Solar energy hot-water heaters,
- Solar lighting tubes for passive daytime operation,
- High-efficiency light bulbs,
- High-efficiency furnaces and air conditioners,
- Solar photovoltaic panels for daytime operation,
- Horizontal windmills for nighttime energy subsidy, and
- Smart grid net metering to sell back excess power.

Smart Appliances

Consumers love new gadgets, and their love is demonstrated every year at one of Las Vegas's most popular trade shows, the Consumer Electronics Show. As the show illustrates, we have the ingenuity required to come up with energy-efficient appliances. Most energy-efficient advances can be achieved just as in the computer industry: by designing new energy efficiencies into our next-generation products, with the goal of 4 percent energy savings per year across new products offered. Enabling these new products to talk to the grid and the energy management network of the facility or home would be a huge energy boon. The windfall of this is that consumers would see such products as must-have, very cool technology; their investments in such products would reduce their carbon footprints within society invisibly and without the draconian pain and suffering that energy conservation opponents always moan about.

Summary

The summary is fairly simple from an economic development perspective. Economic developers are supposed to be guiding the economic growth and health of our local, state, national, and even international economies. The biggest obstacle to economic freedom when it comes to energy is our fear of change and our inability to act on progressive and achievable objectives. We as a society fight changes made to our comfort zones. That is a major hurdle we must overcome to unlock our economic opportunities for the twenty-first century and responsibly address our energy and climate change paradox.

As an industry, economic developers can influence these changes by seeking to invest in industries whose priorities include building and deploying products and services that address energy and climate issues. Alas, since 2008 I have seen little evidence that economic developers are willing to step up and accept their responsibility to lead and advise our elected leaders on restarting our economies appropriately. In fact, there has been quite an absence of leadership; our international partners are commenting that Americans, for the first time, seem lost, unassertive, and so timid in their opinions that it is destabilizing others' beliefs that we can get the global economy back on track. It is time for our leaders to embrace the need for investing in smart industries, which will create jobs and attract new investments. These outcomes will lead to a greater tax base and diversify not only our economy but also our energy supply for the future health, wealth, and quality of life of our communities. As market movers and agents of responsible change, economic developers must be the first adopters of these principles; they must put aside fear, stop squandering their opportunities to recommend bold initiatives, and take decisive steps confidently.

CHAPTER EIGHTEEN

The Battle to Build Competitive and Ecofriendly Communities

Sustainable cities are those that design and manage their form of governance, economies, built environment, transportation systems, energy and water use, food production, and waste in a manner that imposes the smallest footprint upon the environment.

—*Matt Slavin and Ralph Bennett*[1]

O ver the centuries many communities have come and gone. They have done so largely because of a lack of visionary leadership. Each bad decision the leaders made weakened the community until it fell into pieces. Such communities did nothing wrong except to fall prey to their leaders' lack of foresight. Their leaders could not or would not adapt to changing circumstances and conditions that make such places vibrant and vital to humanity. History is littered with examples of failed mega cities and small towns alike; they have all been reclaimed by the earth and are buried by time and obscurity.

Today our community leaders face decisions that will determine whether their own communities will remain relevant, vibrant, and vital to humanity. No matter how large the city or how small the town, a series of bad decisions over time can cascade into a self-destructive course of no return . . . ending in complete failure. Nothing is too big to fail. This is one of the lessons we recently learned from the 2008 meltdown.

---

[1] Slavin, "Sustainability in America's Cities: Creating the Green Metropolis," 2.

How to Remain Competitive

Since our communities must survive and thrive in this chaos of the current economy, they must distinguish themselves from other communities that are vying for the same attention from investors, business expansion opportunists, entrepreneurs, and a highly productive workforce. The competition and incentive wars between states and communities are legendary; there is no end in sight to such battles for innovative new investments and people and market expansions. Since these wars are inevitably going to continue, communities must develop their best offensive strategies to win their campaigns more often than they lose.

Make no mistake: there will be winners and losers in these battles for economic development resources, opportunities, and positive outcomes. Just as in sports, sometimes the best defense (against the erosion of the economic base) is a good offense (by further building the community). The two can complement each other. I think that strategic decisions that improve our communities' opportunities for growth and investments should also be capable of bolstering those who are already there and believe in our communities today. After all, existing businesses have already made the investment. They also have the need to expand their business bases in this highly competitive marketplace. In addition, if we don't nurture and care for businesses, other communities will woo them to their locales, doing what we failed to do. As Lt. Col. Frank McCrady, an American soldier and an economic developer, said:

> Communities without the vision to invest in their own vision of the future they desire for their community should not expect others to invest in their community either. It is required of us today that we lead in our beliefs by making a solid business case with unbiased experts as to why investment in our community is valid and how both the private sector and the public sector will profit

from this newly established joint venture called a public-private partnership.[1]

Today there are many aspects of this green-sensitive economy that offer communities a path to building a distinctive persona that would be attractive to investors, workers, and residents alike. The creation of eco-friendly communities is going to be one of the hottest, most beneficial trends of the twenty-first century; it will generate jobs, spawn new ideas, and, in its totality, result in a vast and productive laboratory that can (and hopefully will) evolve into a model of participatory democracy in the cases of some of our rivals. This trend will include the transformative potential to embrace not merely new, built-from-the-ground-up communities but also older, existing communities. Much as the agricultural technique of precision breeding has produced a new strain of flood-resistant rice that promises to lift farmers in Bangladesh, India, and other places out of abject poverty, the advantages of going clean and green—of making choices and selections that previously may have seemed risky and ill-advised—will now become self-evident. These advantages may convince even many committed skeptics accustomed to denouncing and resisting every opportunity for change; the skeptics will then see that these modifications to their business models can be affordable and, yes, profitable. Those who desire the quality of life that they perceive is offered in these communities will be drawn to places such as Masdar City, Abu Dhabi; Destiny, Florida; Treasure Island, California; and Dongyang, China, as well as places like EarthQuest Village in New Caney, Texas.

How to Build a Green Strategy

So let's examine what normal communities can do to create a competitive posture to build their own green strategies, strategies that will bolster their efforts to draw attention to them as world-class examples of balanced growth and quality lifestyles.

---

[1] McCrady, taken from his public speaking event at the Chamber of Commerce of East Montgomery County, New Caney, Texas, October 2010.

Update Building Codes

There is no dodging the fact that most communities will have to seriously look, first and foremost, at their public policies concerning building codes and restrictive covenants regarding facilities and home construction. The United States could deeply assist in this matter by addressing the woeful status of the current Uniform Building Code and requiring renewable energy practices, energy efficiency standards, and resource conservation requirements as part of the entire system. Given that Congress has failed to act on this type of initiative, it can and does fall to each community to incorporate building codes into their own permit requirements. The first step in creating this new world-class, ecofriendly mind-set is to focus on local building codes and infrastructure to support remodeling and new construction.

Require Energy-Generating Devices

In addition, many communities have disallowed the use of wind generation because wind turbines are ugly and block view corridors. Let me say this bluntly . . . this is foolish and shortsighted. Now let me clarify why these types of outdated rules and local codes are foolish and shortsighted.

First, the industry of wind generation has come a long way since the era of windmills out in the Old West that pumped water to reservoirs for travelers, farms, cattle, and remote homes. With just a smidge of research, most communities could, if they actually tried, find alternative wind generation systems that could be allowed and that are practical in both low wind conditions and low height areas. An example: horizontal turbines that sit on the peak of a roof or on one of the slopes and that are no more unattractive than a satellite dish from Direct TV or Dish Network. When we combine wind turbines with a simple requirement that all new residences employ passive solar energy for lighting, solar hot-water heating, and even solar voltaic panels such as tiles and other structures for regular heating, we could make a significant dent in our energy use in the United States. Such measures could reduce our energy use by 30 to 40 percent if implemented within the next decade. In my opinion, planning for and requiring such retrofits to homes and facilities should be like all of us joining in on the moonshot; we would be doing our fair share in curbing America's energy appetite. Since it is unlikely that Congress will force the retrofits on existing structures as of yet, I think the best solution is to require all new construction to adhere to these standards. As I said earlier, the government should require that when people buy homes, the purchase agreements include the projected energy costs. This way the owners can see with their own eyes the cost of purchasing a facility that has a moderately lower price but is energy inefficient.

Implement Graywater Reuse Systems

The last step in preserving environmental resources is to simply enact a zero-tolerance policy regarding water waste. Every home and facility should be required to have a graywater reuse system. Cities could require that separate meters track buildings and homes to monitor the reuse of water; cities could also provide those who adopt the measure early and voluntarily with a discount on their water purchases based on the cost of the water reclaim and reuse system. Building owners who don't adopt the measure should, on the other hand, pay a premium for their water.

Curb Pollution by Educating the Public and Adjusting Franchise Taxes

The establishment of community pollution control is also essential to a clean environment. In the case of homes and buildings that do not have smokestacks, the requirements should be fairly simple: recycle, separate trash, and reduce electrical and fossil fuel demands by being energy efficient. In the case of polluting industries, any air or water discharges need to be cleaned up or the operations should be shut down. In all of these cases, from the most benign to the most severe, what we owe to our homeowners and building owners is a fair warning of our intentions. I believe every progressive city and town in America should sign a Clean America Resolution that would state something like this:

> As a community that values the environment and wants to protect the integrity of the earth today and in the future, as well as promote the best overall quality of life for our residents and create a more affordable business climate in the future, we are hereby creating a set of standards for all businesses, residents, and property owners to adhere to so that we can achieve these goals. The standards will be phased in over the next ten years and will allow people to plan for the inevitable shift to a more energy-conscious, environmentally sensitive, and business-savvy approach to their livelihoods and their domiciles. We are going to match these requirements with certain financial assistance to make them less financially painful initially and less disruptive to our current situations. Early conformers will get the greatest benefits and as such, each year the benefits will be reduced until they sunset after five years.

So now that we have the compact and charter, how do we pull this off? Good question. All of this is made possible by the current payments we have from putting our own systems in place. For example, almost all communities have franchise taxes on everything from electricity to cable, water, and other services. In order to provide incentives to local property owners, the cities would raise their franchise taxes by 15 percent upon the next contract modification or would implement the taxes by asking the utility and water providers to do so voluntarily. By using these funds, the city could then begin to finance out the changes to those who wished to participate. Immediate conformers would get 100 percent of the maximum benefit the first year, 80% the second year, and so on down to zero percent in year six. Since the sunset on the requirement would still be five years away, many may be faced with making these modifications out of pocket, with no financial assistance. New building construction would automatically qualify for the 100 percent benefit. The local initiative would require the installation of smart water meters and utility meters, alternative energy systems, energy-efficient building materials, and graywater reuse systems. These modifications would be a huge relief in America's energy plight and reduce our strain on the planet, such as on scarce resources like water.

Now we move to phase two. In this phase, world-class communities begin to be much more aggressive as they create an affordable business climate and an environmentally sensitive and energy-efficient city of the future. In this phase, we look at major public works projects that are, in many cases, already on the planning boards. This phase focuses on the percentage of renewable energy being created for use within the grid that services the community, the collection and use of alternative energy sources from new sources such as refuse (waste to energy), and the building of new robust smart infrastructures for delivery of dry and wet services to every property owner. By requiring that all infrastructure be updated and conform to new smart grid technologies within ten years, utility companies will be forced to act; in doing this, we do not have to wait upon the members of Congress to debate the initiative to death and play their blame-game tactics on each other. After all, these are local decisions and therefore we can govern their implementation. By doing so at the local level, we effectively force the United States into this century with our local grassroots strategy to make our nation more competitive and energy efficient. The windfall of this is that there will be ample blue-collar construction jobs created across the country to make all these locally driven changes; therefore, there is no need for us to await for Congress to create a top-down jobs strategy. These are initiatives that our own mayors can advocate and implement and inform us of at our own town hall meetings. This bottom-up method will inevitably save our communities from functional obsolescence.

The last phase is the development of our mobility systems, including bike paths, walking trails, hybrid lanes for vehicles, and high-speed light rail. By creating a dense network of parking-friendly transportation systems and infrastructures that are sensitive to alternative energy, we can a make using ecofriendly vehicles and other green modes of transportation both affordable and time-saving. Want to avoid the traffic jam but don't want to carpool? Just purchase a hybrid and buy a sticker from the city or roads network, and then drive in the fast lane 24/7 and avoid congestion. Paying for alternative transportation is dicier than some of our other choices, but it is still possible: we can place a local carbon tax on our fuels, airport fees, rental cars, and other energy systems related to transportation, and then we can use those funds to build out the infrastructure. Again, these types of projects will create jobs instantly in America, doing what is right and not putting off the pain that future generations would have suffered. The price we pay is worth the tab. The most important factor in all this is to make such changes voluntary and not dictate or mandate them too overtly. If we allow ample time to make this transition, it will occur and the pain will be dissipated over a long enough period that the benefits will outweigh the risks of failing to act. These suggestions allow our communities, our planet, and humanity to be taken off the endangered species list for failing to evolve.

So What Now?

W e have discussed many problems, many solutions, the benefits of implementing those solutions, and the consequences of letting those problems fester. In this concluding section, we will synthesize the information and formulate an action plan that can and must come to fruition if we are to make any headway against the storms that face us now and the storms that are on the horizon. It is time to act.

CHAPTER NINETEEN

Prosperity and Equilibrium in the Economy

It remains to be seen whether the weakness in the American econo-my will lead to a decline in the ability for America to exercise power within the domains of diplomacy and military affairs.
  —*Nicholas Burns, Joseph Nye, and Jonathon Price*[1]

The average American could point to the exact issues that are causing our nation to be dreadfully out of economic balance. It doesn't take a rocket scientist to know what we need to change. We have created a nation that caters to the superwealthy, the people who are almost immune to the economic throes the rest of us are in; the rest of the nation—the majority—are overworked, not in work, and underpaid people, starving for a stable economic future. Truly, though, this is a great irony; we need the superrich to invest funds in our enter-prise system, not tax shelters to avoid taxation. That is the true reality of why we need such a systemic overhaul of our approach to taxation. Those of us who directly work in the economy to spur innovation, sup-port entrepreneurial endeavors, and manage catalyst investments that will lead to more jobs are caught in a very destructive situation. So little heed is given to these economic mavens that they have failed to garner proper public sentiment to support their activities; later we may discover that this lack of respect may have been by their own doing

[1] Burns, *The Global Economic Crisis*, 12.

and an unintended consequence of trying to please everyone (politicians, business owners, and the general public). These individuals are playing it safe to preserve their own economic well-being. As economic developers, they face the challenge of driving hope—in the form of capital—back into the market. Creating a balanced approach to getting the capital back into the gas tank of the economy is difficult. US politics have become so unpredictable that many companies are just sitting on the sidelines with trillions of dollars that could be invested instead placed in a holding pattern. The drivers of a healthy, well-calibrated, and well-modulated economic engine—transparency, accountability, and balance—must receive constant hands-on maintenance and fine-tuning to keep the engine's superchargers humming along. That engine must be kept free from the gunk and pollutants that far too often slow down economies—even causing them to stop, reverse course, and travel backward, as we have recently and unfortunately witnessed. Economic democracy must include opportunities for everyone, providing an economic horn of plenty that is attractive to investors big and small, public and private, domestic and foreign. Economic democracy must do this without, in the process, giving any one economic sector license to dominate any other by turning a blind eye to rule breaking. In this way, investors will view the US economy as a safe haven welcoming innovation—a place to spend money and make money.

In order for the United States to regain its prowess from the standpoint of prosperity, we have to examine the role and size of the government. If we imagine America as a company, we have to view it through a model-driven evaluation of costs versus profits. We just aren't profitable in many of our traditional areas of expertise any longer. The reasons are not just our cost of labor. It is the cost of ridiculous regulations that do not regulate public safety, welfare, and environmental concerns In addition, we have a vacant energy policy with no cost-effective plan for improving clean, reliable power for industries, homes, and other uses. Our education outcomes have slipped so badly that the cost of remedial intervention by companies is one of their greatest expenditures.

The long and short of it is that for the United States to be taken seriously as a great investment, it must have the most educated workforce; the most reliable and cost-effective clean power; the greatest availability of highly productive people; and new innovative patents, products, and services that are on the cutting edge. We will need a robust capital market for all types of business development opportunities, from angels, seed capital, venture capital, public capital, and equity capital to traditional lending and hybrid capitalization from FDI and immigration inflows with capital.

Previously, America had always been the best place to launch and build a business because it possessed all these components. We had readily available capital, workers, intellectual property rights, easy access to licensing, reasonable energy costs, low-cost business taxes, and relatively reasonable regulations. Today we are one of the most expensive and heavily taxed nations on the planet, our people have less discretionary income than twenty years ago, and our energy and labor costs are sky high. The environmental red tape, in addition to the needed cooperation to deploy new technology investments and environmental clean technologies, is so cumbersome many don't even try to wade through it. There are so many disincentives in the capital markets; people end up paying more to the various levels of government than harvesting the fruits of their labor for themselves.

The pillars of providing economic growth include creating reasonable approaches to funding and supporting the innovative concepts and practices that the economic development industry is capable of harnessing, given adequate political support. We have created such a link between short-term, politically motivated decisions on economic development that visionary, over-the-horizon investments are not in style due to political needs (pointing to their outcomes to gain voter approval). So, if the projects can't be realized within the scope of the election cycle, they are simply avoided because they will not pay off in the elected officials' time in office. As Douglas MacArthur said, "A true leader has the confidence to stand alone, the courage to make tough decisions, and the compassion to listen to the needs of others."[1] De-coupling the politics from economic development is necessary, but that said, it does not mean we are going to be able to decouple public sector involvement in spurring economic consideration and thus investment into the local economy. The creation of new models in economic development is necessary if we want to rebuild the capital markets. The models must be market driven and become the proverbial grease between the wheel and the drive shaft so that the car will roll smoothly along. What do I mean by that? I mean that we must learn that investment in an area, company, or community must be balanced for risk versus reward. The riskiest times for any investment are from the time between concept due diligence to validity and then between start-up to sustained operations. These are the times when the company is most at risk. As such, creating a safety net that is both market sensitive and focus on these most vulnerable periods of the company's investment is essential to bolster confidence in speculative investments that target new products, markets, and processes. The creation of capital tools to increase equity and reduce the cost of capital is essential in offsetting these concerns. The politicians say we can't give them a break or it will cost us more to serve the people already here, and that will cause us to raise taxes; it becomes a never-ending, vicious circle in their minds.

In fact, nothing could be further from the truth. Most of these new projects are new money not in the economy yet, what I refer to as "found money." It means that the projects are creating new money not yet claimed by the government. The government claims it needs to get its fair share because it has to pay for the higher costs of providing services. Wouldn't another approach make sense, such as to increase the costs for services based on the demand for them? If the voters feel the costs are too high and thus not merited, then the government should scale back on the services or eliminate them altogether and allow individuals to purchase them if necessary from a private source. Why penalize or depend on new

---

[1] United States Congress, ed., *Congressional Record*, 603.

investments to buy down costs? The questions are what do we want to pay for, and what could we do without paying for in a more competitive market environment? That forces us to decide upon what is most important. The new investments can be modeled so that front-end costs are not penalized and thus are allowed to build up some momentum and much of the initial risks can be repaid to the investors before they start splitting any profits with the government. I have listed some simple changes that could be initiated to provide some deal equilibrium for new investments:

"Found money" deals, like rapid depreciation of capital investment into machinery, equipment, and facilities over the first 3–5 years. Another "found money" deal could be a tax-free status for all machinery, equipment, inventory, and facilities for the first ten years if the operation is sustained for another ten years past the start-up.[2]

A secondary tax credit market for employment jobs, created for jobs that pay above the area's average wage. These credits could be sold on the secondary market each year for the first ten years to repay the investors for part of their capital investments. The profits generated from the tax credit sales would be used to pay off declared start-up costs for land, site improvements, facility design, construction, and initial machinery and equipment purchases. In addition, the cost of inventory production, quality control processes, and R & D could be written off during the first three years. This would spur a massive amount of rolling-forward capital that would be dedicated to reducing operational costs, improving product innovation, and paying for the costs of funding the project.

The establishment of a payroll tax holiday for companies; only payroll taxes would be collected from the new workers so that the taxes would phase into the full rate by year ten. After year seven, the rates would increase by about 25 percent per year until they reached the full rate and normalize in year eleven.

The repealing of all building permit fees, including impact fees, on any projects that will create more than one hundred jobs.

---

[2] Tavakoli, *Structured Finance and Collateralized Debt Obligations*, 371.

The elimination of all corporate income taxes on profits, replacing those taxes with a flat gross receipts tax of 3 to 5 percent. This would give the corporations a modest tax rate with no need to game the system. The use of tax credits and tax holidays would make the rate zero for the first ten years.

Now we can imagine that if we reduced the burden of government on our businesses for the first ten years, there would be a huge push to create new investment projects and thus employ people. The resulting growth would fuel recovery. Furthermore, the long-term, low-tax environment after the tax holiday would bolster confidence in the investor markets, assuring investors that our economy is a very sound place to make new investments and that profits are treated favorably compared to other places around the world.

The best news is that since none of the money would come from existing funds today, businesses would cost the taxpayers virtually nothing. Better yet, businesses would actually create a direct profit, since they would employ people today who are costing the government (and thus the taxpayers) money. This is because these people are currently receiving unemployment assistance or are less gainfully employed because of their wages. Even if the person taking the job moves over from an existing job, the result would be new jobs within the economy. The new job would eventually be filled by someone sitting on the bench. The costs unemployment assistance would decrease, providing direct savings to the taxpayer.

The main idea is that economic developers and public policy makers need to look at "found money" deals as the basis for a massive new hybrid and, yes, preferential economic development strategy to put Americans back to work. Now we can begin rebuilding our industry base, infrastructure, and competitive capabilities, fueled not only by American ingenuity but by funds from investors around the world seeking a safe haven for their economic investments.

Building such an economic development platform needs to be a national, state, and local agreement that is collaborative and that creates

the capacity to get capital flowing back into jobs, facilities, new technologies, processes, and products. We cannot just subsidize loans; we
have to allow investment to work in the most favorable business climate.
Evidence of throwing money at big failing business models can be seen
in TARP (Toxic Asset Relief Program), which bankrolled corporate profits, reinvestments, and acquisitions and failed to reignite the investment
market. It failed to create any meaningful jobs and did not diversify the
economy so that the economy would be less prone to similar pressures
in the future. An additional problem is that TARP has allowed corporations to take the mind-set of "just go for it and if we fail, oh well, Uncle
Sam will bail us out." We set a series of bad precedents with the 2008–
2009 TARP intervention, and we did not build or reboot the belief that
the capital markets had new knowledge of how to better handle their financial affairs. Bringing equilibrium to the markets means that risk must
be less than reward. Confidence in the capital markets and the business
climate must be restored. Much of what I have mentioned in this chapter is easily attainable and would positively affect job creation and new
capital investments, but the various levels of governments must give
up their attempts to replicate how we did business before; they should
stop trying to seize their share of new investments for bloated governmental costs. Creating equilibrium means that government must learn
from this period of history and reexamine its own size, scope of services,
and cost of doing business. Government must simultaneously encourage a more highly profitable business climate and provide a world-class
quality of life. This can and should be done. In fact, in my opinion we
need to be capitalistic and allow businesses that have made poor decisions to fail and be consumed by industry leaders with proper business
acumen. How will we know if leaders have made poor decisions? They
expose themselves by asking for and receiving deregulation; they ex-
ploit their industries and financial markets; and they lack proper management of risk evaluations, not employing proper safeguards to build
their businesses responsibly. Propping up these poorly run businesses
is not capitalistic; it instead is a slippery slope toward big government

and eventually socialism. Today, I believe capitalism can be properly regulated and given parameters of socially acceptable norms without artificially supporting it and thus degrading its value. Capitalism is an agent of progress and, sometimes, the destructive change that advances innovation, profits, and services to humanity.

CHAPTER TWENTY

Capitalists Can Have Hearts Too

Each of us has the potential to contribute. . . . You have a great
opportunity to make a new shape of the world.
    —*Dalai Lama Tenzin Gyatso, in a Speech to US Students*[1]

Capitalists are often accused of being greedy and oblivious to the needs of others around them. This laundry needs to be aired and discussed. While altruism and charity are not dead, they all too often appear to be on life support; the conservatives and liberals are both at fault for the morass of inept governance. Indeed, far too many of us throughout the world can afford to do something positive with our own wealth (spurring innovation, job creation ventures, collaborative partnerships, and other opportunities that also increase our wealth) but choose to remain uninvolved. To put it even more bluntly, indifference rules.

The members of this apathetic group seem uninterested in how posterity will judge them; they have no planned legacies for the future other than for their own families, and as such, they are rather fixated on wealth accumulation. I do think that preservation of wealth is not an unfair goal to have. There are many examples of wealthy people who have used their wealth to benefit the whole country and yet remain very, very wealthy. Bill and Melinda Gates created the Bill and Melinda Gates

---

[1] Bernton, "Dalai Lama Urges Students," May 15, 2001.

Foundation, one of the most respected charities in the world. They run the charity like a business, and they are getting fantastic results.

Now, I don't believe in sharing wealth without requiring hard work from the recipient of the wealth. But I do believe in giving people the opportunity to rise out of squalor and better themselves to make their own wealth. They then can take the majority of that wealth home to their families without being forced to give it to the various governments or others that feel entitled to the wealth without working or risking at the same level. The fruits of a labor should go to the person who achieved success and wealth by his or her own toils. That person can then decide to give back to the community in ways he or she desires, doing it freely and without Big Brother forcing him or her to share the pennies. The government's responsibility (as well as our own) is to give people the tools to better themselves so they can create their own futures; we do not owe anyone else part of our own fruits, but we should be enticing those who have an abundance to reinvest in our society and reap the profits for doing so.

> *The time is now near at hand which must probably determine whether Americans are to be freemen or slaves. . . . The fate of unborn millions will now depend, under God, on the courage and conduct of this army.*
> —*George Washington, in an Address to the Continental Army before the Battle of Long Island, August 27, 1776*[1]

After reviewing the example of our very first elected leader, who was truly a national hero for the ages, how can we believe that big government must surely equate to better government? I believe Washington's objectives were clear. It takes the courage of many to topple the enslaving practices of leaders with socialist tendencies. Sometimes it takes drastic action. For Washington, it took the Revolutionary War. We don't need another war, however; we just need to stand together and make hard choices together.

---

[1] Sparks, *The Writings of George Washington*, 449.

CHAPTER TWENTY-ONE

The Economic Outlook for 2020 and Beyond

Uncertainty is the refuge of hope.
—*Henri Frederick Amiel*[2]

The outcomes from which our future will be determined are not set in stone. It will soon be determined whether the United States will remain the great economic power it once was or whether it will follow the path of many great empires of the past and deteriorate into oblivion. The decisions we make in 2012 will be critical in determining which path our nation goes down, for good or for bad. This chapter features two imaginary bulletins about the American economy regarding choices taken or not taken. Let me be clear on this—I think this economic transition will require nearly a decade for us to properly reposition ourselves. Only then will we begin to realize the fruits from the necessary investments that will sustain America as the greatest economic show on earth. That clock to fruition starts once we begin to make good decisions to make needed investments; as of the writing of this book, indications of such decisions have not appeared, so real recovery is beyond 2020 as of now.

Future News Flash 2020: Path 1

"As the world's leader in climate-change research and in the development, marketing, and application of cutting-edge technologies designed

---

[2] Harvey, *Achieve Anything in Just One Year*, 181.

to measure and cope with atmospheric changes (on scales ranging from the micro and local to continent-wide and beyond), the United States has reaped the benefits economically and in prestige for the giant leaps forward it has taken to save the planet from self-destruction. The millions of domestic jobs created have far outpaced the jobs lost in fossil fuel industries—which still exist, but in smaller, more compact forms according to the nonrenewable nature of the fossil fuels themselves.

"The broad-based research on climate change has expanded into other areas, including water conservation and enhanced antipollution filtering devices; some of these devices are simple to purchase, use, and maintain, thus allowing individuals and small groups to inexpensively conserve and reuse this most precious of vital resources. Working with the UN and private humanitarian groups, as well as using direct grants, the United States has invested billions in enhanced water purification, conservation, and reuse kits, sending them to countries around the world. US companies have gained prestige, thus adding value to their brands, by distributing kits and selling them at cost, and then using the resulting tax credits to increase net profits. The end result has been that America as a manufacturing and innovation leader has been well established.

"In addition, the energy conservation and enhanced capabilities of the modern smart grid, along with major new clean fuel technologies, renewable energy platforms, and energy efficiency modifications, have enabled the United States to reduce its carbon footprint by 50 percent over the last ten years and reduce it fossil fuel consumption by over 30 percent over that same time period. With these advances, the American economic juggernaut seems well poised to lead the global revolution in the energy century. Americans now have formed the most competitive labor force with the most cost-effective, environmentally sensitive business processes and the highest amount of discretionary income on the planet. The United States has reached full employment, and the flow of bright, productive, and legal immigrants to its shores is helping to meet the once-again resurgent demand for workers caused by the economic growth of the overall economy. American ingenuity and products are considered the crème de la crème of the market place."

"The US has promoted enhanced Internet use domestically and abroad so that millions of new users, especially those residing in rural and poorer communities, are now connected to the World Wide Web. The last mile of the digital infrastructure (the proverbial golden spike of the digital age) has been built into the information highway once and for all. Congress has passed laws reforming immigration policies while at the same time enacting legislation that protects the nation's borders and operates effectively. Reform in these two areas also has resulted in parallel legislation that further protects and strengthens citizens' rights while allowing America to attract the world's best and brightest to come to the country and achieve their ultimate economic dreams.

"The resulting immigration and homeland security network has made America highly productive and safe from terrorism without restricting the citizens' civil liberties. The American energy policy of reducing fossil fuels has had the economic impact of exponentially reducing the funds available to terrorists, and as such, terrorist threats have declined to inconsequential levels. The future looks bright."

Future News Flash 2020: Path 2

"Having gone through yet another round of reducing benefits to the elderly and working-class citizens, the United States faces rising mortality rates. Affordable health care is unavailable to millions of citizens, and the United States is still the only country among the world's developed nations that has no functional form of national health care. Most of those caught in the recent throes of additional layoffs from America's still-declining manufacturing sector cannot afford and have no access to healthcare. This unemployment leaves well over 100 million Americans without healthcare; one in three Americans is uninsured, and most of these uninsured are not (yet) eligible for Social Security, even though they were very productive workers. This has caused personal bankruptcies to continue to rise exponentially each year. Most of these folks have lost their jobs, dignity, and homes, and they are virtually economically worthless in their middle-age years, the most productive years of former generations' lives.

"Environmental devastation continues to ravage the land, rendering millions more acres unsuitable for farming. The costs of food and energy are astronomical; water is strictly rationed; the industrial base continues to shrink; and the cost of higher education means shouldering a lifetime financial commitment for students who, upon graduation, must cope with bleak job prospects.

"Tens of thousands of wealthier Americans continue the trend of moving to countries with lower living costs and with more abundant economic opportunities. The rolling brownouts and power outages from the grid breaking down have hampered the reliability of power to both residents and industries, making just-in-time delivery promises the fantasy of a bygone era.

"Likely corrective actions for continued business-as-usual efforts will get more difficult to make and much more severe in their economic disruption of accepted norms. The average American now faces economic restrictions on virtually every cent he or she makes. The unemployment rate continues to loom over 10 percent, and in many areas it is approaching 15 percent; meanwhile, the underemployed and those who have already exhausted their unemployment benefits push the actual unemployment and underemployment numbers to well above 25 percent. The amount of discretionary income for the average American has created a bleak outlook for consumer goods for the tenth year in a row. American buying power has been so eroded and foreign sales to America have been so restricted that new technologies are no longer launched in America but in Asia. American consumers are finding that the everyday technologies of just ten years ago—televisions, appliances, cars, cellular phones, computers, and furniture—are simply not within economic reach of most Americans today. The American share of global GDP has shrunk from 30 percent ten years ago to less than 15 percent today. Things are looking bleaker and bleaker."

Choosing Path 1

Most of us know the truth; we just don't want to face it. As our forebears said, we hold certain truths to be self-evident. We all knew when the 2008 election heated up that this was a pinnacle moment in American history, and not because we were considering the election of a woman; an ethnic minority; or a non–computer-literate, last generation politician (who eventually was paired with one of the most inept politicians ever from a standpoint of overall knowledge, acumen, and polish—it was down right embarrassing). I do believe our political system is not the realm of elitists, but it should be and could be the realm of our best and brightest minds that should be focused more on resolving America's problems, crafting a working bipartisan compromise that could be put to work, and then putting Americans back to work, protecting and rebuilding our quality of life and putting the respect back into our foreign policy so that we are once again the lighthouse of hope to the rest of the world.

The problem with 2008 is that all the rhetoric was used and no action came out of it—that is, no action that had any long-lasting, significant impact on our overall problem. We bandaged the problem and just exacerbated the wound by putting off the tough decisions that would rebuild trust in our financial markets and bring consumer and voter confidence back.

> *Victory belongs to the most persevering.*
> —*Napoleon Bonaparte*[1]

Yes, I think we squandered the faith that we were ready to place back in our politicians, hoping they would get us back on track. Instead, they proved that they just tell us what we want to hear and then do whatever they please once elected. Truly, the politicians showed that their true masters are the icons of commerce, not the people who elect them.

---

[1] Esdaile, *Napoleon's Wars*, Chapter 10.

If we do not push for real structural changes in our government, taxes, trade, education, workforce benefits, homeland security, civil liberties, immigration, climate change, and energy policies, our country will not be the better for this delay. We are eroding our values; capabilities; quality of life; fiscal solvency; and individual, civil, and economic liberties. The much-discussed tipping point is actually upon us. We passed peak production in about 2003, passed peak oil this past decade, passed peak population in 2010, and now we are setting the stage to surpass peak taxes in 2011 by further going after those who might actually have the funds to invest in our recovery (if we could produce some meaningful tax revisions that would encourage them to do so). These are the elements of the perfect storm that will destroy our country if we refuse the call this last time.

This future can and must be avoided. We have constructed a country today not by our own devices but rather our failure to be accountable for our actions, where the government no longer works for the people but rather the people work for the government. We have created a massive Byzantine government that is so bloated that most have no idea where to start to manage our programs and their expenditures. We have created such a beast that even the masters of the beast, our own Congress, have no real idea how to tame it.

However, pundits and hopeful politicians are no better; they start their campaigns to redirect our attention to irrelevant minutia and use scare tactics. Any discussion of change is immediately sensationalized as anticapitalistic, antipatriotic, or partisan driven. The first thing we must overcome is the media behind the confusion—confusion sown by those who want no real change because of their own special interest–driven purposes. We must look out for the best interests of our people, not the best interests of corporations or government itself. In the end, if the people are healthy, wealthier, and wisely educated they will spend more on products, produce more innovative products and services, and pay a fair share of their discretionary income in taxes. They will make better, more informed choices on energy, technology, employment, education, retirement, health care, transportation, housing, and other services and products offered by a robust economy. Restoring faith in our elected leaders to make good decisions that lead to Path 1 means that they must learn how to compromise and make uniformly positive decisions in the best interest of their constituents, not their reelection campaigns.

CHAPTER TWENTY-TWO

The W6 Approach: An Action Plan

Two of the gravest general dangers to survival are the desire for comfort and a passive outlook.

—*US Army Survival Manual*[1]

In this final chapter, it is most important that we discuss the implications of the suggestions in this book and the future actions that you, the reader, can decide to take. Marvelous changes can be made when we act together according to a plan.

The W6 approach is a process used by businesses, governments, and anybody else who is laying out a plan of action. The questions we will use are the following:

- What's your message?
- Why should I care?
- What are you asking me to do?
- What's in this for me?
- When is my deadline for these actions?
- What happens if I don't act?

It is wonderful to finish a book and feel satisfied; however, I would like you to finish this book and feel powerfully motivated to act on the crucial points brought up in this book. Only then can we make

---

[1] US Department of the Army, *US Army Survival Manual*, 1.

meaningful changes that will keep us on the right path to prosperity and happiness.

What's Your Message?

Americans cannot continue to accept unrealistic views that the good times will come back if we just wait this storm out. Unless we take action individually and collectively to create systemic and dynamic changes despite our political paralysis, unless we hold our leaders accountable, and unless we stop waiting for the nation to fix itself, we will not get our nation back on track. Profound change and, yes, even some economic chaos can be the springboard to reignite the American ideal and raise the global bar on economic outcomes once more.

Why Should I Care?

It's your country. Failure to participate means that your civic power is turned over to those who would corrupt and pillage our system. The American people themselves are the whistle-blowers. It is the responsibility of all citizens to participate in civic government; the concept of civilization signifies that we humans have reached a stage of social development that is advanced, that we are willing to work together to create something better than individuals could do on their own. You may not be affected by some of the government's bad decisions, but eventually something will affect you personally. Being civically watchful means that you help keep your community strong and free of corruption. Being economically wise means that you have the knowledge that will help you make good financial decisions as you participate in various civic duties (going to town hall meetings, voting for people and referendums, participating in school board meetings, etc.).

You have to be accountable yourself for the situation our nation is in. We have tolerated and allowed this cancer to erode the strength of our great republic. So be accountable by exercising your rights while you still have some. Invest in your own skills, vote for leaders who will lead, and hold those leaders accountable. Seek to learn how you can create more value for your family, your community, and your profession, and then do something about it. Political and economic issues will affect you or someone you love sooner or later, and you should want to participate so that you and your loved ones will be affected positively.

What Are You Asking Me to Do?

This section contains a summarized list of fifteen suggestions to remake America. Details of these suggestions are laid out in the specific chapters of this book, cross-referenced for your convenience. We can start making these changes by telling our politicians that these possibilities, if enacted, will make our nation great once more. Most Americans, when I discuss these principles and ideas during public forums or lectures, almost always agree with the changes that need to be made. The problem is that the average American has no idea how to get control of our country again, how to wrest the power from special interests, from the elite, and from the benevolent ruling class (mostly made up of lawyers) who are elected to Congress through their own chicanery and then fail to keep their campaign promises. So let these changes begin with us. We must start at the grassroots level.

Fifteen Legislative Changes to Make within the American Government

1. Legislate a Congressional Overhaul Act. Set term limits on all state and congressional elections, permitting no more than three terms of service at each level of elected government. Change terms to shorter limits: five years in the case of the Senate, four years for the state legislature, and four years for the House of Representatives. Finally, require that those elected, as well as all public servants, must live like the rest of us citizens, with vouchers for their workforce benefits, not more lavish retirements or paid junkets by special interest groups. Every citizen and public servant should be given the same access to benefits, case

closed. If our elected officials must live like us, they will feel the sting of their bad decisions and feel the benefits of the good ones. We should prohibit them and their families from lobbying during and after their terms in office for a minimum of five years. This is essential if we want to reduce indirect favors and the demonetizing from the political election system. In addition, we must call for the elimination of special interest campaign donations and the return of one person, one vote; campaign funding must come from the people, not corporations. Corporations are not citizens; they are an "it" or an entity. We are people, sentient and thus worthy of our politicians' full attention. We must require politicians' honorable service to us as they act as public servants, not lap dogs to their funders. (See p. 13, "Suggested Changes to Limit Corruption.")

2.   Call for the abolishment of the current tax code and implement a new national tax code based on consumption and use taxes (a modified fair tax). Stop penalizing wealth. In addition, income taxes should be used only for the four needs of the worker (retirement, health care, unemployment, and disabilities) through a private, self-directed (but federally regulated) voucher system. (See p. 27, "The Power of the Tax Code.")

3.   Reduce frivolous programs and nonessential entitlements. Sunset Social Security, Medicaid, and Medicare as declining benefits over the next thirty years. Replace this with an American Choice Workforce Benefits System, which would use a fully self-directed voucher system for retirement, health care, unemployment, and disabilities. This system would require a flat 15 percent of earnings. This also would require that 1099 paid service contractors must have the 15 percent self-employment tax withheld by those

who pay them, putting the monies into their own private tax trust accounts. Those funds cannot be used for anything else but to purchase these benefits. The government would regulate that companies need to provide some guaranteed minimum threshold for each category. (See p. 28, "Why Raising Taxes Won't Help Us.")

4.   Legislate a national Fair Corporate Tax Act. Create a tax code that rewards innovation, investments, and savings as well as R & D investments, community development, and economic development investments. This tax code would require a gross receipts tax on all businesses of 3 to 5 percent. If corporations make qualified investments, they can deduct them from their gross receipts tax. This should be the only method for deducting from corporate tax burdens. I am a strong advocator of P3s, and I believe that investment in these partnerships should qualify a corporation for an additional deduction. These P3 models could provide the source for attracting such funding from the private sector to fulfill long-term projects that would benefit both the public and private sectors. (See p. 40, "Questions and Solutions.")

5.   Abolish property taxes, and implement a national local consumption tax for police, fire, parks, recreation, and civic administration. Most other local services, like water, sewer, electricity, gas, cable, and telephone, could be based on user taxes. If we use a 5 percent local sales tax, a 5 percent national sales tax, and a 4 percent state sales tax as the average (and everyone pays them), we would have enough cash to rebalance our country. Even the black market service wages would also pay into the system. This gives us a combined flat tax of around 29 percent that everybody pays. This percentage does

exclude gasoline and carbon taxes and other user fees, which would equate with a flat tax of approximately 35 percent, but the 29 percent is clean, understandable, and not so daunting for many to fulfill. No more dreading April 15th. (See p. 39, "Property Taxes.")

6. Modify TARP and bankruptcy rules to become the National Home Ownership Preservation Act. Allow homeowners to write off second mortgages and reduce first mortgages to 80 percent of their homes' appraised values in order to reform banking. This would rebuild the home as a sacred source of middle-class wealth once more instead of a revolving credit card for frivolous spending. (See p. 54, "Financial Markets and Banking.")

7. Formulate a law called the National Workforce and Education Outcomes Act. This act would implement a national skills assessment test every five years within the workforce and include curriculum to maintain and improve skills. This act would also require skills assessments for freshman and seniors in high school. This intervention would greatly enhance the flexibility of our workforce to respond to business needs; it would also motivate and provide an avenue for those who are under-employed to reach their potential and stave off the loss of critical skills. It would allow us to provide direction to students on their workforce options and inform employers about potential hiring prospects. By doing this we will make education and business very compatible and accountable to each other. (See p. 59, "Continuing Education for Our Workforce.")

8. Require military training and civic service to retain US citizenship. Although this might be considered

radical, I believe it would help our youth if they were required to serve the community either by enrolling in the military reserves or rendering another type of civic service (or both). By requiring at least two years of community service and forty hours of annual community service, we could improve our communities and have a well-trained reserve force to help our full-time troops. (See p. 61, "Military Training.")

9. Create a public and private school voucher program. All individuals should get a portion of their local and state sales tax expenditures for use to purchase their children's education. Since education is a major point of controversy, the voucher system will allow everyone to make choices as to what schools they use and force competition into the public school system for kids. (See p. 62, "Paying for Education.")

10. Provide college, university, and technical school grants for 100 percent of all books, tuition, and technology tools as long as the student maintains a 3.0 GPA. By rewarding good students with funds to go to school and not putting the students into debt for the rest of their lives, we will free up our people to become the best and brightest on the planet. In addition, this reward would encourage people to excel at their studies and, when coupled with the voucher system, the funding would greatly rejuvenate educational attainment within our society. (See p. 62, "Paying for Education.")

11. Require inspections on 100 percent of imports to the United States. This reduces harmful items from being slipped into this country; it will also level the playing field to begin manufacturing within the United States again. A

nation has to make things to be great, and to compete globally we must reignite manufacturing in America. By forcing 100 percent inspections, paid for by the exporter upon arrival to our country, we could spur reinvestment in the United States. There are two positive outcomes from this: our homeland security will be much better and thus we will be safer as a whole. (See p. 101, "Myth 4.")

12.   Rebuild and expand America's infrastructure and mobility. Build/expand/improve American roads, rails, airports, and bike paths for greater mobility. This includes light rail in all major metropolitan statistical areas and new high-speed rails between all metropolitan statistical areas. In addition, we can strengthen and update our water, sewer, telecommunications, transmission, and seaport systems. Our transportation choices and quality of utilities, as well as their affordability, should rival the rest of the world, not be the laughing stock of the global community. Mobility is especially important; updating our systems would reward us with clean, safe, and high-speed mobility, free of major congestion. This mobility would greatly enhance our options to transport things more cost-efficiently and effectively, thus saving time, energy, and money. (See p. 178, "Five-Year Hiatus on Profits for Job-Creating Investments.")

13.   Create a national Energy Policy Agency to guide America toward energy independence and energy efficiency, with high levels of aggressive, green, and sustainable guidelines. This policy, when carried out, would reduce our appetite for fossil fuels and foreign energy supplies. Reward the expansion and installation of clean technologies and renewable energy (especially in automobiles and fleets) with 100 percent deductibility for clean technology

and renewable energy purchases. The deduction would come from local real estate taxes in the case of facilities and state and local income taxes with regard to corporations. (See p. 207, "More Technology.")

14.   Rebuild and update US infrastructure and capabilities by putting in a new smart grid, from generation to consumption—all the way into the home. Allowing technological devices to communicate quickly is just one of the many features of the smart grid that will give us tremendous energy savings. (See p. 208, "More Infrastructure.")

15.   Implement PACE (Property Assessed Clean Energy) loans nationwide. Create local, self-imposed loan pools for homeowners and business property owners to update their existing facilities so that the facilities are energy efficient and conserve resources. Require mandatory energy savings certificates during the disclosure of property sales. Giving people access to pools of money allows them to have the funds to make retrofits to their facilities and homes. Since 93 percent of our facilities can and should use both passive and direct solar energy, as well as other renewable energy sources, implementing PACE bonds will drastically cut down our nation's addiction to fossil fuels. (See p. 209, "Smart Recovery.")

I am asking you to act within your capacity and within your sphere of influence to introduce these changes into our legislative processes at the local, state, national, and international levels of government. If you are in local government, start there. If you have access to the higher echelons of government, start there. Begin with what you have and what you can do. See where it will take you . . . and our country.

What's in This for Me?

Many of the benefits of the changes I am asking you to make are behind-the-scenes; you enjoy many freedoms now, and the changes I am asking will help you keep those freedoms. However, some benefits are very visible:

You can regain your ability to compete and make a dignified wage, thus increasing the quality of life of your family and your own self-esteem. You can do these things by expanding your investment in yourself and your skills for competing in the workplace; you can also do this by investing in your families' educational needs.

You can save money in the long run, stave off the effects of global warming and carbon-based pollution, and reduce the funds for violent terrorists to use against us. You can accomplish these things by investing in hybrid and other clean and renewable energy platforms for your home, your workplace, and your choices for transportation.

You can see your will being done as you and like-minded individuals collectively vote and educate those who seek public election about your needs. But if you don't vote, you don't get to complain; that is reserved for those of us who are active citizens. You can have the satisfaction that your leaders represent you by understanding the voting record of all the incumbents and refusing to reelect those who don't perform to your expectations. You can hold them accountable for partisanship and failure to lead. In short, your voice can be powerful.

You can get out of debt and stay out of debt. It is a wonderful, freeing feeling. You can escape the slavery that so many Americans feel by striving to be fiscally conservative and investing in your home, energy efficiency, retirement, and education. These priorities must be ahead of frivolous material items. You will have less stress and lower blood pressure if you don't spend more than you make, period. Cash will be king in this new transitional economy, so have plenty of it and you will do well, in spite of the pack of others who might remain foolish and continue to be spendthrifts.

When Is My Deadline for These Actions?

Since we have already reached peak production, peak oil, and peak population, it is our responsibility to formulate ways to act carefully and appropriately. And soon. All of these pieces of legislation can be enacted in the near future, but they should be enacted as soon as possible because it will take a decade to fully reap the benefits, thus pushing our ultimate recovery well beyond 2020 even if we started tomorrow.

What Happens If I Don't Act?

It is hard for us to recognize our own denial of what has transpired over the past five decades, since the country first introduced the income tax and ushered in Big Government on February 3, 1913. With that decision and others that have followed, we have eroded the original intentions of our founders, the intentions to help us pursue life, liberty, and happiness. Worse yet, most of us feel totally powerless to change the way things are. The final blow to all of this is if we continue to perpetuate the transformation of our great republic by our lack of focus, commitment, and action, we will soon become a Nanny State and a socialistic democracy. We will no longer live with the true spirit of a free republic that is held together by ideals, protected by laws, and governed by our peers.

The America we know could be lost forever if in this generation we don't act to reestablish it as the best business climate with the best quality of life, making it balanced by fiscal, environmental, technological, educational, and energy-based policies that are sustainable and profitable. Our capitalistic approach should not be forced down the slippery slope of big government and socialism.

CHAPTER TWENTY-THREE

American Ideals and Reality

Freedom is a fragile thing and is never more than one generation away from extinction. It is not ours by inheritance; it must be fought for and defended constantly by each generation, for it comes only once to a people.

—Ronald Reagan, from California Gubernatorial Inauguration Speech[1]

Since these are my concluding thoughts, I want to make sure that I clearly articulate to you, the reader, my reasoning for such a drastic call to action for such major changes in our nation. The evidence of what has elicited this radical approach appears all around us today. Our families are breaking down from economic stress. Our financial coffers are being robbed regularly by bright Wall Street and corporate schemers. Our elected officials have sold us out and have put us in harm's way, hindering our ability to live a dignified existence and pursue life, liberty, and happiness. Politicians have failed to maintain the public trust and have put us into the position of being a debtor nation with a massive and exponentially growing deficit. And because we have no functional energy policy we are forced to deal with despotic, warlord-like energy barons.

---

[1] University of Texas Library System, "Ronald Reagan." Speech given on January 5, 1967.

Our course seems clear to me: we must scrutinize, discuss, adapt, revamp, amend, and transform the way we do things. Who must supervise these changes? Who have the most to lose and the most to gain from these adjustments in our government? We, the people.

I hope this book has been a springboard for your thoughts on how you and I, along with others who are concerned for the welfare of our country, can cause a grassroots movement to restore our nation, a nation that has no limits on what we can achieve. This will require personal sacrifice during our lifetimes, fearless and visionary leadership, and purposeful focus as a people. It is our space shot in an era where the space program has been shut down because of too many problems at home. So let's fix those problems.

Veritas vos liberabit
The truth shall set you free.

Don A. Holbrook

APPENDIX

10 Amendments for Freedom, Inc. *America's Freedom Amendments*. Accessed July 4, 2011, http://www.10amendments.org/PDF/Freedom%20Amendments%20Plan%20-%20February%202011.pdf.

ACT. "Workforce Development." Accessed August 31, 2011, http://www.act.org/workforce/.

Aldonas, Grant, Robert Lawrence, and Matthew Slaughter. *Succeeding in the Global Economy: A New Policy Agenda for the American Worker. The Financial Services Forum*. Washington, DC: Financial Services Forum Policy Research Group, 2007.

Annandale, David. *Making Profits, Protecting Our Planet: Corporate Responsibility for Environmental Performance in Asia and the Pacific*. Manila, Philippines: Asian Development Bank, 2005.

Archer, Peter. *The Quotable Intellectual: 1,417 Bon Mots, Ripostes, and Witticisms for Aspiring Academics, Armchair Philosophers*. Avon: Adams Media, 2010.

Barber, Dean. "A New Lost Generation." Barber Biz Newsletter. Accessed September 25, 2011, https://deanbarber.wordpress.com/2011/09/25/a-new-lost-generation/.

Barber, William. "In the Interest of Sensibility." Accessed June 20, 2011, http://intheinterestofsensibility.wordpress.com/2011/06/19/presumptions-and-assumptions/.

Basile, Ralph, Tory Dowling, and Tony Saloman. "Scorecard." *Economic Development Journal* 10, no. 1 (Winter 2011): 50–56.

Bernton, Hal. "Dalai Lama Urges Students to Shape World." *Seattle Times*, May 15, 2001. Accessed September 29, 2011, http://community.seattletimes.nwsource.com/archive/?date=20010515&slug=dalai15m0.

Bingham, Amy. "Herman Cain's 9-9-9 Plan: Buy Less, Pay Less." ABC News. Accessed Oct 1, 2011, http://abcnews.go.com/blogs/politics/2011/09/herman-cains-9-9-9-plan-buy-less-pay-less/.

Bishop, Matthew, and Michael Green. *The Road to Ruin*. New York: Random House, 2010.

Bok, Derek Curtis. *Universities and the Future of America*. Durham, NC: Duke University Press, 1990.

Brunnermeir, Mark K., Stefan Nagel, and Lasse Petersen. "Carry Trade & Currency Crashes." Washington, DC: National Bureau of Economic Research, 2009. Accessed Sept 11, 2011, http://www.princeton.edu/~markus/research/papers/carry_trades_currency_crashes.pdf.

Bureau of Economic Analysis. *Foreign Direct Investment in the United States: New Investment in 2006*. Washington, DC: U.S. Printing Office, June 2007.

Burke, Edmund. *The Works of the Right Hon. Edmund Burke*. London: Samuel Holdsworth, 1837. Accessed September 13, 2011, http://books.google.com/books?id=RZJjAAAAMAAJ&printsec=frontcover&source=gbs_ge_summary_r&cad=0#v=onepage&q&f=false.

Burns, R. Nicholas, Joseph S. Nye Jr., and Jonathon Price. *The Global Economic Crisis and Potential Implications for Foreign Policy and National Security*. Washington, DC: Aspen Institute, 2010.

Campos, J. Edgardo., and Sanjay Pradhan. *The Many Faces of Corruption: Tracking Vulnerabilities at the Sector Level*. Washington, DC: World Bank Publications, 2007.

Carafano, Jay. "How to Fix the 100 Hours Homeland Security Bill." The Heritage Foundation. Accessed October 1, 2011, http://www.heritage.org/Research/Reports/2007/02/How-to-Fix-the-100-Hours-Homeland-Security-Bill.

Churchill, Randolph S., and Martin Gilbert, eds. *Winston S. Churchill: Young Statesman, 1901-1914*. Vol. 2. Michigan: Houghton Mifflin, 1967. Accessed June 23, 2011, http://books.google.com/books?id=NiAaAAAAMAAJ.

Cisneros, Henry. *Interwoven Destinies: Cities and the Nation*. American Assembly. New York: W. W. Norton Company, 1993.

Commonwealth of Australia, Infrastructure Australia (Department of the Attorney General). "Public Private Partnerships." Accessed

September 9, 2011, http://www.infrastructureaustralia.gov.au/ public_private/.

Corrigan, Mary Beth, Jack Hambene, William Hudnut III, Rachelle L. Levitt, John Stainback, Richard Ward, and Nicole Witenstein. *10 Principles for a Successful Public Private Partnership.* Washington, DC: Urban Land Institute, 2005.

Crapo, Mike. "Budget & Fiscal Responsibility." Accessed Oct 2, 2011, http://crapo.senate.gov/issues/budget/budget.cfm.

Data360. "Share of Global GDP by Country." Accessed August 31, 2011, http://www.data360.org/dsg.aspx?Data_Set_Group_Id=804.

Deuch, Roni Lynn. *Surviving the Coming Tax Disaster: Why Taxes Are Going Up, How the IRS Will Be Getting More Aggressive, and What You Can Do to Preserve Your Assets.* Dallas, TX: BenBella Publishing, 2010.

Esdaile, Charles. *Napoleon's Wars: An International History, 1803–1815.* New York: Penguin Publishing, 2009.

Evenett, Simon J., Bernard M. Hoekman, and Olivier Cattaneo. *Crisis Response and Openness: Implications for the Trading System.* London: CEPR, 2009.

Federal Reserve Board of San Francisco, *Globalization: Threat or Opportunity for the U.S. Economy.* FRBSF Economic Letter, 2004.

Florida, Richard. "The Road Map to a High Speed Recovery." *The New Republic.* Accessed June 25, 2010, http://www.tnr.com/article/economy/76961/richard-florida-reset-recovery-economy-future.

Friedman, Milton. "Economic Freedom, Human Freedom, Political Freedom." University of Wisconsin–Whitewater. Accessed June 25, 2011, http://facstaff.uww.edu/mohanp/theory9.html.

Friedman, Thomas. "Really Unusually Uncertain." *The New York Times.* Accessed July 4, 2011, http://www.nytimes.com/2010/08/18/opinion/18friedman.html.

Friedman, Thomas. "The First Law of Petropolitics." *Foreign Policy.* May 2006, 154.

Frisch, Max, and Rolf Kieser. *Novels, Plays, Essays.* New York: Continuum Publishing, 1989.

Forbes, Steve. "PBS New Hour Interview of Steve Forbes." PBS. Accessed June 25, 2011, http://www.pbs.org/newshour//bb/congress/forbes_flat_tax.html.

Ford, Paul Leicester, ed. *The Writings of Thomas Jefferson*. 10 vols. New York: G. P. Putnam's Sons, 1892–1899.

Garmise, Shari. *People and the Competitive Advantage of Place: Building a Workforce for the 21st Century*. Armonk, NY: M. E. Sharpe, 2006.

Garmise, Shari, and Ann Berlin. *International Economic Development Council—Primer on Globalization*. Washington, D.C: International Economic Development Council, May 2008.

Gevorkian, Peter. *Large-Scale Solar Power System Design (GreenSource): An Engineering Guide*. New York: McGraw Hill Professional, 2011.

Glover, Peter C., and Michael J. Economides. *Energy and Climate Wars: How Naive Politicians, Green Ideologues, and Media Elites Are Undermining the Truth about Energy and Climate*. London: Continuum International Publishing Group, 2010.

Goldstein, David B. *Invisible Energy: Stratagies to Rescue the Economy and Save the Planet*. Point Richmond: Bay Tree Publishing, 2009.

Gratz, Donald B. "The Peril and Promise of Performance Pay: Making Education Compensation Work." Lanham, MD: R & L Education, 2009.

Griffith, William. *Historical Notes of the American Colonies and Revolution, 1754–1775*. Burlington: His Executors, 1843. Accessed September 12, 2011, http://books.google.com/books?id=NjgvAAAAYAAJ&printsec=frontcover&source=gbs_ge_summary_r&cad=0#v=onepage&q&f=false.

Hale, David. "Brave New Economy." *Wall Street Journal*. February 22, 2008.

Hamilton, Daniel S., and Joseph Quinlan. "Winners and Losers: Europe Is a Big Winner from Globalization, If Only Politicians Would Say So." Economist.com. Accessed August 29, 2011, http://www.economist.com/node/10765186.

Hardman, J. B. S., ed. *Rendezvous with Destiny: Addresses and Opinions of Franklin Delano Roosevelt*. Kila: Kessinger Publishing, 2005.

Harvey, Jason. *Achieve Anything in Just One Year: Be Inspired Daily to Live Your Dreams and Accomplish Your Goals!* Halifax: Amazing Life Press, 2009.

Hoekstra, Peter. "Bringing Education Reform Back Home." The Heritage Foundation. Accessed October 1, 2011, http://www.heritage. org/Research/Commentary/2011/03/Bringing-Education-Reform- Back-Home.

Hofmeister, John. *Why We Hate the Oil Companies: Straight Talk from an Energy Insider.* New York: Palgrave McMillan, 2010.

IBM Global Services. *Global Location Trends: Annual Report.* Somers, NY: IBM, 2007.

Jacobs, Paul. "Who Creates Jobs?" Common Sense Newsletter. Accessed October 1, 2011, http://thisiscommonsense.com/?p=6608.

Jones, Bruce D., Carlos Pascual, and Stephen John Stedman. *Global Risks 2008: A Global Risk Network Report.* World Economic Forum. Geneva, Switzerland: Brookings Institution Press, 2008.

Juhasz, Antonia. *The Tyranny of Oil: The World's Most Powerful Industry — and What We Must Do to Stop It.* New York: Harper Collins Publishing, 2009.

Kerry, Mark. *Tigers of the Tigris.* Indianapolis: Dog Ear Publishing, 2008.

Ketchum, Richard M. *Will Rogers, His Life and Times.* New York: McGraw-Hill, 1973.

Kooper, Robert, Zhi Wang, and Shang-jin Wei. "How Much of Chinese Exports Is Really Made in China? Assessing Foreign and Domestic Value-Added in Gross Exports." US International Trade Commission. Accessed November 1, 2011, www.usitc.gov/publications/332/working.../ec200803b_revised.pdf.

Krieger, Richard Alan. *Civilization's Quotations: Life's Ideal.* New York: Algora Publishing, 2002.

Law Offices of Rajiv S. Khanna, PC. "EB-5 Investment Green Card." Immigration.com. Accessed June 30, 2011, http://www.immigration. com/greencard/eb5-green-card/eb-5-investment-green-card.

Legal Language Services. "The New Colossus." Accessed June 25,

2011, http://www.legallanguage.com/resources/poems/statue-libertypoem/.

Mandaville, Michael. *Citizen-Soldier Handbook: 101 Ways Every American Can Fight Terrorism*. Indianapolis: Dog Ear Publishing, 2009.

Marler, Jenny. "Underemployment 19.8% in February, on Par with January." Gallup News. Accessed June 30, 2011, http://www.gallup.com/poll/126272/underemployment-february-par-january.aspx.

Maxwell, William Earl, Earnest Crain, and Adolfo Santos. *Texas Politics Today, 2009–2010*. Boston: Cengage Learning, 2009.

McKinsey & Company. "An Economy That Works: Job Creation and America's Future." Accessed June 29, 2011, http://www.mckinsey.com/mgi/publications/us_jobs/index.asp.

McMorris-Santoro, Evan. "Gingrich Calls for Federal Law Banning Shariah Law in US." TPM. Accessed June 25, 2011, http://tpmdc.talkingpointsmemo.com/2010/09/gingrich-calls-for-federal-law-banning-shariah-law-in-us.php.

National Academy of Engineering. *Real Prospects for Energy Efficiency in the United States*. Washington, DC: National Academies Press, 2010.

National Science Foundation. *Science and Engineering Indicators*. Arlington, VA: National Science Foundation, 2008.

Novogradac, Michael J. *New Markets Tax Credit Handbook*. San Francisco, CA: Novogradac & Company LLP, 2006.

O'Neill, Meaghan. "84 Ways You Can Help the Planet." *New York Times*. Accessed November 1, 2011, http://www.nytimes.com/2007/11/18/health/18iht-18planet.8378813.html?pagewanted=2.

OECD. *Establishing a Framework for Evaluation and Teacher Incentives*. Paris, France: OECD Publishing, 2011.

OpenSecrets.org. "Lobbying: US Oil." Accessed June 25, 2011, http://www.opensecrets.org/lobby/clientsum.php?id=D000058081&year=2010.

Palmisano, Samuel J. "The Globally Integrated Enterprise." *Foreign Affairs* 85, no. 3 (2006): 127–136.

Polina, Ron. *Selling Out a Superpower: Where the U.S. Economy Went Wrong and How We Can Turn It Around*. Amherst, MA: Prometheus Books, 2010.

PR Newswire. "Congress Is Looting Federal Worker, Military Retirement Funds, Says William Fruth, Founder of 10 Amendments for Freedom." Accessed June 3, 2011, http://www.prnewswire.com/news-releases/congress-is-looting-federal-worker-military-retirement-funds-says-william-fruth-founder-of-10-amendments-for-freedom-84465732.html.

Rajan, Raghuram. "Bernanke Must End Era of Ultra-Low Rates." *Financial Times*. Accessed August 10, 2011, http://www.ft.com/intl/cms/s/0/2a19a706-9a7a-11df-87fd-00144feab49a.html#axzz1UZY5PKcP.

Rawson, Hugh. *The Unofficial Rules of Life as Handed Down by Murphy and Other Sages*. Edison, New Jersey: Book Sales, 2002.

Robinson, Eugene. "Sharia as the New Red Menace?" *Washington Post*. Accessed June 25, 2011, http://www.washingtonpost.com/wp-dyn/content/article/2010/09/20/AR2010092004257.html.

Rogers, Betty. *Will Rogers*. Norman: University of Oklahoma Press, 1941.

Roosevelt, Theodore. "The Man with the Muck-Rake." Accessed October 2, 2011, http://www.americanrhetoric.com/speeches/teddy-rooseveltmuckrake.htm.

Santayana, George, and James Seaton. *The Genteel Tradition in American Philosophy and Character and Opinion in the United States*. New Haven, CT: Yale University Press, 2009.

Scott, Richard. *I Don't Have Time*. London: Filament Publishing, 2010.

Semas, Leonard A. *Reason, Justice, and Common Sense: A Collection of Essays from the Sierra Sage*. Genoa: Sierra Sage, 2009.

Slavin, Matt and Ralph Bennett. "Sustainability in America's Cities: Creating the Green Metropolis." Washington, DC: Island Press, 2011.

Sparks, Jared, ed. *The Writings of George Washington: Correspondence and Miscellaneous Papers Relating to the American Revolution*. Cambridge, MA: American Stationers' Company, 1834.

Spencer, Christopher. "Global Issues of the Twenty-First Century and United Nations Challenges: A Guide to Facts and View on Major or Future Trends." Accessed November 1, 2011, http://www.global-challenges.org/.

Steele, Michael. *Right Now: A 12-Step Program for Defeating the Obama Agenda*. Washington, DC: Regnery Gateway, 2009.

Strategy Unit. "Tom Friedman on 'Being Green Is the New Red White and Blue.'" Accessed June 25, 2011, http://strategyunit.blogsome.com/2006/01/08/tom-friedman-on-being-green-is-the-new-red-white-and-blue/.

Summers, Larry. "Rethinking Globalization." Livemint.com and *The Wall Street Journal*. Accessed Oct, 1, 2011, http://www.livemint.com/2008/05/12000358/Rethinking-globalization.html.

Szenberg, Michael. *Eminent Economists: Their Life Philosophies*. New York: Cambridge University Press, 1993.

Tavakoli, Janet M. *Structured Finance and Collateralized Debt Obligations: New Developments in Cash and Synthetic Securitization*. New York: John Wiley & Sons, 2008.

Tayor, Dorceta E. *Environment and Social Justice: An International Perspective*. Bingley, UK: Emerald Group, 2010.

Thompson, Dennis F. *Just Elections: Creating a Fair Electoral Process in the United States*. Chicago: University of Chicago Press, 2004.

United States Congress, ed. *Congressional Record, January 4 to January 17, 2007*. Washington, DC: Government Printing Office, 2010.

US Department of the Army. *US Army Survival Manual*. Washington, DC: Smithmark Publishing, 1991.

University of Texas Library System. "Ronald Reagan Governor of California Inauguration Speech, Sacramento, California." Accessed June 24, 2011, www.reagan.utexas.edu/archives/speeches/govspeech/01051967a.htm.

United States Patent and Trademark Office. "Table of Issue Years and Patent Numbers for Selected Document Types Issues Since 1836." Accessed September 15, 2011, http://www.uspto.gov/web/offices/

ac/ido/oeip/taf/data/issuyear.htm.

Wadhwa, Vivek, AnnaLee Saxenian, Ben Rissing, and Gary Gereffi. *America's New Immigrant Entrepreneurs*. Durham and Berkeley: Duke University and the University of California, 2007.

Washington, Henry Augustine, ed. *The Writings of Thomas Jefferson: Being His Autobiography, Correspondence, Reports, Messages, Addresses, and Other Writings, Official and Private*. Washington, DC: H. W. Derby, 1859.

Washington, George. "George Washington Farewell Address." Archiving Early America. Accessed June 25, 2011, http://www.early-america.com/earlyamerica/milestones/farewell/text.html.

Washington, George. *Maxims of Washington: Political, Social, Moral, and Religious*. New York: D. Appleton Company, 1855.

Weiner, Eric. "Prosecutors: Congressman Took $400K in Bribes." NPR. Accessed October 24, 2011, http://www.npr.org/templates/story/story.php?storyId=10712500.

White, Sammis B., Richard D. Bingham, and Edward W. Hill. *Financing Economic Development in the 21st Century*. Armonk, NY: M. E. Sharpe, 2003.

World Bank. *Global Economic Prospects 2008: World Trade*. Washington, DC: World Bank Publications, 2008.

Yale Law School, Lillian Goldman Law Library. "First Inaugural Address of Dwight D. Eisenhower." Accessed June 24, 2011, http://avalon.law.yale.edu/20th_century/eisen1.asp.

Yorck von Wartenburg (Graf), Maximilian. *Napoleon as a General, Volume 2*. London: K. Paul, Trench, Truebner & Co., Ltd., 1902.

INDEX

A

B

C

Don A. Holbrook

Certified Economic Developer and Fellow Member of the International Economic Development Council

A resident of Las Vegas, Nevada, Don Allen Holbrook is a private consultant/practitioner involved in the major elements of economic development public policy, site location, and strategic destination tourism development. He is one of the most influential and recognized subject matter experts in the field of economic development and is the most published and quoted in the field. During his twenty-year career, he has worked on a wide variety of projects representing billions of dollars in capital investment and generating more than fifty thousand jobs.

Don has specialized in creating customized incentive policies, such as equity funding, specialized tax increment funding, tax abatements, workforce tax credits, specialized state legislation to increase equity and reduce operational costs to attract and finance projects, creative hybrid capital development by communities, and targeted incentives that reduce the overall cost to his clients and/or help his public sector clients close deals. Don has worked with economic organizations worldwide in developing strategic plans; core market assessment; target industry analysis; business-attraction incentives; publicly backed strategic business investments in capital formation; and permanent convertible, subordinated debt financing. He focuses on creating public-private partnerships that are built on real-world economic realities and tied to well-balanced capabilities that reward risk taken by both sectors.

Don is recognized for his prowess in the economic development industry; for his pioneering of site locations and technology-based, community-profiling infrastructures; and for his work in establishing the data standards used by the International Economic Development Council.

A highly respected and renowned speaker on world-class economic development projects, Don is one of the most sought-after advocates in economic development and takes his simple message to communities around the world. Some call him the Johnny Appleseed of economic development. His wit, message, and charm have made him highly popular as a keynote speaker on local economic development strategies. He speaks frequently on the topics of "The Art of the Deal Today" and surviving and thriving in today's economic turbulence. Don has written two books: His first, *The Little Black Book of Economic Development*, was released in 2007 and is still the best-selling book in the economic development industry. His second book, released in 2008, is titled *Who Moved My Smoke Stack?*

www.ingramcontent.com/pod-product-compliance
Lightning Source LLC
Chambersburg PA
CBHW071359170526
45165CB00001B/116